Lecture Notes in Computer Science   15230

Founding Editors

Gerhard Goos
Juris Hartmanis

W0079670

The series Lecture Notes in Computer Science (LNCS), including its subseries Lecture Notes in Artificial Intelligence (LNAI) and Lecture Notes in Bioinformatics (LNBI), has established itself as a medium for the publication of new developments in computer science and information technology research, teaching, and education.

LNCS enjoys close cooperation with the computer science R & D community, the series counts many renowned academics among its volume editors and paper authors, and collaborates with prestigious societies. Its mission is to serve this international community by providing an invaluable service, mainly focused on the publication of conference and workshop proceedings and postproceedings. LNCS commenced publication in 1973.

Susanne Graf · Paul Pettersson · Bernhard Steffen

Editors

Real Time and Such

Essays Dedicated to Wang Yi
to Celebrate His Scientific Career

 Springer

Editors
Susanne Graf (iD)
Université Grenoble Alpes, VERIMAG
Grenoble, France

Paul Pettersson (iD)
Mälardalen University
Västerås, Sweden

Bernhard Steffen (iD)
TU Dortmund University
Dortmund, Germany

ISSN 0302-9743   ISSN 1611-3349 (electronic)
Lecture Notes in Computer Science
ISBN 978-3-031-73750-3   ISBN 978-3-031-73751-0 (eBook)
https://doi.org/10.1007/978-3-031-73751-0

Preface

This Festschrift is dedicated to Wang Yi of Uppsala University, Sweden. Wang's career has been marked by many important contributions to the fields of real-time and embedded systems, with a particular focus on model-checking of real-time systems, embedded systems design, real-time scheduling, and multicore systems.

We have worked with Wang since the middle of the 1990s. His academic journey began a few years earlier with a Ph.D. in Computer Science from Chalmers University of Technology in 1991. Since 2000, he has held the Chair in Embedded Systems at Uppsala University, where he has significantly advanced the understanding and capabilities of his research fields. His work has not only pushed the boundaries of theoretical research but also led to practical implementations in several software tools that have had a profound impact on both academia and industry.

Among many accolades, Wang was awarded a KAW Grant from the Knut and Alice Wallenberg Foundation in 2020 and an ERC Advanced Grant from the European Research Council in 2019. His contributions have been recognized with Uppsala University's Rudbeck Medal for achievements in science in 2022, and the IEEE TCRTS Award for technical achievement and leadership in real-time computing in 2019. Notably, his development of UPPAAL earned him the CAV Award in 2013. Wang is a Fellow of both the ACM and IEEE, a member of the Royal Society of Sciences in Uppsala, and Academia Europaea in London. His leadership roles include serving on the ERC Panel, the IEEE Fellow Evaluation Committee, and the Executive Committees of ACM SIGBED and IEEE TCRTS. His guidance and mentorship have shaped the careers of many young researchers and professionals in the field.

It is with great pleasure that we present this collection of papers in honor of Wang's profound impact on the field of real-time and embedded systems. We hope that these contributions will inspire scientists in our community towards future research and innovation, continuing the research paths that Prof. Wang Yi has so brilliantly illuminated.

August 2024

Susanne Graf
Paul Pettersson
Bernhard Steffen

Organization

Program Committee

Susanne Graf	Verimag, Grenoble, France
Paul Pettersson	Mälardalen University, Sweden
Bernhard Steffen	TU Dortmund, Germany

Reviewers

Bjorn Andersson	Carnegie Mellon University, USA
Elena Fersman	KTH Royal Institute of Technology, Sweden
Susanne Graf	Verimag, Grenoble, France
Bengt Jonsson	Uppsala University, Sweden
Kim G. Larsen	Aalborg University, Denmark
Paul Pettersson	Mälardalen University, Sweden
Philipp Ruemmer	University of Regensburg, Germany
Cristina Seceleanu	Mälardalen University, Sweden
Tiberiu Seceleanu	Mälardalen University, Sweden
Aneta Vulgarakis Feljan	Ericsson, Sweden

Contents

All About Time 1
    Susanne Graf, Paul Pettersson, and Bernhard Steffen

Wang at MDU in a Nutshell 8
    Hans Hansson, Christer Norström, and Cristina Seceleanu

To Sifu - Supervision, Mentorship and Lifelong Bond 12
    Elena Fersman and Paul Pettersson

Research in One Area Benefits Another 18
    Bjorn Andersson

Verifying PLC-Automata Against Counterexample Formulas Using Timed
Automata 23
    Ernst-Rüdiger Olderog

Nudging Strategies for User Journeys: Take a Path on the Wild Side 42
    Einar Broch Johnsen, Paul Kobialka, Andrea Pferscher,
    and Silvia Lizeth Tapia Tarifa

Adaptive Task Planning and Formal Control Synthesis Using Temporal
Logic Trees 64
    Yulong Gao, Can Zhou, Alessandro Abate, and Karl H. Johansson

Trading Space for Simplicity in Stateless Model Checking 79
    Parosh Aziz Abdulla, Mohamed Faouzi Atig, Sarbojit Das,
    Bengt Jonsson, and Konstantinos Sagonas

Performance Analysis of Stochastic Digraph Real-Time Task Model 98
    Martin Kristjansen and Kim Guldstrand Larsen

A Closer Look at Pseudo-polynomial Time and Its Use in Real-Time
Scheduling Theory 120
    Sanjoy Baruah and Pontus Ekberg

Voting-Based Shortcuts through Random Forests for Obtaining
Explainable Models 135
    Alnis Murtovi, Maximilian Schlüter, and Bernhard Steffen

xii   Contents

Reminiscences of a Real-Time Researcher 154
    Thomas A. Henzinger

Author Index 165

All About Time

Susanne Graf[1,2], Paul Pettersson[3], and Bernhard Steffen[4(✉)]

[1] CNRS, Grenoble INP, VERIMAG, University Grenoble Alpes, Grenoble, France
susanne.graf@imag.fr
[2] Uppsala University, Uppsala, Sweden
[3] Mälardalen University, Västerås, Sweden
paul.pettersson@mdu.se
[4] TU Dortmund University, Dortmund, Germany
steffen@cs.tu-dortmund.de

Abstract. Timing is a central concern in critical embedded systems. Such systems must interact with a physical environment in a timely fashion. The critical point here is not average performance but guaranteed performance which must be good enough for the given environment. In this introduction to the Festschrift dedicated to Wang Yi on the occasion of his 60th birthday, we give an overview on the contributions of Wang Yi to the analysis and the construction of real-time systems and to the related contributions to this volume.

Keywords: Timed CCS · Timed Automata · UPPAAL · Task Automata · Timed Systems · Real-time Systems · Embedded Systems · Cyber-physical Systems · Model-checking · Real-time Scheduling · Real-time System Design

1 Formal Methods, Time and Tools

We met Wang Yi for the first time in the beginning of the 1990s. Perhaps the first time we all met him at a conference was at the first International Conference on Tools and Algorithms for the Construction and Analysis of Systems (TACAS) in 1995 in Aarhus, Denmark. A few years earlier Wang had moved to Uppsala University in Sweden after defending his PhD thesis on "A Calculus of Real-time Systems" [1] at Chalmers University of Technology in 1991. He had enrolled his first PhD student in 1993 and they had started to work on verification of timed automata (TA) [2, 3] and initiated collaboration with Kim G. Larsen's group at Aalborg University in 1995.

At TACAS 1995, Wang presented their tool, which they had just named UPPAAL after UPPsala and AALborg. And its algorithm used at the time that was based on an on-the-fly backwards symbolic reachability analysis approach in combination with efficient data structures based on difference bounded matrices [6]. He also demonstrated that UPPAAL could verify a version of Philips audio control protocol in less than one minute [4]. At the time this was a breakthrough as it demonstrated that timed automata technology could be applicable and time-saving in an industrial setting.

In the following years, the academic collaboration on UPPAAL was intense. The theory was further developed [4, 7], the underlying algorithms and data structures were improved [8, 10, 11], and the tool was applied to solve a great number of verification problems [5, 11, 12]. In contrast to many other academic tools at the time, effort was spent on making the tool user friendly with a graphical user interface including an editor for systems of timed automata, a simulator with support for diagnostics, an editor for requirements, etc. This made UPPAAL accessible to industrial users and popular in education, often in courses on formal methods or real-time systems.

The scientific importance of Wang's work on UPPAAL was acknowledged by the computer aided verification community in 2013 when he was awarded the CAV Award 2013:

> *"Kim G. Larsen, Paul Pettersson and Wang Yi received the CAV Award in 2013 "For developing UPPAAL which is the foremost tool suite for the automated analysis and verification of real-time systems."*

In 2002, Wang et al. presented a theory that extended the model of timed automata with asynchronous processes (or tasks) [13, 14]. The theory was formed as a model, later named the model of task automata, that used timed automata to describe task release patterns, and decidability results showing how the associated scheduling problem could be analyzed for a large set of real-time scheduling policies [13, 15, 16]. As such, the theory of task automata constitutes a very general way of specifying and analyzing scheduling problems of real-time, embedded, and cyber physical systems [16–18]. The theory was also accompanied by a tool, named TIMES [14], that could be used for graphical editing, simulation, debugging with diagnostic traces, etc. This work was first awarded at its first introduction with a best tool paper/demo award of ETAPS 2002.

2   Real-Time Systems and Tools

After having started his research career in the Formal Methods community, Wang slowly moved to the real-time and scheduling community, without forgetting his strong background on formal methods which allowed him to come up with excellent results. He always looked for the narrow path on the ridge of the optimal compromise between expressivity and analyzability. As an illustration, the TIMES tool [14] was initially based on the expressive TA, improving analyzability led to Task Automata [18]. In the extension called CATS [20], concepts of Real-Time Calculus are integrated by allowing the user to describe arrival patterns of tasks either by timed automata or by arrival curves. Abstraction of TA by arrival curves allows for efficient verification of expressive models. The TIMES-Pro tool [33] extends to hybrid systems. It uses the Digraph Real-Time (DRT) task model [26, 29] to represent discrete components and differential equations for physical ones. DRT is used to approximate continuous components for analysis.

We mention here only a part of Wang's work, mostly published, and often rewarded, at RTSS. Right from the start, he has been interested in scheduling on multiprocessor platforms, for example, in [19, 21–25, 34] where he and his students explore new analysis methods and new scheduling approaches [34]. They introduce the expressive yet analysable Digraph model [26], and come up with new results for mixed critical systems [27, 28, 30] by proposing new scheduling methods [27] or by improving the shape of the demand function [28, 30] for example. They got also interested in the analysis of systems with sporadic tasks, where they have obtained a number of interesting hardness results [30–32, 35]. But this is only a subset of Wang's work in this domain over almost the last 20 years.

Wang has always been interested in going a step further, and the idea of generating actual implementations from analyzed models has already been present in UPPAAL, and strengthened in TIMES [14] and TIMES-Pro [33]. A few years back, he started thinking about a design approach for Real-Time Embedded Systems with languages for the specification of functionality and timing aspects, (separate) analysis of each aspect, and finally code generation for a given platform. Like for the synchronous approach, the fundamental properties, such as determinism, would be guaranteed by construction, analysis would be compositional, and everything for implementations on multi-core platforms. This has led to the definition of an ERC project which has been presented at RTSS [36] and received with enthusiasm. In [37] we define the semantics underlying the MIMOS language, based on an extended version of timed Kahn Process Networks. In the MIMOS tool [40], still under active development, there are three levels of languages: the (graphical) MIMOS language defining a hierarchical network, a task model onto which nodes are mapped, and the "action language" defining the actual data transformations is for the moment "any" programming language, but there is also a dedicated language under work, more appropriate for analysis. For the analysis at scheduling level, a tool DATooR [39] is being developed. This work is under active development, and it is extremely promising. And we know Wang, we are sure that he and his group will get something solid and useful, as Wang says, the SCADE for multi-core.

3   Contributions of This Festschrift

This volume is a collection of papers in honor of Wang's research and impact. The papers are either personal notes [41–43, 51] or more scientific contributions [44–50]. In the following we give a short overview of the papers in the order they appear in the volume:

In *Wang at MDU in a nutshell* [41], Hans Hansson, Christer Norström and Cristina Seceleanu describe the impact of Wang Yi's tenure at Mälardalen University from 1999 to 2000. In *To Sifu - Supervision, Mentorship and Lifelong Bond* [42], Elena Fersman and Paul Pettersson, explore the relationship between themselves and their computer science mentor Wang Yi. In *Research in one Area Benefits Another* [43], Björn Andersson highlights Wang's significant contributions to bridge the gap between the Formal Methods and Real-Time Scheduling Theory domains.

Several contributions in this volume are related to model-checking, timed automata, or UPPAAL. In *Verifying PLC-Automata against Counterexample Formulas using Timed Automata* [44], Ernst-Rüdiger Olderog describes that timed automata are primarily used for verifying real-time systems but are not directly implementable. He shows how PLC-Automata, which can be implemented on Programmable Logic Controllers, can be translated into timed automata for verification purposes using tools like UPPAAL.

In *Nudging Strategies for User Journeys: Take a Path on the Wild Side* [45], Einar Broch Johnsen, Paul Kobialka, Andrea Pferscher, Silvia Lizeth, and Tapia Tarifa discusses the use of automata learning algorithms to create behavioral models of user journeys from data, enriched with time and cost variables. They explore how these models can be used to nudge user behavior, demonstrated through a case study with a music streaming application.

In *Adaptive Task Planning and Formal Control Synthesis using Temporal Logic Trees* [46], Yulong Gao, Can Zhou, Alessandro Abate, and Karl H. Johansson, discusses Temporal Logic Trees (TLT) as a solution to the challenges of formal control synthesis under temporal logics, particularly for uncertain infinite systems and complex real-time task planning. TLT, derived from Linear Temporal Logic (LTL) formulae, enables adaptive task planning and formal control synthesis for both finite and infinite systems, with a focus on dynamic online updates.

In *Trading Space for Simplicity in Stateless Model Checking* [47], Parosh Aziz Abdulla, Mohamed Faouzi Atig, Sarbojit Das, Bengt Jonsson, and Konstantinos Sagonas, introduces a simpler technique for managing sleep sets in Dynamic Partial Order Reduction (DPOR) algorithms, which, despite having exponential worst-case space consumption, offers better average-case performance compared to the previous method. Experimental results show that this new approach is faster and uses similar memory for average programs.

The next two papers in this volume are in the area of Real-Time Systems Scheduling. In *Performance Analysis of Stochastic Digraph Real-Time Task Model* [48], Martin Kristjansen and Kim G, Larsen, discusses the expansion of the Digraph Real-Time (DRT) Task Model to the Stochastic Digraph Real-Time (SDRT) Task Model, incorporating stochastic behavior for soft deadlines. The authors use UPPAAL SMC to simulate SDRT tasks and analyze performance metrics like utilization and missed deadlines.

In *A Closer Look at Pseudo-Polynomial Time and its Use in Real-Time Scheduling Theory* [49], Sanjoy Baruah and Pontus Ekberg discusses how Professor Wang Yi and his collaborators have advanced real-time computing by developing task models that allow schedulability analysis using pseudo-polynomial time algorithms. The paper reviews these contributions in the context of recent work and explores potential extensions.

In *Voting-Based Shortcuts through Random Forests for Obtaining Explainable Models* [50], Alnis Murtovi, Maximilian Schlüter, and Bernhard Steffen, presents new voting-based pruning strategies to aggregate Random Forests into more explainable decision tree-like models, aiming to control size growth while maintaining accuracy. Four strategies are explored, balancing pruning aggressiveness and fidelity, with experiments demonstrating their effectiveness on various datasets.

In *Reminiscences of a Real-Time Researcher* [51], Thomas A. Henzinger highlights the productive convergence of Formal Methods, Real Time, and Control Theory in the late 1980s, leading to significant developments such as Timed Automata, the UPPAAL toolkit, and the Hybrid Systems conference. The essay offers a personal retrospective on the early years of this emerging research field.

References

1. Yi, W.: A calculus of real time systems, Doctoral thesis, Chalmers University of Technology, ISBN 91–7032–589–8 (1991)
2. Yi, W., Pettersson, P., Daniels, M.: Automatic verification of real-time communicating systems by constraint-solving. In: Formal Description Techniques VII: Proceedings of the 7th IFIP

WG 6.1 international conference on formal description techniques (pp. 243-258). Boston, MA: Springer US (1995)

3. Alur, R., Dill, D.: A theory of timed automata. Theor. Comput. Sci. **126**(2), 183–235 (1994)
4. Laxsen, K.G., Pettersson, P., Yi, W.: Diagnostic Model-Checking for Real-Time Systems, pp. 575–586. Springer, Berlin Heidelberg (1996)
5. Larsen, K.G., Pettersson, P., Yi, W.: Model-checking for real-time systems. In: Fundamentals of Computation Theory: 10th International Conference, FCT'95 Dresden, Germany, August 22–25, 1995 Proceedings 10 (pp. 62-88). Springer Berlin Heidelberg (1995).
6. Johan Bengtsson, W., Griffioen, D., Kristoffersen, K.J., Larsen, K.G., Larsson, F., Pettersson, P., Yi, W.: Verification of an Audio Protocol with Bus Collision Using UPPAAL. In: Alur, R., Henzinger, T.A. (eds.) Computer Aided Verification, pp. 244–256. Springer Berlin Heidelberg, Berlin, Heidelberg (1996). https://doi.org/10.1007/3-540-61474-5_73
7. Larsen, K.G., Pettersson, P., Yi, W.: UPPAAL in a Nutshell. Int. J. Softw. Tools Technol. Transf. **1**(1–2), 134–152 (1997)
8. Larsen, K.G., Pettersson, P., Yi, W.: UPPAAL: Status & developments. In Computer Aided Verification: 9th International Conference, CAV'97 Haifa, Israel, Proceedings 9 (pp. 456-459). Springer Berlin Heidelberg (1997)
9. Larsen, K.G., Larsson, F., Pettersson, P., Yi, W.: Efficient verification of real-time systems: Compact data structure and state-space reduction. In: Proceedings Real-Time Systems Symposium (pp. 14-24). IEEE (1997).
10. Lindahl, M., Pettersson, P., Yi, W.: Formal Design and Analysis of a Gear Controller. In: Steffen, B. (ed.) Tools and Algorithms for the Construction and Analysis of Systems, pp. 281–297. Springer Berlin Heidelberg, Berlin, Heidelberg (1998). https://doi.org/10.1007/BFb0054178
11. Larsson, F., Pettersson, P., Yi, W.: On Memory-Block Traversal Problems in Model-Checking Timed Systems. In: Graf, S., Schwartzbach, M. (eds.) Tools and Algorithms for the Construction and Analysis of Systems, pp. 127–141. Springer Berlin Heidelberg, Berlin, Heidelberg (2000). https://doi.org/10.1007/3-540-46419-0_10
12. Seabrook, J.: Now. In: The Refuge and the Fortress, pp. 153–225. Palgrave Macmillan UK, London (2009). https://doi.org/10.1057/9780230235014_5
13. Amnell, T., Fersman, E., Pettersson, P., Sun, H., Yi, W.: Code synthesis for timed automata. Nord. J. Comput. **9**(4), 269–300 (2002)
14. Fersman, E., Pettersson, P., Yi, W.: Timed Automata with Asynchronous Processes: Schedulability and Decidability. In: Katoen, J.-P., Stevens, P. (eds.) Tools and Algorithms for the Construction and Analysis of Systems, pp. 67–82. Springer Berlin Heidelberg, Berlin, Heidelberg (2002). https://doi.org/10.1007/3-540-46002-0_6
15. Amnell, T., Fersman, E., Mokrushin, L., Pettersson, P., Yi, W.: TIMES b— A Tool for Modelling and Implementation of Embedded Systems. In: Katoen, J.-P., Stevens, P. (eds.) Tools and Algorithms for the Construction and Analysis of Systems, pp. 460–464. Springer Berlin Heidelberg, Berlin, Heidelberg (2002). https://doi.org/10.1007/3-540-46002-0_32
16. Fersman, E., Mokrushin, L., Pettersson, P., Yi, W.: Schedulability Analysis Using Two Clocks. In: Garavel, H., Hatcliff, J. (eds.) Tools and Algorithms for the Construction and Analysis of Systems, pp. 224–239. Springer Berlin Heidelberg, Berlin, Heidelberg (2003). https://doi.org/10.1007/3-540-36577-X_16
17. Fersman, E., Yi, W.: A generic approach to schedulability analysis of real-time tasks. Nord. J. Comput. **11**(2), 129–147 (2004)
18. Fersman, E., Mokrushin, L., Pettersson, P., Yi, W.: Schedulability analysis of fixed-priority systems using timed automata. Theor. Comput. Sci. **354**(2), 301–317 (2006)
19. Fersman, E., Krcál, P., Pettersson, P., Yi, W.: Task automata: Schedulability, decidability and undecidability. Inf. Comput. **205**(8), 1149–1172 (2007)

20. Krcal, P., Stigge, M., Yi, W.: Multi-processor Schedulability Analysis of Preemptive Real-Time Tasks with Variable Execution Times. In: the proc. of 5th Int Conference on Formal Modeling and Analysis of Timed Systems, Salzburg, Austria, LNCS 4763: 274–289 (2007)
21. Krcal, P., Mokrushin, L., Yi, W.: A tool for compositional analysis of timed systems by abstraction. In: Proc, of 19th Nordic workshop on programming theory, Oslo (2007)
22. Guan, N., Yi, W., Gu, Z., Yu, G.: New schedulability test conditions for non-preemptive scheduling on multiprocessor platforms. In: The proc. of the 29th IEEE Real-Time Systems Symposium, Barcelona (2008)
23. Guan, N., Stigge, M., Yi, W., Yu, G.: Cache-aware scheduling and analysis for multicores. In: Proceedings of the seventh ACM international conference on Embedded software (pp. 245-254) (2009).
24. Guan, N., Stigge, M., Yi, W., Yu, G.: New response time bounds for fixed priority multiprocessor scheduling. In: 2009 30th IEEE Real-Time Systems Symposium (pp. 387-397). IEEE (2009).
25. Guan, N., Stigge, M., Yi, W., Yu, G.: Fixed-Priority Multiprocessor Scheduling with Liu & Layland's Utilization Bound. In: the proc. of RTAS10, 16th IEEE Real-Time and Embedded Technology and Applications Symposium Stockholm, Sweden (2010)
26. Lv, M., Nan, G., Yi, W. and Yu, G.: Combining Abstract Interpretation with Model Checking for Timing Analysis of Multicore Software. In: the proc. of the 31th IEEE Real-Time Systems Symposium, San Diego, CA, USA (2010)
27. Stigge, M., Ekberg, P., Guan, N., Yi, W.: The digraph real-time task model. In: 2011 17th IEEE real-time and embedded technology and applications symposium (pp. 71-80). IEEE (2011).
28. Guan, N., Ekberg, P., Stigge, M., Yi, W.: Effective and efficient scheduling of certifiable mixed-criticality sporadic task systems. In: 2011 IEEE 32nd Real-Time Systems Symposium (pp. 13-23). IEEE (2011).
29. Ekberg, P., Yi, W.: Bounding and shaping the demand of mixed-criticality sporadic tasks. In: the proc of the 24rd Euromicro Conference on Real-Time Systems. Pisa, Italy (2012)
30. Stigge, M., Yi, W.: Combinatorial abstraction refinement for feasibility analysis. In: 2013 IEEE 34th Real-Time Systems Symposium (pp. 340-349). IEEE (2013).
31. Ekberg, P., Yi, W.: Bounding and shaping the demand of generalized mixed-criticality sporadic task systems. Real-Time Syst. **50**(1), 48–86 (2014)
32. Ekberg, P., Yi, W.: Uniprocessor feasibility of sporadic tasks with constrained deadlines is strongly coNP-complete. In: 2015 27th Euromicro Conference on Real-Time Systems (pp. 281-286). IEEE (2015).
33. Ekberg, P., Yi, W.: Uniprocessor feasibility of sporadic tasks remains coNP-complete under bounded utilization. RTSS (2015)
34. Abdullah, J., Dai, G., Guan, N., Mohaqeqi, M., Yi, W.: Towards a tool: times-pro for modeling, analysis, simulation and implementation of cyber-physical systems. Models, Algorithms, Logics and Tools: Essays Dedicated to Kim Guldstrand Larsen on the Occasion of His 60th Birthday, 623-639 (2017)
35. Jiang, X., Guan, N., Long, X., Yi, W.: Semi-federated scheduling of parallel real-time tasks on multiprocessors. In 2017 IEEE Real-Time Systems Symposium (RTSS) (pp. 80-91). IEEE (2017).
36. Ekerg, P., Yi, W.: Fixed-priority schedulability of sporadic tasks on uniprocessors is NP-hard, RTSS (2017)
37. Yi, W.: Design and dynamic update of real-time systems. RTSS (2019)
38. Yi, W., Mohaqeqi, M., Graf, S.: Mimos: A deterministic model for the design and update of real-time systems. In International Conference on Coordination Languages and Models (pp. 17-34). Cham: Springer Nature Switzerland (2022).

39. Roozkhosh, S., Hoornaert, D., Mancuso, R., Athanassoulis, M.: Hardware data re-organization engine for real-time systems. In: Proceedings of the Open Demo Session of the 43rd Real-Time Systems Symposium (RTSS@ Work) (2022).

40. Mohaqeqi, M., Yi, W.: DATooR, white paper: A DAG Design and Analysis Tool, see https://user.it.uu.se/~mormo492/datoor/DAG_Tool.pdf, under development

41. Dai, G., Khodabandeloo, B., Mohaqeqi, M., Yi, W. et al.: MIMOS tool, see https://akhoda256.github.io/agency-jekyll-theme/, under development

42. Hansson, H., Norström, C., Seceleanu, C., Wang at MDU in a nutshell. In this volume

43. Fersman, E., Pettersson, P.: To Sifu - Supervision, Mentorship and Lifelong Bond. In this volume

44. Andersson, B.: Research in one Area Benefits Another. In this volume

45. Olderog, E-R.: Verifying PLC-Automata against Counterexample Formulas using Timed Automata. In this volume

46. Johnsen, E.B., Kobialka, P., Pferscher, A., Tarifa, S.L.T.: Nudging Strategies for User Journeys: Take a Path on the Wild Side. In this volume

47. Gao, Y., Zhou, C., Abate, A., Johansson, K.H.: Adaptive Task Planning and Formal Control Synthesis using Temporal Logic Trees. In this volume

48. Abdulla, P.A., Atig, M.F., Das, S., Jonsson, B., Sagonas, K.: Trading Space for Simplicity in Stateless Model Checking. In this volume

49. Kristjansen, M., Kim, G., Larsen, Performance Analysis of Stochastic Digraph Real-Time Task Model. In this volume

50. Baruah, S., Ekberg, P.: A Closer Look at Pseudo-Polynomial Time and its Use in Real-Time Scheduling Theory. In this volume

51. Murtovi, A.: Maximilian Schlüter, Bernhard Steffen, Voting-Based Shortcuts through Random Forests for Obtaining Explainable Models. In this volume

52. Henzinger, T.A.: Reminiscences of a Real-Time Researcher. In this volume

Wang at MDU in a Nutshell

Hans Hansson$^{(\boxtimes)}$, Christer Norström, and Cristina Seceleanu

School of Innovation, Design, and Engineering,
Mälardalen University, Västerås, Sweden
{hans.hansson,christer.norstrom,cristina.seceleanu}@mdu.se

The Facts

In the labyrinthine world of real-time systems, few names resonate as powerfully as that of Prof. Wang Yi. As the co-inventor of the UPPAAL model checker, alongside Prof. Kim G. Larsen and Prof. Paul Pettersson, Wang has charted new territories in computer science, setting a benchmark that stands as a testament to excellence. His contributions are legendary, his standards unwavering, and his influence in the academic world is nothing short of monumental. UPPAAL has become the cornerstone for verifying real-time systems, ensuring that everything from automated trains to biological models operates with the precision of a Swiss watch.

From May 1999 to December 2000, Prof. Wang Yi served as a visiting professor at Mälardalen University (MDU). During this time, he collaborated closely with several researchers within the realms of Computer Science and Computer Engineering at the Mälardalen Real-Time Research Centre. Wang's impactful research, both during and surrounding this period, has left an indelible mark on the development of research at MDU. His influence has contributed to the growth of the Computer Science and Computer Engineering research environment, which expanded from approximately 25 members during Wang's tenure to a vibrant community of about 200 researchers and PhD students. This environment was further strengthened by the recruitment of Wang's first PhD student, Paul Pettersson, as a full professor in Real-Time Systems in 2006. Altogether, over 200 publications and nearly 20 PhD theses produced by MDU researchers have leveraged on Wang's scientific contributions, notably UPPAAL and its derivatives. Detailing how MDU has harnessed Wang Yi's scientific excellence would require a work far more extensive than this "Festschrift," so here, we will turn to some more personal reflections...

Hans Hansson's Personal Note:

A Curious Mind and Lifelong Friend

I know Wang since the early 1990ies when we both completed our PhD-theses; Wang's thesis contributed with a continuous time process algebra providing a key basis for UppAal and my thesis included a discrete time process algebra. I was surely on the losing side...

S. Graf et al. (Eds.): Festschrift Wang Yi, LNCS 15230, pp. 8–11, 2025.
https://doi.org/10.1007/978-3-031-73751-0_2

Fig. 1. The person being honored and the authors in alphabetical order. Pictures from the 1999 Mälardalen Real-Time Research Centre annual report, apart from the picture of Cristina, which is from a different source and a (much) later date.

At that time, I was working at the Swedish Institute of Computer Science in Stockholm and Wang did his PhD at the other side of Sweden, at Chalmers University of Technology in Gothenburg. As we completed our theses at about the same time on similar topics we did have some interaction, including providing feedback on our respective thesis drafts, but it was not until Wang got a position at Uppsala University (my Alma Mater) we became friends.

In 1997 I was offered a chair in Computer Engineering at one of Sweden's University Colleges, Mälardalen University, with main task to strengthen the scientific profile of the Computer Science/Computer Engineering research. Wang was one of the friends that I involved in this, resulting in Wang getting a part-time employment at Mälardalen. What strikes me about Wang is that he is an unusually innovative and curious researcher. There are many examples of this, but what I particularly remember is a curiosity-driven question that he asked to a few of our industrial collaboration partners: "How much do you earn?". Although he never got an answer (except for a pair of raised eyebrows), I think asking questions that others do not ask is part of being a great scientist, which Wang surely is!

Although Wang has now reached a respectable age, I'm sure he has many productive years ahead of him. I wish him the best on his continued journey and thank him for his contributions to science, as well as for being a great friend and fun person to work with.

Christer Norström's Personal Note:

On Sportsmanship and Academic Excellence Across East and West

I first met Wang in the 90s and we became good friends almost instantly. We've done some research together, but this text will focus on Wang's social skills and interests outside of research.

In 2001, our families met for a big event in my hometown-the yearly show by Volvo Construction Equipment. The world-leading producer of yellow machines that move dirt. At the annual show, they allow kids, and sometimes their parents, to test these big machines, of course supervised by a professional driver. Wang's son and my son are about the same age, and this event was something they, and we, really appreciated. The memory of these rides ended up on a big poster at Mälardalen University, featuring our sons and highlighting the collaboration between Mälardalen University and Volvo, where both Wang and I were active. The following year, our families met in Uppsala for the annual air show, which was also a success! Additionally, I remember when Wang proudly showed us his new BMW. Conclusion: Wang is interested in vehicles! (And YES, these days he is driving a claimed to be self-driving one...)

In 2017, I was invited by Wang to participate in a high-level conference in Shenyang, China. Shenyang is in the northeast of China, close to the border to North Korea. The conference included leading Chinese researchers and top-level industrialists in embedded systems, along with some very prominent researchers from the US, South Korea, and Europe.

My lasting memory of this event is Wang's ability to combine excellent hospitality—such as having dinner around a hot pot and telling stories—with bringing guests to play badminton together with students and himself. He embodies the belief that what people do is more important than where they are born, and he combines his love for sports, socializing, and excellent research seamlessly in a unique and very impressive way. I played some really challenging badminton matches with Wang and his students and enjoyed every moment, though I did end up with terrible muscle soreness.

During a walk by the river together with Wang, we saw people playing table tennis. We stopped to watch, and suddenly, I was invited to play and Wang of course pushed me to play. When they learned that I came from Sweden, the country of the world-renowned table tennis player J-O Waldner, we quickly became friends.

Both Wang and I know that sports and science unite people!

Cristina Seceleanu's Personal Note:

The Man, The Myth, The Model Checker

This is a personal note that draws on my experience with various encounters with Wang, who became a friend throughout the years. I first heard of Wang during my Ph.D. studies at the Turku Centre for Computer Science, in Finland, when my supervisor Prof. Ralph Back wanted to appoint Wang as the external examiner of one of his Ph.D. student's dissertation. There was debate in the group if the thesis was strong enough, that it did not use model checking, and what could one expect as questions. After much discussion Wang was appointed external examiner and all went well. However, Wang's name in a Ph.D. committee sent shivers down the spines of both seasoned researchers and fledgling students, standing as a testament to Wang's high standards.

After that, I got to meet Wang in person at various conferences throughout the world, as well as at Mälardalen University and Uppsala University, when we both served in grading committees for Ph.D. students. If you have ever faced Wang at a Ph.D. defense, you know what it feels like to be a knight confronting a dragon. Armed with a seemingly endless supply of tough, probing questions, Wang ensures that only the most resilient candidates pass through the academic gauntlet. Here is a classic Wang moment during a Ph.D. defense:

- Candidate: "Our model guarantees a 99.9% reliability."
- Wang: "And the remaining 0.1%? Should we expect it to fail on Leap Day?"

I remember discussing research with Wang during the breaks of a formal methods conference, in 2010. At that time, I was working on research with a different model checker from UPPAAL, and I was sharing the encountered challenges with Wang. After listening carefully, Wang looked at me and concluded: "Only UPPAAL works, this is the truth."

Despite his rigorous standards and formidable questioning, Wang is beloved by his students and colleagues. His sense of humor is as sharp as his intellect, often diffusing tense moments with a well-timed joke or a humorous remark. His ability to balance seriousness with levity makes him not just a model scientist but a fun companion too. My most vivid memories are in connection to various instances of ISoLA, the International Symposium On Leveraging Applications of Formal Methods, Verification and Validation, which take place on wonderful islands. These gatherings are more than just academic events. They are arenas of intellectual sparring, storytelling, and the occasional bout of uproarious laughter. Sharing the dinner table with Wang at ISoLA conferences bears the promise of some truly memorable moments, in a joyful and relaxed atmosphere together with the other participants.

As we celebrate Wang's contributions to the field of real-time systems and his indelible impact on generations of students, we acknowledge that his legacy is one of relentless pursuit of excellence, tempered with kindness and humor. Here it is to a scholar, a mentor, and a legend whose work will continue to inspire and challenge us all.

From Us All

Wang, may your models always check out, your questions always challenge, and your laughter always light up the room. We are looking forward to enjoying your friendship for many years to come.

Happy Festschrift, Wang!

To Sifu - Supervision, Mentorship and Lifelong Bond

Elena Fersman[1]([⊠]) and Paul Pettersson[2]

[1] Ericsson Inc, 2755 Augustine Dr, Santa Clara, CA 95054, USA
elena.fersman@ericsson.com
[2] Mälardalen University, Box 883, 721 23 Västerås, Sweden
paul.pettersson@mdu.se

Abstract. The term 'Sifu' in Chinese denotes a 'teacher' or 'master' and is used to describe an individual who has attained significant expertise and mastery in a specific field, often within martial arts. In this paper, we describe the bond between us and our sifu in computer science, Professor Wang Yi.

Keywords: Real-time Systems · Embedded Systems · Cyber-physical Systems · Modelling · Model-checking · Real-time Scheduling · UPPAAL

1 Introduction

Working on a PhD thesis in computer science shares many similarities with practicing martial arts. Both endeavors require a high level of discipline and dedication. In martial arts, consistent practice is essential to master techniques and forms, while in a PhD program, sustained effort is needed to conduct research, write, and revise the thesis work over several years. Continuous learning and improvement are crucial in both fields. Martial artists constantly learn new techniques and refine their skills, just as PhD students continuously learn new concepts, refine their hypotheses, and improve their research methodologies. Both pursuits involve overcoming significant challenges. Martial artists face physical and mental challenges, including rigorous training and sparring with opponents. PhD students encounter intellectual and practical challenges, such as solving complex problems, conducting experiments, analyzing data and battling with fellow PhD students.

Patience and perseverance are essential in both martial arts and completing a PhD thesis. Mastery in martial arts takes years of practice, while completing a thesis is a long-term endeavor requiring patience and perseverance. Both fields demand intense focus and concentration. Martial artists need to concentrate to execute techniques effectively and remain aware of their surroundings. Similarly, PhD students need sustained focus to conduct in-depth research and ensure accuracy in their work.

Goal setting and achievement are integral to both martial arts and a PhD program. Martial artists set goals such as earning belts or mastering specific techniques, while PhD students aim to publish papers, complete experiments, and ultimately defend their thesis. Additionally, both disciplines emphasize balance and harmony. Martial arts focus on the

S. Graf et al. (Eds.): Festschrift Wang Yi, LNCS 15230, pp. 12–17, 2025.
https://doi.org/10.1007/978-3-031-73751-0_3

balance of body and mind and the harmony between offensive and defensive techniques. In a PhD program, students must balance different aspects of research, such as theory and application, and find harmony between work and personal life (Fig. 1).

Fig. 1. Professor Wang Yi leading his research group in the 2000s. Photo by Leonid Mokrushin.

Mentorship and supervision is a central element in both PhD studies and martial arts. Martial arts students learn under the guidance of a master or *sifu*, who provides training, feedback, and support. Sifu is a Chinese term that translates to "teacher" or "master" and is used to refer to someone who has achieved a high level of expertise and mastery in a particular discipline, especially in martial arts. The term sifu can be broken down into two characters: "si" (師) meaning "teacher" or "master," and "fu" (父) meaning "father". This reflects the dual role of a sifu as both an instructor and a mentor, similar to a parental figure in guiding and nurturing their students. The bond between a sifu and their students is often lifelong, emphasizing the importance of the transmission of knowledge from one generation to the next. In this paper, we will describe how this bond has been created between us and our sifu, Professor Wang Yi, through various techniques, challenges, and decisions.

2   Excellence

Coming into Wang's research group was a steep curve. Wang has a tradition of shooting only for the moon (and even if you miss, you land among the stars), which is hard for a new PhD student who just wants to produce a result and get published, no matter where.

Looking back to what felt like a very long time, but turned out to be just a year or so of struggle, resulted in us publishing in prestigious venues such as ETAPS and CAV, which definitely paved the way to a more successful way ahead. This approach of course also ensured that the research conducted under his guidance reached prestigious and recognized research communities, and enhanced the visibility of the work (Fig. 2).

Fig. 2. Wang Yi at team building activity in the 2000s. Photo by Leonid Mokrushin.

Working with a supervisor who strives for excellence offers many advantages for graduate students. It encourages critical thinking, attention to detail, and a commitment to thoroughness that can distinguish a student's work. In addition, a supervisor who demands high standards often has a strong professional network, providing students with opportunities to connect with experts in their field all over the world. This can lead to collaborative projects and postdoctoral opportunities, which we both have experienced through working with industrial partners such as ABB and Philips, and doing our postdocs at Aalborg University in Denmark, and École normale supérieure Paris-Saclay in France.

3   Team

Paul had the privilege of being Wang's first PhD student in 1993, while Elena came into a well-established team of PhD students at Uppsala University in 1999, who had already been working together on UPPAAL [2], the underlying theories, algorithms, data structures, tool development, and case studies for years.

Being part of a high-performing research group enhances a PhD student's visibility in the academic community. Publishing in top-tier venues often translates into better job prospects, higher research funding success rates, and greater academic recognition. This rigorous training environment prepares students not only to excel in their academic careers but also equips them with the resilience and skills needed to tackle complex challenges in any professional setting. Wang's research group (commonly known as the UPPAAL group at Uppsala University) consisted of a set of diverse profiles, with each PhD student having unique skills. All of us delveded into the underlying theory, and in addition we had a mix of brilliant programmers, both for frontend and backend, researchers who put together great lab assignments for undergraduate students and people doing modeling and verification of industrial case studies.

4   Leading by Example

Every PhD student knows the feeling of working hard just before a paper submission deadline, after weeks of writing and polishing. Wang has been a role model for us in many aspects, from ideation to writing and presenting the research results, but staying up at nights in the office supporting his students with their papers before deadline was something special. We were working alongside each other for long hours, figuring out all the details in the long theorem proofs and putting them down in writing.

A PhD supervisor who leads by example always serves as a source of inspiration for his students. Wang always actively engaged in our research demonstrating intellectual curiosity. This supervision style not only sets a high standard but also instills these values in his PhD students. It was great to have a role model who not only talks the talk but walks the walk. At the same time, Wang was always fair about the original ideas, and the work put into them by team members. We recall that after every long pre-deadline sprint of work, he would leave the final touches and the actual submission of the paper to the corresponding author.

Another strong quality of Wang was to know when to let go. When we wrote the "Two-clock" paper [4] he was very clear that after discussing the scientific contribution of the paper he was confident that we would be able to write it in a pedagogical manner without his help. In addition, even though we are talking about strong scientific sides of Wang as supervisor, he did not forget to show that the value of producing a PhD thesis is in the learning process. This was very clear when Elena figured out that unnecessarily complex clock subtraction can be substituted with a more straight-forward clock addition in order to prove schedulability. It made her both happy for the result and sad due to the insight that the new finding would make her previous work obsolete. Wang explained however that the research path is rarely straight, and all findings on the way are of value to the research community (Fig. 3).

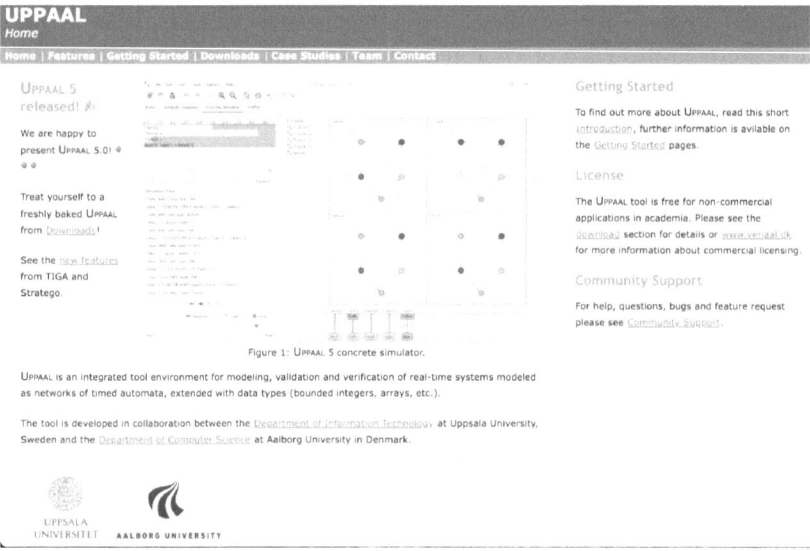

Fig. 3. The UPPAAL tool web page www.uppaal.org. Captured on August 10, 2024.

5   Business Savviness

Even though Wang's area of science is theoretical computer science, he was always striving at seeing practical applications of his research. Case study papers describing experiments done together with industrial partners, using tools built by the research team, have been a necessary component of each of the PhD thesis coming out of the team. In the beginning of her PhD studies Elena said to Wang with a slight degree of shame in her voice: "I also have a degree in business management, but that's irrelevant for my PhD". "It's relevant", Wang replied, "one day you will want to make money".

From the early days, the UPPAAL team experimented on their science by implementing model-checking algorithms in a predecessor of the UPPAAL tool. When the

UPPAAL tool was founded in collaboration with Kim Larsen's group at Aalborg University in 1995, the platform was further used for experimentation in the team, for solving industrial case studies in collaboration with industrial partners, and as a pedagogical tool for computer science students taking a course on real-time systems.

Later, after Wang got the idea of extended timed automata with tasks and their schedulability the TIMES tool [3] was born. TIMES used a version of UPPAAL as a backend, but gave the user of the tool the opportunity to augment the timed automata with real-time tasks.

Several other tools have been created since then, using various underlying theories. The beauty of making it practical was in stream-lining the actual tool code to make the tool most efficient and relevant for industrial applications. The students who used the tools in their classes and later joined industrial companies often came back to the research team asking for a license to use the tool in an industrial setting, which led to the formation of the company UPP4ALL International AB that delivers UPPAAL software licenses to various companies and organizations.

6   Conclusion

For us, Professor Wang Yi is a great sifu. His unique style of leadership and mentorship has brought us together and shaped us as researchers, supervisors and managers in our careers and life in general. Thank you so much Wang! Looking forward to many future years of friendship and collaboration.

References

1. DALL-E 2, https://openai.com/index/dall-e-2/, last accessed 2024/07/15
2. UPPAAL in a nutshell. K.G. Larsen, P Pettersson, W Yi. International Journal on Software Tools for Technology Transfer 1. Springer, pp 134–152 1997
3. TIMES: a tool for schedulability analysis and code generation of real-time systems. Formal Modeling and Analysis of Timed Systems: First International Workshop. Springer: Cham. pp 60–72 (2004)
4. Schedulability analysis using two clocks. Elena Fersman, Leonid Mokrushin, Paul Pettersson, Wang Yi. Tools and Algorithms for the Construction and Analysis of Systems: 9th International Conference. Springer, pp 224–239 (2003)

Research in One Area Benefits Another

Bjorn Andersson[✉]

Software Engineering Institute, Carnegie Mellon University, Pittsburgh, USA
baandersson@sei.cmu.edu

Abstract. Wang Yi at Uppsala University in Sweden is well-known for his contributions to formal methods (FMs), creating the most widely used model checker for timed automata. I imagine most participants at ISoLA 2024 view him from that perspective. However, with this note, I want to highlight another perspective: his contributions to real-time scheduling (RTS) theory, how his research in FMs benefits RTS theory, and how he serves as a bridge between FMs and RTS theory. The aim of this note is neither to cover all of Wang Yi's scientific contributions (which are numerous) nor to present his most famous (or most highly cited) works nor to present the works that he had done as a single author; instead, the aim is to present the bridge between FM and RTS theory.

Keywords: Formal methods · real-time scheduling

1 Difference Between FMs and RTS

1.1 The Difference: Course-Grained View

FMs differs from RTS theory in that the former is general whereas the latter is specific; the latter is for proving timing correctness considering contention for shared resources.

1.2 FMs

The FMs research community tends to create languages for describing a system and describe run-time behavior as a sequence of states. Rules describe (possibility of) change from one state to another. Some systems produce output. Most systems take input which may influence how the rules effect change. Correctness properties may be described with a special language. There is a procedure to determine whether a correctness property holds for a system. There are different methods for describing state (e.g., finite state machine, timed automata, hybrid systems, programming languages, concurrent processes) and there are different methods for proving (or disproving) correctness properties (e.g., model checking, theorem proving, abstract interpretation).

© The Author(s), under exclusive license to Springer Nature Switzerland AG 2025
S. Graf et al. (Eds.): Festschrift Wang Yi, LNCS 15230, pp. 18–22, 2025.
https://doi.org/10.1007/978-3-031-73751-0_4

1.3 RTS Theory

A real-time system is a (software/computer) system where correctness depends not only on computed value but also on the time at which the value is computed. Real-time systems exist in many products and sectors of society; e.g., spacecraft, aircraft, ground vehicles, ships, medical devices, factories, drilling/boring machines, and autonomous robots. The research community of real-time systems considers a wide range of challenges but the one that tends to attract the most attention is analyzing the effect of contention for shared resources on timing of software—RTS theory deals with that.

RTS theory considers a system comprising a set of *tasks* where each task generates at run-time a sequence of *jobs*. When a job is requested to execute, it is said to *arrive*. A job may execute and eventually *finish*. A job does not re-appear after it has finished but a new job of the same task may arrive. A task τ_i is described with parameters stating (i) bounds on possible arrival times of jobs of task τ_i, (ii) bounds on amounts of resource that jobs of task τ_i need, and (iii) latest acceptable finishing time of a job of task τ_i relative to its arrival.

The parameters used to describe tasks, and the interpretation of the parameters are called a *task model*; assigning values to these parameters yields a *taskset*. An example of a task model is: A task τ_i is described with a period T_i, a deadline D_i, and a worst-case execution time C_i with the interpretation that (i) each job (except the first) of task τ_i arrives at time T_i after the preceding job of task τ_i, (ii) each job of task τ_i has worst-case execution time C_i, and (iii) if a job of task τ_i finishes at most D_i time units after its arrival, then we say that the job *meets its deadline*. An example of a taskset is: $T_1 = 10$, $D_1 = 10$, $C_1 = 4$, $T_2 = 14$, $D_2 = 14$, $C_2 = 6$.

Note that different task models may use the same parameters, but they may be interpreted differently. For example, in one task model, the T parameter may be interpreted as a period and for each task the arrival time of its first job is zero; in another task model, the T parameter may be interpreted as a period and for each task the arrival time of its first job is non-deterministic; in yet another task model, the T parameter may be interpreted as a minimum inter-arrival time.

RTS theory considers resources (e.g., CPU, memory bus, critical sections) and rules arbitrating access to resources. For example, for CPU scheduling, it is common to assume each task is assigned a priority and a job inherits the priority of its task; at run-time, at each time, the CPU scheduler selects (among the jobs that are eligible for execution) the job with the highest priority; this is called *fixed-priority scheduling*. The rules that arbitrate access to resources may need to specify tie-breaking; for example, in a computer with a single CPU and there are two tasks with jobs eligible and both have the same priority, which job should be selected?

RTS theory often considers non-determinism of some of the following forms: (i) non-determinism of arrival times, and (ii) non-determinism of amount of resource needed, and (iii) non-determinism due to lack of tie-breaking specification. The non-determinism of arrival times is motivated by the need to model systems that are *event triggered* (e.g., the system must respond to an incoming message but before run-time we do not know exactly when the message will arrive). The non-determinism of resource needed is motivated by the need to model that the amount of resource needed at run-time depends on circumstances at run-time (e.g., the data payload of a message received influences the execution of a job). The non-determinism due to lack of tie-breaking specification is motivated by lack of exact information about how a CPU scheduler works. Thus, before run-time, one does not know exactly which execution or schedule will be generated at run-time.

A taskset is said to be *schedulable* if it holds that for all executions/schedules, for each task, for each job of the task, the job meets its deadline. Before run-time, we typically want to know if a taskset is schedulable. A *schedulability test* is a procedure that determines whether a taskset is schedulable. A schedulability test is a mathematical procedure that proves (or disproves) a property of a system—it is not just testing.

Important research challenges in RTS theory are (i) develop more expressive task models, and (ii) given a task model, develop an algorithm that performs schedulability testing.

1.4 The Difference: Fine-Grained View

As already mentioned, FMs tend to be general; hence the algorithms used to determine whether a property holds tend to have high time and space complexity (e.g., exponential time complexity in the worst case, or undecidable). In contrast RTS theory requires a system is described with a task model; this is more restrictive. However, this restrictiveness comes with the advantage that schedulability tests have traditionally had very low time-complexity. For example, one result states that for a certain type of restrictive task model, if a taskset has CPU utilization at most 69% then it is schedulable. This schedulability test has linear time complexity: if the taskset has n tasks, then the schedulability test has time complexity $O(n)$. Note that this schedulability test provides no information on tasksets with CPU utilization greater than 69% although we know that there are many tasksets with CPU utilization greater than 69% that are schedulable (i.e., the schedulability test is pessimistic). Other results in RTS theory use task models that are a bit more expressive, less pessimistic, and perform schedulability testing in pseudo-polynomial time.

In RTS theory, the starting point has been restrictive task models and sometimes high pessimism; the research has aimed to reach more expressive models and decrease pessimism. Note that this starting point is the opposite of FM which provides high expressiveness and low pessimism. So, in this sense, one can say that RTS theory has moved towards FM. Wang Yi and his collaborators have made major contributions in this direction. Two results are particularly noteworthy.

1. Encoding schedulability analysis as reachability computation of timed automata. This was presented in the paper [1].
2. Extending traditional real-time scheduling theory to a task model where each task is described in a way that is similar to an automaton. This was presented in the paper [2].

Details about these are provided below.

2   Encoding Schedulability Analysis as Reachability Computation of Timed Automata

Consider non-preemptive Earliest-Deadline-First (EDF) scheduling on a single processor. EDF means that at each instant, among the jobs eligible for execution, the job selected for execution is the one that has the earliest deadline (the absolute time—not relative to its arrival).

The main idea of encoding schedulability analysis as reachability is as follows:

1. For each task, construct an extended timed automaton with tasks (TAT); that is, for each task, do the following:
   a. Introduce one timed automaton so that each transition represents that a job of the task arrives.
   b. Assign an action symbol to each transition between locations.
   c. For each action symbol, specify two numbers: one is the execution time of the job that is generated; the other is the relative deadline of the job that is generated.
2. Create a semantics of TAT; this is achieved by extending the semantics of the state of a timed automaton so that it includes a sequence of pending jobs where each job is characterized by remaining execution time and remaining time to deadline.
3. Perform parallel composition of these TAT.
4. Introduce an error state so that if the TAT is unschedulable, then it is possible to reach the error state.
5. Show that the problem of deciding whether the error state in the TAT is reachable is decidable. This proof relies on the observation that if a taskset is schedulable, then there is an upper bound on the number of tuple elements in the TAT for each action symbol.

This led to a new research direction [3] to identify decidability and undecidability of schedulability analysis for different task models with different assumptions.

3   Extending Traditional Real-Time Scheduling Theory to a Task Model Where Each Task is described in a Way that is Similar to an Automaton

Consider the preemptive variant of EDF instead of the non-preemptive variant. Consider a single processor. For this case, RTS theory provides a framework that introduces a notion called *demand-bound function* (dbf) of a task and states that if for each positive real number t it holds that the sum of dbf of t over all tasks is at most t, then the taskset is schedulable.

Wang Yi extended this framework so that each task is described with a labelled directed graph so that each node corresponds to a job and each edge corresponds to a decision on which job arrives next. Hence, there can be a non-deterministic decision what job a task generates next. Wang Yi's paper [2] showed (i) a dynamic programming approach to compute the dbf for a given task and given value of t, and (ii) how to compute a set of values of t such that dbf only needs to be evaluated for values of t in this set (schedulability of the taskset is not affected by other values of t).

The time complexity of the schedulability test is pseudo-polynomial; this is not higher time complexity than previous works. But when it comes to job arrivals, deadlines, and execution times, this task model generalized almost all previously known task models in RTS theory.

Follow-on work introduced additional expressiveness to consider mixed criticality, mutually exclusive resources [4], and dependencies between tasks.

References

1. Norström, C., Wall A., Yi W.: Timed automata as task models for event-driven systems. In: 6th International Workshop on Real-Time Computing and Applications Symposium. IEEE, Hong Kong, China, pp. 182–189 (1999)
2. Stigge, M., Ekberg P., Guan N., Yi W.: The digraph real-time task model. In: 17th IEEE Real-Time and Embedded Technology and Applications Symposium. IEEE, Chicago, pp. 71–80 (2011)
3. Fersman, E., Krcál, P., Pettersson, P., Yi, W.: Task automata: schedulability, decidability and undecidability. Inf. Comput. **205**(8), 1149–1172 (2007)
4. Guan, N., Ekberg, P., Stigge, M., Yi, W.: Resource sharing protocols for real-time task graph systems. In: 23rd Euromicro Conference on Real-Time Systems, IEEE, Porto, Portugal, pp. 272–281 (2011)

Verifying PLC-Automata Against Counterexample Formulas Using Timed Automata

Ernst-Rüdiger Olderog[✉]

Carl von Ossietzky University of Oldenburg, Oldenburg, Germany
olderog@informatik.uni-oldenburg.de

Abstract. Timed automata due to Rajeev Alur and David Dill are the primary model for verifying properties of real-time systems with a continuous time domain. UPPAAL developed by Kim G. Larsen and Wang Yi and their collaborators is the main tool for practically performing such verifications. However, timed automata are in general not implementable. An automata model that enables implementation on the platform of Programmable Logic Controllers are PLC-Automata introduced by Henning Dierks. By translating them into timed automata, properties of PLC-Automata can be verified. We show this for properties formulated by counterexample formulas. The presentation is based on our book "Real-Time Systems" with Henning Dierks.

Keywords: real-time systems, verification, timed automata, PLC-Automata, counterexample formulas, Duration Calculus

1 Introduction

We consider real-time systems with the continuous time domain of non-negative real numbers. *Timed automata* due to Rajeev Alur and David Dill [2] are the primary formal model for verifying properties properties of such systems. This is because despite of having an infinite set of timed configurations, the reachability of (constraints at) locations of timed automata is decidable thanks to a reduction to finitely many regions or zones. Today, UPPAAL developed by Kim G. Larsen and Wang Yi and their collaborators is the main tool for practically performing such verifications [3,16]. In 2013, Kim G. Larsen, Paul Petterson, and Wang Yi received the CAV award of the international conference series "Computer-Aided Verification" for developing UPPAAL as "the foremost tool suite for the automated analysis and verification of real-time systems"[1].

However, when it comes to the implementation of real-time systems, timed automata have the disadvantage that they are in general not implementable [4, 22]. This is because they allow for instantaneous updates and zero-time message exchange [9].

---

[1] see: i-cav.org/cav-award

S. Graf et al. (Eds.): Festschrift Wang Yi, LNCS 15230, pp. 23–41, 2025.
https://doi.org/10.1007/978-3-031-73751-0_5

A different automata model of real-time systems, called *PLC-Automata*, has been introduced by Henning Dierks [5]. It enables the implementation on the widespread and standardized platform of Programmable Logic Controllers [12], abbreviated PLCs. PLCs have a built-in operating system that performs a cycle consisting of three phases. *Polling*: the values of the input busses are read; *computing*: the application program on the PLC is performed once and thus updates the internal state taking the values read in the polling into account, it can set, read, and reset timers; *updating*: the values of the output busses are set by copying values from a reserved memory location. Each cycle takes time. So instantaneous reactions are excluded here. PLC-Automata provide a formal model for specifying the behavior of a PLC. In particular, they include an upper bound for the cycle time. How to verify behavioral properties of PLC-Automata? Dierks has shown that PLC-Automata can be given a semantics in terms of timed automata [5,7]. This ensures verifiability.

Talking of verification, we have to fix a requirement language. We take here so-called *counterexample formulas*, abbreviated CEX formulas, taken as a subset of the Duration Calculus [23,25]. Each CEX formula specifies a pattern of a single behavior that the real-time system should *not* exhibit. In this paper, we recall the approach of verifying PLC-Automata against CEX formulas using timed automata described in the book [19] and illustrate it by a new example.

This paper is organized as follows. In Sect. 2, we define timed automata as used in this paper. In Sect. 3, we define PLC-Automata and introduce a running example. In Sect. 4, we introduce counterexample formulas and use them to specify the desired behavior of the running example. In Sect. 5, we detail an approach to the verification of PLC-Automata against counterexample formulas by representing both in terms of timed automata. In Sect. 6, we conclude the paper. Appendix A shows the UPPAAL timed automata used in the verification.

Dedication. We dedicate this paper to Wang Yi. His research on real-time systems has led to the tool UPPAAL that is now the backbone of many verifications performed in this area. In our group at Oldenburg, we have successfully applied UPPAAL both in research and teaching.

2   Timed Automata

Timed automata were introduced by R. Alur and D. Dill as an operational model of real-time systems [2]. Timed automata extend finite automata by clock variables ranging over the continuous time domain, represented by the non-negative real numbers: $\mathsf{Time} = \mathbb{R}_{\geq 0}$. Constraints on the values of the clock variables serve as guards of the transitions and as invariants in the finitely many control states. Timed automata can be combined into networks by using parallel composition and restriction operators of the process algebra CCS [18]. The most important result on timed automata is that it is decidable whether a given control state is reachable. This led to the development of several tools for the automatic verification of behavioral properties of timed automata. Of these, UPPAAL [16] is the currently the most widespread one. Whereas in [2] timed automata served to recognize real-time languages via Büchi acceptance conditions, later a simplified definition of timed automata, originally called *timed safety automata* [10], replaced the Büchi acceptance condition by location invariants enforcing progress. This version is now widespread and is adopted in UPPAAL, which uses timed automata extended with committed locations and urgent channels as well as data variables.

To define these automata, we need the following sets of symbols. Chan is a set of *channels*, with typical elements a, b. The idea is that inside a network, timed automata can communicate via channels. To this end, for each channel a there are two *visible actions*: $a?$ denotes an *input* and $a!$ the corresponding *output* on the channel a, where $a?, a! \notin$ Chan. Furthermore, $\tau \notin$ Chan represents an *internal action*, not visible from outside. The set of all *actions* is given by $Act = \{a? \mid a \in \text{Chan}\} \cup \{a! \mid a \in \text{Chan}\} \cup \{\tau\}$, with typical elements α, β. *Alphabets* B are sets of channels: $B \subseteq$ Chan. For each alphabet B we define the corresponding action set by $B_{?!} = \{a? \mid a \in B\} \cup \{a! \mid a \in B\} \cup \{\tau\}$. Note that $B_{?!} \subseteq Act = \text{Chan}_{?!}$ holds.

Let $\mathbb{X}$ be a set of clock variables, with typical elements x, y, z, and V be a set of data variables, with typical element v. The set $\Phi(\mathbb{X})$ of *clock constraints* over $\mathbb{X}$, with typical element φ_{clk}, is defined as follows:

$$\varphi ::= x \sim c \mid x - y \sim c \mid \varphi_1 \wedge \varphi_2$$

where $x, y \in \mathbb{X}$, $c \in \mathbb{Q}_{\geq 0}$, and $\sim \in \{<, >, \leq, \geq\}$. Constraints $x - y \sim c$ are called *difference constraints*. Further constraints like true or $x = c$ are considered as abbreviations. Constraints which are conjunctions of comparisons of the form $x \preceq c$ with $\preceq \in \{<, \leq\}$ are called *downward closed* because whenever they are satisfied for some clock values then also for smaller clock values.

The set $\Phi(V)$ *integer* or *data constraints over* V, with typical element φ_{int}, is defined as the set of Boolean expressions with a suitable syntax. The set $\Phi(\mathbb{X}, V)$ of *guards*, with typical element φ, is defined as follows:

$$\varphi ::= \varphi_{\text{clk}} \mid \varphi_{\text{int}} \mid \varphi_1 \wedge \varphi_2,$$

where $\varphi_{\text{clk}} \in \Phi(\mathbb{X})$ and $\varphi_{\text{int}} \in \Phi(V)$. Let $R(\mathbb{X}, V)$ denote the set of *reset* operations, with typical element r. For clocks $x \in \mathbb{X}$, the resets are simply $x := 0$, but for variables $v \in V$, the resets are assignments of the form $v := \psi$ for a suitable data expression ψ.

Definition 1 (Timed Automaton). *An* (extended) *timed automaton* $\mathcal{A}$ *is a structure* $\mathcal{A} = (L, C, B, U, \mathbb{X}, V, I, E, \ell_{\text{ini}})$, *where:*

- *L is a finite set of* locations *or* control states, *with typical element* ℓ.
- *$C \subseteq L$ is the set of* committed locations.
- *$B \subseteq$ Chan is a finite alphabet of* channels, *with typical elements* α, β.
- *$U \subseteq B$ is the set of* urgent channels.
- *$\mathbb{X}$ is a finite set of* clocks *and* V *is a finite set of* data variables.
- *$I : L \rightarrow \Phi(\mathbb{X})$ is a mapping that assigns to each location a downward closed clock constraint, its* invariant.

– $E \subseteq L \times B_{?!} \times \Phi(\mathbb{X}, V) \times R(\mathbb{X}, V)^* \times L$ *is the finite set of directed edges.*
An element $(\ell, \alpha, \varphi, \boldsymbol{r}, \ell') \in E$ *describes an edge from location* ℓ *to location* ℓ'
with action α, *guard* φ, *and a list* $\boldsymbol{r}$ *of reset operations on clocks in* $\mathbb{X}$ *and*
data variables in X. *If* $(\ell, \alpha, \varphi, r, \ell') \in E$ *and* chan$(\alpha) \in U$ *then* $\varphi = $ true.
This condition prevents that urgent actions are prohibited by guards.
– $\ell_{\mathrm{ini}} \in L$.

Timed automata can be graphically represented as annotated state transition diagrams. For examples, we refer to the Figs. 2, 3 and 4 in Sect. 5.

Real-time systems are typically modelled by networks of timed automata built up from single timed automata by the composition operators of parallel composition and restriction inspired by Milner's Calculus of Communicating Systems (CCS) [18]. The idea of CCS is that parallel processes, here timed automata, communicate in a one-to-one fashion via handshake communication. To this end, complementary actions $a!$ and $a?$ of two parallel automata can synchronize to yield the internal action τ but they can also be performed individually to be prepared for a later synchronization. This is important for parallel composition to be an associative binary operator on timed automata. For more details see [19]. We write $\mathcal{C}(\mathcal{A}_1, \ldots, \mathcal{A}_n)$ for a *closed* network of extended timed automata $\mathcal{A}_1, \ldots, \mathcal{A}_n$, where all channels are declared local to the network so that synchronization between the component automata is enforced. These networks can be represented in the tool UPPAAL (which additionally offers broadcast communication). To restrict the nondeterminism arising from the interleaving semantics of parallel composition, UPPAAL uses the following concepts.

Committed Locations. If at least one automaton of a network is in a committed location, time is not allowed to pass and the next transition must involve an outgoing edge of at least one of the committed locations. Committed locations serve to model *atomic regions* consisting of several transitions that should be executed without interference by transitions of any other automaton.

Urgent Channels. Once a synchronization between two automata along an urgent channel is enabled, a transition must happen without delay. Note that this transition does not necessarily synchronize over the urgent channel.

Semantics of Networks. Let $\mathcal{A}_i = (L_i, C_i, B_i, U_i, \mathbb{X}_i, V_i, I_i, E_i, \ell_{\mathrm{ini},i})$ be extended timed automata, for $i = 1, \ldots, n$. In the closed network $\mathcal{C}(\mathcal{A}_1, \ldots, \mathcal{A}_n)$ each component automaton $\mathcal{A}_i$ has its own control location ℓ_i. For the whole network a *control vector* $\boldsymbol{\ell} = (\ell_1, \ldots, \ell_n)$ collects these control locations. Then the operational semantics of the network is defined by a labelled transition system

$$\mathcal{T}_e(\mathcal{C}(\mathcal{A}_1, \ldots, \mathcal{A}_n)) = (\mathit{Conf}, \mathsf{Time} \cup \{\tau\}, \{\xrightarrow{\lambda} \mid \lambda \in \mathsf{Time} \cup \{\tau\}\}, C_{\mathrm{ini}}),$$

where for $\mathbb{X} = \bigcup_{k=1}^n \mathbb{X}_k$ and $V = \bigcup_{k=1}^n V_k$

– $\mathit{Conf} = \{\langle \boldsymbol{\ell}, \nu \rangle \mid \ell_i \in L_i \wedge \nu : \mathbb{X} \longrightarrow \mathsf{Time} \wedge \nu \models \bigwedge_{k=1}^n I_k(\ell_k)\}$ is the set of *configurations* of $\mathcal{C}(\mathcal{A}_1, \ldots, \mathcal{A}_n)$.
– For each $\lambda \in \mathsf{Time} \cup \{\tau\}$ the transition relation $\xrightarrow{\lambda} \subseteq \mathit{Conf} \times \mathit{Conf}$ has one of the following three types: it can be

(i) an *internal transition* $\langle \ell, \nu \rangle \xrightarrow{\tau} \langle \ell', \nu' \rangle$ involving only one component automaton $\mathcal{A}_i$,

(ii) a *synchronization transition* $\langle \ell, \nu \rangle \xrightarrow{\tau} \langle \ell', \nu' \rangle$ involving two component automata $\mathcal{A}_i$ and $\mathcal{A}_j$ with $i \neq j$, or

(iii) a *delay transition* $\langle \ell, \nu \rangle \xrightarrow{t} \langle \ell, \nu + t \rangle$ advancing the time of every clock in ν by $t \in \mathsf{Time}$, expressed as $\nu + t$,

- $C_{\mathrm{ini}} = \{\langle \overrightarrow{\ell_{\mathrm{ini}}}, \nu_{\mathrm{ini}} \rangle\} \cap \mathit{Conf}$ is the set of *initial* configurations. The vector $\overrightarrow{\ell_{\mathrm{ini}}}$ consists of the initial locations $\ell_{\mathrm{ini},i}$ of all component automata $\mathcal{A}_i$ and the valuation ν_{ini} assigns 0 to all clocks and data (here: integer) variables in the set $\mathbb{X} \cup V$.

Committed locations and urgent channels require special attention in this definition. For example, in case (iii) it is required that there is *no* $i \in \{1, \ldots, n\}$ with $\ell_i \in C_i$, i.e., no automaton is in a committed location. For full details we refer to [19]. There we required pairwise disjoint sets $\mathbb{X}_i$ of clocks for the component automata $\mathcal{A}_i$ in the definition of the semantics, but thanks to the restriction to downward closed clock constraints as location invariants we do not need disjointness.

3   PLC-Automata

Programmable Logic Controllers, abbreviated PLCs, are often used in industry to control real-time systems [12]. A reason for the relevance of PLCs in real-time applications is that each PLC has a built-in real-time operating system. This cannot be disturbed by application programs to guarantee a minimal functionality in case of a program failure.

Given an application program, the operating system executes the following non-terminating cycle consisting of three phases. *Polling*: the values of the sensors are read; *computing*: the application program on the PLC is performed once and thus updates the internal state taking the values read in the polling into account, it can set, read, and reset timers; *updating*: the values of the actuators are set by copying values from a reserved memory location. This is summarized by the following loop:

while true **do**
  • poll sensors: input;
  • compute next state (possibly using timers);
  • update actuators: output
od

Each cycle takes time. So instantaneous reactions are excluded here. This guarantees implementability on a real hardware.

PLC-Automata introduced by H. Dierks provide an abstraction specifying the behavior of an application program on a PLC [5]. The syntax of these automata is defined as follows.

Definition 2 (PLC-Automaton). *A PLC-Automaton is a structure* $\mathcal{A} = (Q, \Sigma, \delta, q_0, \varepsilon, S_t, S_e, \Omega, \omega)$, *where:*

- *Q is a non-empty, finite set of* states, *with typical element q;*
- *Σ is a non-empty, finite set of* inputs, *with typical element σ;*
- *$\delta : Q \times \Sigma \longrightarrow Q$ is the* transition function;
- *$q_0 \in Q$ is the* initial state;
- *$\varepsilon > 0$ is an* upper time bound *for the execution of a cycle;*
- *$S_t : Q \longrightarrow$ Time is a function that assigns a* delay time *to each state;*
- *$S_e : Q \longrightarrow 2^\Sigma$ is a function that assigns a* set of delayed inputs *to each state;*
- *Ω is a non-empty, finite set of* outputs; *and*
- *$\omega : Q \longrightarrow \Omega$ is a function that assigns an* output *to each state.*

PLC-Automata extend Moore machines by the components ε, S_t and S_e. They can be graphically represented as annotated state transition diagrams.

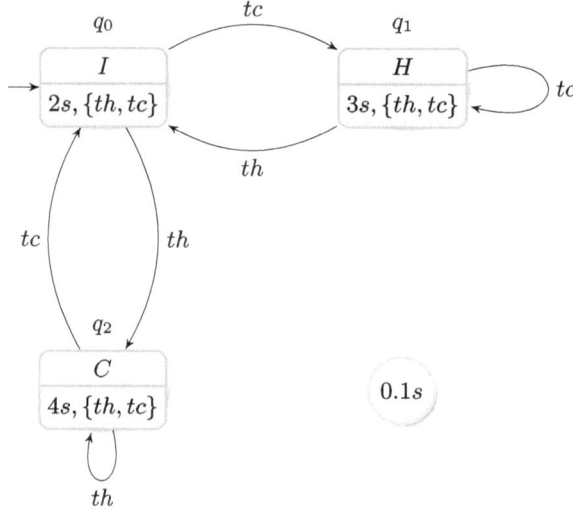

Fig. 1. PLC-Automaton $\mathcal{A}_t$ for temperature control

Example 1. Figure 1 shows a PLC-Automaton, called $\mathcal{A}_t$, for controlling the temperature in a water tank. It reacts to the inputs tc (too cold) and th (too hot). Its task is to heat up the water tank when the temperature sinks below some threshold and to cool it down if the temperature raises above another threshold. It has three states named q_0, q_1 and q_2, with q_0 as its initial state. Each state q is drawn as a box with two compartments. The upper compartment displays the output $\omega(q)$. Here we see the outputs I (Idle), H (Heating), and C (Cooling). The lower compartment exhibits the delay time $S_t(q)$ and the set $S_e(q)$ of delayed inputs. For instance, in state q_0 with output I the automaton does not react for $2s$ to any input. A transition $\delta(q, \sigma) = q'$ is represented by an arrow from state q to state q' labelled with the input σ. The time bound for the cycle is shown in a separate circle, here it is $0.1s$. The automaton ensures that the input values are read once within this time bound. Input changes that occur faster than the cycle time may not be recognized.   □

Each PLC-Automaton can be implemented using the programming language ST (Structured Text) dedicated for PLCs [12, 17] as shown in [5]. Formal semantics of PLC-Automata have been defined both in terms of logic (Duration Calculus) and in terms of timed automata [5]. Their relationship has been investigated in [7].

4   CEX Formulas

Logics for reasoning about the behavior of real-time systems are mostly extensions of temporal logics for reactive systems. For the continuous-time domain, MTL (Metric Temporal Logic) [14] and TCTL (Timed Computational Tree Logic) [1] have been proposed. These are point-based temporal logics.

By contrast, the *Duration Calculus*, abbreviated DC, is an interval-based temporal logic for real time [23, 25]. Interval-based reasoning allows for an intuitive specification of the successive phases of a real-time computation [19]. Often, the DC enables a succinct expression of properties due to the use of integrals, with the integration bounds are hidden in the semantics. The price is that the satisfiability of the DC is in general undecidable [23, 24]. This led to the definition of subsets of the DC that are closer to an implementation level and where the satisfiability is decidable. In particular, A.P. Ravn introduced the subset of DC implementables [21]. They come with different patterns that model initialization, sequencing, stability, and synchronization with external inputs.

In this paper, we use a uniform pattern for the specification of properties of real-time systems called *counterexample formulas* [19]. The idea is that each formula describes a single behavior that must *not* occur [11]. Except for initialization, the DC implementables can be rewritten into equivalent counterexample formulas.

Definition 3 (Counterexample Formulas). *A counterexample formula, abbreviated* CEX *formula, has the following form:*

$$\text{true}\,;\,(\lceil \pi_1 \rceil \wedge \ell \in I_1)\,;\,\ldots\,;\,(\lceil \pi_k \rceil \wedge \ell \in I_k)\,;\,\text{true} \tag{1}$$

where for $i \in \{1, \ldots, k\}$ the π_i are state assertions and the I_i are non-empty time intervals of the form (b, e) or $[b, e)$ or $(b, c]$ or $[b, c]$ with $b, c \in \mathbb{Q}_{\geq 0}$ and $e \in \mathbb{Q}_{\geq 0} \cup \{\infty\}$, Intervals (b, ∞) and $[b, \infty)$ denote the unbounded sets $\{t \in \text{Time} \mid b < t\}$ and $\{t \in \text{Time} \mid b \leq t\}$, respectively. For intervals $I_i = (0, \infty)$ we drop the part "$\wedge \ell \in I_i$" constraining $\lceil \pi_i \rceil$ in (1).

Intuitively, the formula (1) specifies that the following behavior is *undesirable*. After some arbitrary finite interval (the initial true) it follows a sequence of k

non-point intervals, starting with the state assertion π_1 that holds for a duration ℓ inside the interval I_1 and ending with the state assertion π_k that holds for a duration ℓ inside the interval I_k, finally followed by some arbitrary finite interval (the final true). These time intervals can be visualized as follows:

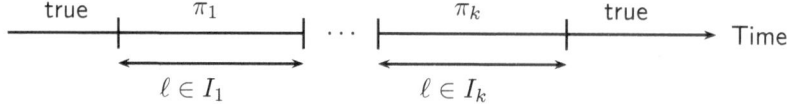

Inside the formula (1) we use operators of the Duration Calculus. A *state assertion* is a Boolean expression π build up from equations $X = d$, where X is a time-dependent *state variable* or *observable* that is interpreted as a function from Time to a domain of finitely many values, with d being one of these values. Semantically, state assertions yield values 0 or 1. Given a time interval $[b, e] \subseteq$ Time, the symbol ℓ denotes the length of that interval, i.e., $e - b$. An interval with $\ell = 0$ is called a *point interval*. The notation $\lceil \pi \rceil$ abbreviates $\int \pi = \ell \wedge \ell > 0$ and asserts that π holds *almost everywhere* in the considered time interval, which has to be a non-point interval. This is expressed using the integral $\int \pi$, which is the accumulated time when π evaluates to 1 in the considered interval. For $\lceil \pi \rceil$ to hold, this integral should yield the length ℓ of the considered interval. Since the integral $\int \pi$ is insensitive to changes of the value of π at single time points, the equation $\int \pi = \ell$ expresses only that π holds *almost everywhere*. The symbol ; denotes the *chop operator* of interval logic: a formula $F \, ; G$ holds on a given interval $[b, e]$ if this can be "chopped" into two adjacent subintervals $[b, m]$ and $[m, e]$ such that F holds on $[b, m]$ and G holds on $[m, e]$. In the visualization the chop points are marked by vertical bars.

Example 2. We give examples of CEX formulas specifying properties of the thermostat in Fig. 1. Let Out denote the output observable and In the input observable for the thermostat. We take $\lceil C \rceil$ as a shorthand for $\lceil \text{Out} = C \rceil$ and $\lceil C \wedge th \rceil$ as a shorthand for $\lceil \text{Out} = C \wedge \text{In} = th \rceil$, and analogously for other values.
    The CEX formula

$$\text{(Seq-2)} \qquad \text{true} \, ; \, \lceil C \rceil \, ; \, (\lceil \neg (C \vee I) \rceil) \, ; \, \text{true}$$

specifies that the following is undesirable. After some arbitrary finite interval (true) it follows a non-point interval where the output is C ($\lceil C \rceil$), after which we see a non-point interval where the output is neither C nor I ($\lceil \neg (C \vee I) \rceil$). Informally, this formula expresses the *Sequencing* requirement that after an output C of non-point duration the subsequent output should be C or I.
    The CEX formula

$$\text{(UbStab-2)} \qquad \text{true} \, ; \, \lceil \neg C \rceil \, ; \, \lceil C \wedge th \rceil \, ; \, \lceil \neg C \rceil \, ; \, \text{true}$$

specifies that the following is undesirable. After some arbitrary interval (true) and an interval where the output is $\neg C$ ($\lceil \neg C \rceil$) we see an interval where the output is C and the input is th ($\lceil C \wedge th \rceil$), after which the output is $\neg C$ again.

Informally, this formula expresses the *Unounded Stability* requirement that under the input *th* the output C should be *stable*. The initial change from $\neg C$ to C is needed to catch the begin of the phase where the output is C.

The CEX formula

$$\text{(BdStab-4)}\qquad \mathsf{true}\,;\,\lceil \neg C\rceil\,;\,(\lceil C\wedge tc\rceil\wedge\ell<4)\,;\,\lceil \neg C\rceil\,;\,\mathsf{true}$$

specifies that the following is undesirable. After some arbitrary interval (true) and an interval where the output is $\neg C$ ($\lceil \neg C\rceil$) we see an interval of a length smaller than 4 where the output is C and the input is tc ($\lceil C\wedge tc\rceil\wedge\ell<4$), after which the output is $\neg C$ again. Informally, this formula expresses the *Bounded Stability* requirement that under the input tc the output C should be *stable* for at least $4s$. The initial change from $\neg C$ to C is needed to catch the begin of the phase where the output is C.

The CEX formula

$$\text{(Syn-1)}\qquad \mathsf{true}\,;\,(\lceil C\wedge tc\rceil\wedge\ell=4.5)\,;\,\lceil C\rceil\,;\,\mathsf{true}$$

specifies that the following is undesirable. After some arbitrary interval (true) and an interval of length 4.5 where the output is C and the input is tc ($\lceil C\wedge tc\rceil$) we see that the output continues to be C. Informally, this formula expresses the *Synchronization* requirement that after output C and input tc has been observed for $4.5s$, the output should change to a value different from C. $\qquad\square$

For the PLC-Automaton $\mathcal{A}_t$ for temperature control we require that it does not satisfy any of the CEX formulas in Table 1.

5   Verification

We wish to show that a real-time system $\mathcal{S}$ *satisfies* a requirement P, abbreviated

$$\mathcal{S} \text{ sat } P. \tag{2}$$

Here, $\mathcal{S}$ is given by a PLC-Automaton and P by a CEX formula. Our approach is automatic verification based on (extended) timed automata (using the model checker UPPAAL). To this end, we proceed in three steps:

1. Represent $\mathcal{S}$ as a network $\mathcal{C}(\mathcal{A}_1,\ldots,\mathcal{A}_n)$ of (extended) timed automata.
2. Represent P as a *test automaton* $\mathcal{T}(P)$ together with a formula $\mathcal{F}(P)$ (in the logic of UPPAAL). The purpose of a test automaton is to act as an observer of the system and thereby simplify the formula $\mathcal{F}(P)$ that remains to be checked by UPPAAL. The test automaton should react to the observed system's behavior such that the following equivalence holds:

$$\mathcal{S} \text{ sat } P \qquad \text{iff} \qquad \mathcal{C}(\mathcal{A}_1,\ldots,\mathcal{A}_n,\mathcal{T}(P)) \models \mathcal{F}(P), \tag{3}$$

where $\models$ is the satisfaction relation between networks of timed automata and TCTL formulas as admitted in the logic of UPPAAL.

Table 1. CEX formulas for PLC-Automaton $\mathcal{A}_t$ of Fig. 1 for temperature control

Sequencing:	
(Seq-1)	true; $\lceil H \rceil$; $\lceil \neg(H \vee I) \rceil$; true
(Seq-2)	true; $\lceil C \rceil$; $\lceil \neg(C \vee I) \rceil$; true
Unbounded stability:	
(UbStab-1)	true; $\lceil \neg H \rceil$; $\lceil H \wedge tc \rceil$; $\lceil \neg H \rceil$; true
(UbStab-2)	true; $\lceil \neg C \rceil$; $\lceil C \wedge th \rceil$; $\lceil \neg C \rceil$; true
(UbStab-3)	true; $\lceil \neg I \rceil$; $\lceil I \wedge th \rceil$; $\lceil \neg(I \vee C) \rceil$; true
(UbStab-4)	true; $\lceil \neg I \rceil$; $\lceil I \wedge tc \rceil$; $\lceil \neg(I \vee H) \rceil$; true
Bounded stability:	
(BdStab-1)	true; $\lceil \neg I \rceil$; $(\lceil I \wedge th \rceil \wedge \ell < 2)$; $\lceil \neg I \rceil$; true
(BdStab-2)	true; $\lceil \neg I \rceil$; $(\lceil I \wedge tc \rceil \wedge \ell < 2)$; $\lceil \neg I \rceil$; true
(BdStab-3)	true; $\lceil \neg H \rceil$; $(\lceil H \wedge th \rceil \wedge \ell < 3)$; $\lceil \neg H \rceil$; true
(BdStab-4)	true; $\lceil \neg C \rceil$; $(\lceil C \wedge tc \rceil \wedge \ell < 4)$; $\lceil \neg C \rceil$; true
Synchronization:	
(Syn-1)	true; $(\lceil C \wedge tc \rceil \wedge \ell = 4.5)$; $\lceil C \rceil$; true
(Syn-2)	true; $(\lceil H \wedge th \rceil \wedge \ell = 3.5)$; $\lceil H \rceil$; true
(Syn-3)	true; $(\lceil I \wedge tc \rceil \wedge \ell = 2.2)$; $\lceil I \rceil$; true
(Syn-4)	true; $(\lceil I \wedge th \rceil \wedge \ell = 2.2)$; $\lceil I \rceil$; true

3. Check $\mathcal{C}(\mathcal{A}_1, \ldots, \mathcal{A}_n, \mathcal{T}(P)) \models \mathcal{F}(P)$ using the model checker UPPAAL.

Typically, $\mathcal{T}(P)$ has a distinguished *bad location* called q_{bad} and the formula $\mathcal{F}(P)$ is defined as follows:

$$\mathcal{F}(P) \iff \forall\Box \neg \mathcal{T}(P).q_{\text{bad}}. \tag{4}$$

Thus combining (3) with (4) yields: $\mathcal{S}$ sat P iff in the context of the network $\mathcal{C}(\mathcal{A}_1, \ldots, \mathcal{A}_n, \mathcal{T}(P))$ the test automaton $\mathcal{T}(P)$ never reaches its bad location.

For the interaction of the test with the system, the test automaton $\mathcal{T}(P)$ will have edges labelled with the input action *step?* that synchronize with corresponding output actions *step!* inserted in the timed automata $\mathcal{A}_1, \ldots, \mathcal{A}_n$ of the system that must not effect the behavior of the system as far as P is concerned.

5.1   Representing PLC-Automata

The intended semantics of a PLC-Automaton $\mathcal{A}$ can be represented by a network $\mathcal{T}(\mathcal{A})$ of two extended timed automata $\mathcal{T}(\mathcal{A}) = \mathcal{C}(\mathcal{A}_{\text{In}}, \mathcal{A}_{\text{Out}})$, one for the input variable In and one for the output variable Out. The network uses

- a clock x to measure the time that the current input is stable,
- a clock y to measure the time spent in current state,
- a clock z to measure the time elapsed in current cycle.

We illustrate this for the PLC-Automaton $\mathcal{A}_t$ of Fig. 1. The timed automaton $\mathcal{A}_{\mathsf{In}}$ is very simple: see Fig. 2. It just generates all possible values of the input variable In, here $\mathsf{In} = tc$ and $\mathsf{In} = th$, and with each new value it resets the clock x to measure (for use in $\mathcal{A}_{\mathsf{Out}}$) how long this value is stable. The guards $x \geq 1$ ensure that the input values are stable for a small amount of time. Before each change of the input value, $\mathcal{A}_{\mathsf{In}}$ offers from its initial *committed* location ℓ^c (indicated by the prefix $c :$) a communication *step*! for the interaction with the test automaton for the requirement given as a CEX formula, to be explained in Sect. 5.2.

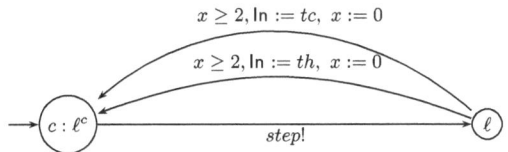

$$x \geq 2, \mathsf{In} := tc, \ x := 0$$
$$x \geq 2, \mathsf{In} := th, \ x := 0$$
$$c : \ell^c \qquad step! \qquad \ell$$

Fig. 2. $\mathcal{A}_{\mathsf{In}}$ with committed *step*! communication

The timed automaton $\mathcal{A}_{\mathsf{Out}}$ determines the value of the output variable Out by modelling the phases polling, computing, possibly with delays, and updating of the PLC cycle. To this end, it uses all three clocks x, y, z mentioned above. For the PLC-Automaton $\mathcal{A}_t$ of Fig. 1 it is shown in Fig. 3. It has also committed locations where a communication *step*! for the interaction with the test automaton is offered. These are shown by the shaded areas.

We see that for $i \in \{0, 1, 2\}$ each state q_i of the PLC-Automaton $\mathcal{A}$ gives rise to five locations in $\mathcal{A}_{\mathsf{Out}}$: the *committed* location $q_{i,p}^c$ with a *step*! communication leading to the location $q_{i,p}$ for polling, the location $q_{i,c}$ for computing with the location $q_{i,d}$ for handling delays, and the location $q_{i,u}$ for updating the output variable Out. In the initial location $q_{0,p}^c$, the clocks y and z are assumed to be at 0. In each location (except the committed ones) the invariant $z \leq \varepsilon$ checks whether the cycle time ε of $\mathcal{A}$, here $\varepsilon = 0.1$, is not exceeded. From the polling location $q_{i,p}$ the new input value is stored a local variable In_P (for "polled In") for inspection in the current cycle. Since checking the inputs is delayed in all states in the PLC-Automatonby values much beyond the cycle time, we can expect some looping through the locations $q_{i,p}^c, q_{i,p}, q_{i,c}$ and $q_{i,d}$ before the clock y exceeds the thresholds 2, 5, and 25, respectively. Only then the value of the polled input In_P results in a (possibly new) value of the output variable Out and a move to the next (possibly new) location committed location $q_{i,p}^c$.

The general definition of $\mathcal{A}_{\mathsf{Out}}$ together with statements of its semantic properties can be found in [19]. The original definition of the timed automata semantics of PLC-Automata is due to [5]. Its relation to the logical semantics based on Duration Calculus has been investigated in [7].

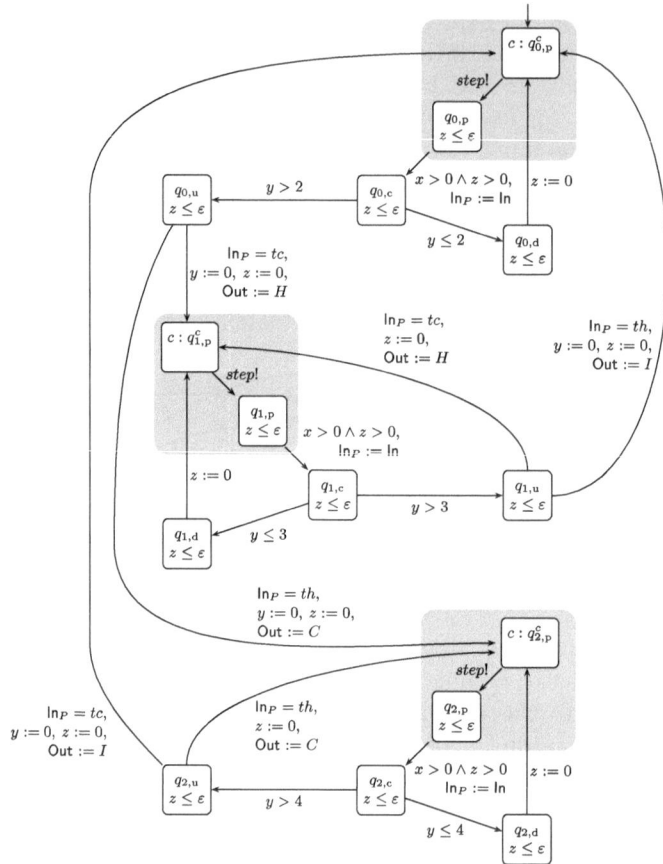

Fig. 3. $\mathcal{A}_{\mathsf{Out}}$, with committed *step!* communications highlighted

5.2 Representing CEX Formulas

Next, we represent CEX formulas as extended timed automata that serve as test automata running in parallel with the timed automata representing the given PLC-Automaton. We illustrate this first for the CEX formula

$$(\text{Syn-1}) \qquad \mathsf{true}\,;\,(\lceil C \wedge tc \rceil \wedge \ell = 4.5)\,;\,\lceil C \rceil\,;\,\mathsf{true}$$

of Example 2. The corresponding test automaton $\mathcal{T}(\text{Syn}-1)$ is shown in Fig. 4. Its aim is to reach the location q_{bad} when a counterexample satisfying the sequence (Syn-1) has been observed.

$\mathcal{T}(\text{Syn}-1)$ uses input actions *step?* to synchronize with corresponding output actions *step!* in the timed automata representing the PLC-Automaton under test. In its initial location q_0, the test automaton accepts arbitrary behavior until it nondeterministically decides to switch to the location q_1, provided the output is C and the input is tc. At this transition the clock z_1 is reset to measure the

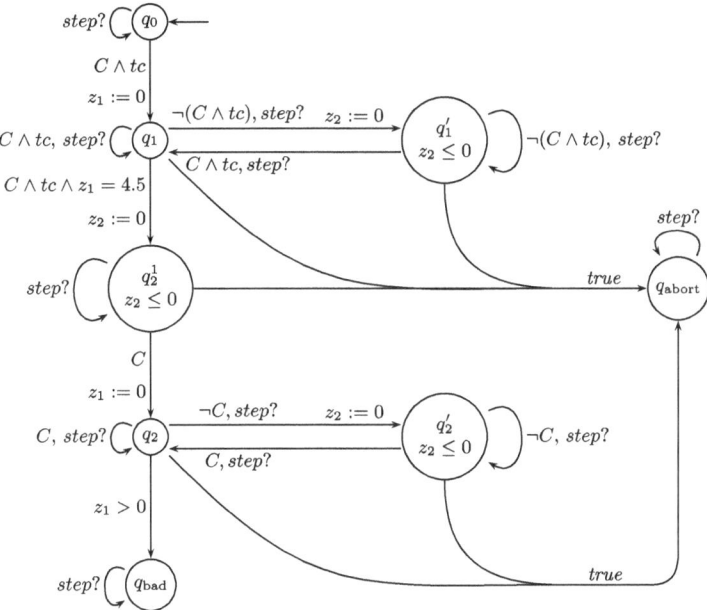

Fig. 4. Test automaton $\mathcal{T}(\text{Syn} - 1)$ for the CEX formula (Syn-1)

duration of the phase $\lceil C \wedge tc \rceil$. When z_1 shows exactly 4.5, a move from q_1 to q_2^1 is enabled. Taking this move, the clock z_2 is reset to make the location q_2^1 urgent by the invariant $z_2 \leq 0$, i.e., it has to be left before the time advances. If the output is still C, the location q_2^1 can be left towards the location q_2, thereby resetting clock z_1. If in q_2 the output remains C and the clock z_1 measures a value beyond 0, the bad location q_{bad} is reachable. This shows that the sequence (Syn-1) has been observed, i.e., a counterexample has been found.

The moves from the location q_1 to q_1' and back take care of the possibility that the state assertion $C \wedge tc$ is *not* valid for a point interval within the phase $\lceil C \wedge tc \rceil$ of (Syn-1). Since the semantics of $\lceil C \wedge tc \rceil$ is insensitive against changes at individual time points, these point intervals must not disturb the overall observation of (Syn-1). Analogously, the moves from q_2 to q_1' and back take care of the possibility that the state assertion C is *not* valid for a point interval within the phase $\lceil C \rceil$ of (Syn-1).

The purpose of $\mathcal{T}(\text{Syn} - 1)$ is to find a sequence of phases satisfying the counterexample (Syn-1). However, the test automaton might fail to do so because it might choose a time point to switch to q_1 when no counterexample can be observed. To avoid a blocking behavior of the test automaton there are unconstrained edges from all appropriate locations towards q_{abort}. One "successful" run of $\mathcal{T}(\text{Syn} - 1)$ to q_{bad} is sufficient for establishing the counterexample (Syn-1).

To deal with the other CEX formulas in Table 1 we applied the pattern of a test automaton for a CEX formula in its general form (1) displayed in Fig. 5.

5.3   Verification using Timed Automata

The verification of $\mathcal{A}_t$ against the CEX formula (Syn-1) then amounts to checking that the network of timed automata

$$\mathcal{C}(\mathcal{A}_{\mathsf{In}}, \mathcal{A}_{\mathsf{Out}}, \mathcal{T}(\mathrm{Syn}-1))$$

never reaches the bad location q_{bad} of $\mathcal{T}(\mathrm{Syn}-1)$. We performed this verification with UPPAAL, Version 5.0. We used a factor 10 for the times in $\mathcal{T}(\mathrm{Syn}-1)$ and the PLC-Automaton $\mathcal{A}_t$ of Fig. 1, so that the cycle time ε becomes 1. In Appendix A, the Figs. 6 and 7 show the UPPAAL timed automata corresponding to $\mathcal{A}_{\mathsf{Out}}$ and $\mathcal{T}(\mathrm{Syn}-1)$ used in the verification.

Also all other 13 CEX formulas of Table 1 have been represented by corresponding timed test automata, following the pattern shown in Fig. 5. In each case, UPPAAL verified that the bad state of the test automaton is never reached. As a further example, we show the somewhat larger UPPAAL timed automaton representing the CEX formula (BdStab-4) in Fig. 8 of Appendix A.

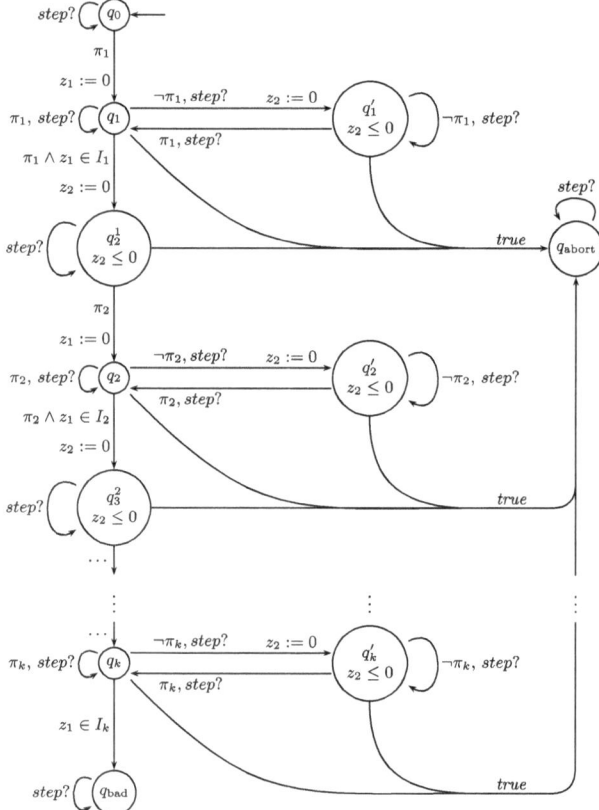

Fig. 5. The pattern of a test automaton for a CEX formula in its general form (1). It is a slightly revised version of the pattern in [19], p.257.

We remark that these positive verification results subtly depend on the choices of the timing conditions. For example, an attempt to verify the modified synchronization requirement

$$(\text{Syn-4}')\qquad \mathsf{true}\,;\,(\lceil I \wedge th \rceil \wedge \ell = 2.1)\,;\,\lceil I \rceil\,;\mathsf{true}$$

with time 2.1 instead of 2.2 in (Syn-4) led to a negative result. As an explanation, we refer to the bounded stability requirement

$$(\text{BdStab-1})\qquad \mathsf{true}\,;\,\lceil \neg I \rceil\,;\,(\lceil I \wedge th \rceil \wedge \ell < 2)\,;\,\lceil \neg I \rceil\,;\mathsf{true}$$

and the tight time bound of $0.1s$ for the cycle of the PLC-Automaton $\mathcal{A}_t$ (see Fig. 1), which is not enough for the desired reaction. In more detail, the CEX formula (BdStab-1) expresses that under the input th, the output I should be stable for at least $2s$, whereas (Syn-4') expresses that after output I and input th have been observed for $2.1s$, the output should change to a value different from I (to avoid the counterexample specified by (Syn-4')). This is not a contradiction to (BdStab-1), but with its cycle time of $0.1s$, the PLC-Automaton $\mathcal{A}_t$ does not guarantee to change the output quickly enough.

For the specific case study in this paper, every verification result, positive or negative, was generated in a few seconds. Thus we did not find the need to use advanced features of UPPAAL, Version 5.0, like randomized algorithms [13].

6 Conclusion

PLC-Automata were inspired by the project UniForM Workbench, where Jan Peleska and Bernd Krieg-Brückner of the University of Bremen collaborated with the author and Alexander Baer of the company Elpro LET in Berlin [15]. The application area was railway control for trams driving in Berlin. The engineers at Elpro used the programming language ST (Structured Text) dedicated for Programmable Logic Controllers (PLCs). In this project, Henning Dierks developed PLC-Automata as an abstract formal model of PLC behavior, having a formal semantics amenable for real-time model checking [5].

The running example in this paper shows that each PLC-Automaton requires in its representation as network of timed automata three clocks. It is well-known that the complexity of verifying timed automata grows exponentially with the number of clocks. So is this approach realistically applicable?

The primary case study in the UniforM project was called "Single-tracked line segment" (SLS): controllers implemented on PLCs had to guarantee that trams driving in opposite directions and sharing a longer segment of a single track obey mutual exclusion. Also other phenomena like the stuttering of sensors had to be taken into account. In [8], several models of SLS in terms of PLC-Automata were verified by representing the timed automata semantics in UPPAAL, augmented with an automatic loop for performing counterexample guided abstraction refinement (CEGAR).

The largest case study using PLC-Automata dealt with an industrial controller of a tramway in the city of Jena, Germany. It was called "Jena Steinweg" after the street where the control was situated and allowed for various movements of trams in that area. The distributed controller was modelled by a network of 114 PLC-Automata [6]. It was not possible to model check the whole system in an acceptable time, but some properties could be checked, for instance that the controller never gives admissions to a piece of track for more than one direction.

For real-time systems with parallel and sequential composition operators, structural transformations may be used to simplify their verification [20]. Applying this approach to PLC-Automata could be of interest for future work.

Acknowledgement. The author thanks Christopher Bischopink for suggesting the example in Sect. 3.

A   UPPAAL Timed Automata

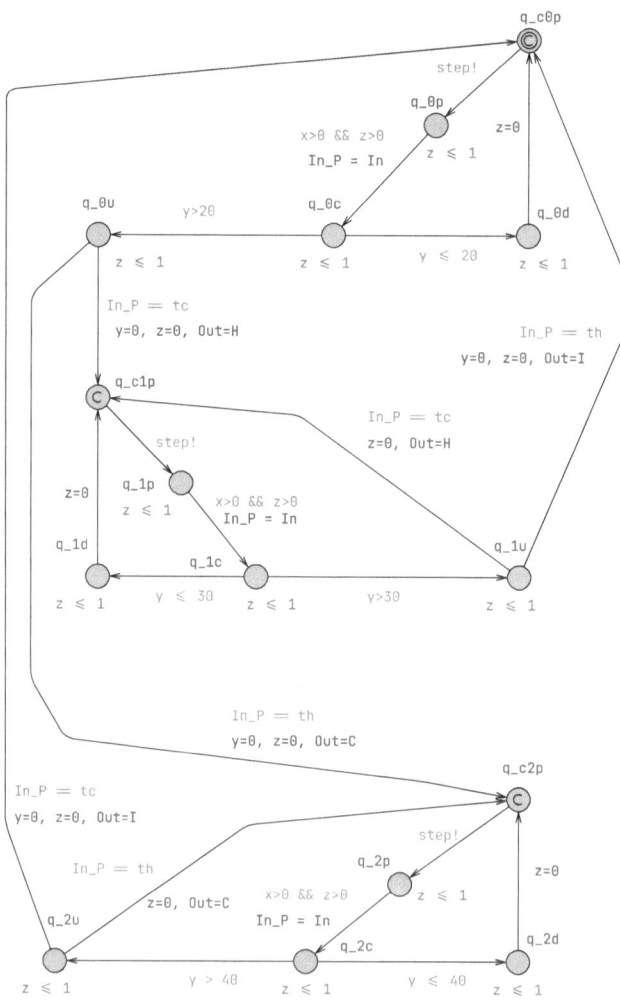

Fig. 6. $\mathcal{A}_{\mathsf{Out}}$ as UPPAAL timed automaton

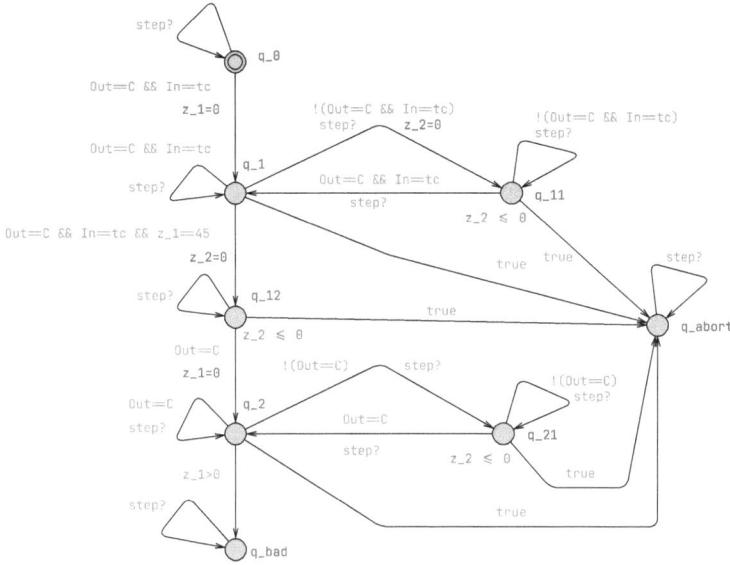

Fig. 7. $\mathcal{T}(\text{Syn} - 1)$ as UPPAAL timed automaton

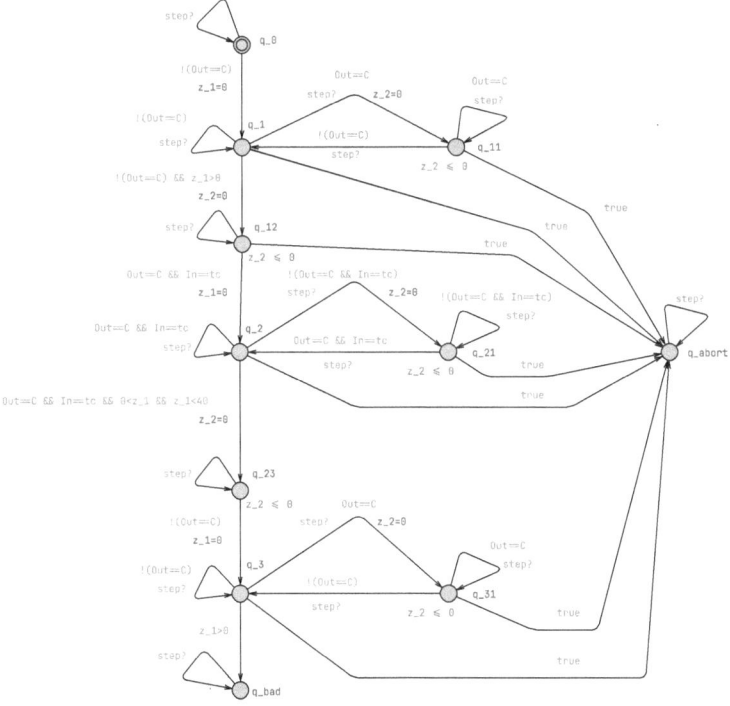

Fig. 8. The CEX formula (BdStab-4) represented as UPPAAL timed automaton

References

1. Alur, R., Courcoubetis, C., Dill, D.L.: Model-checking in dense real-time. Inf. Comput. **104**, 2–34 (1993). https://doi.org/10.1006/INCO.1993.1024
2. Alur, R., Dill, D.L.: A theory of timed automata. Theor. Comput. Sci. **126**, 183–235 (1994). https://doi.org/10.1016/0304-3975(94)90010-8
3. Bengtsson, J., Yi, W.: Timed automata: semantics, algorithms and tools. In: Desel, J., Reisig, W., Rozenberg, G. (eds.) Lectures on Concurrency and Petri Nets, Advances in Petri Nets. LNCS, vol. 3098, pp. 87–124. Springer, Cham (2003). https://doi.org/10.1007/978-3-540-27755-2_3
4. Cassez, F., Henzinger, T.A., Raskin, J.: A comparison of control problems for timed and hybrid systems. In: Tomlin, C.J., Greenstreet, M.R. (eds.) Hybrid Systems: Computation and Control, 5th International Workshop, HSCC 2002, Proceedings. LNCS, vol. 2289, pp. 134–148. Springer (2002). https://doi.org/10.1007/3-540-45873-5
5. Dierks, H.: PLC-automata: a new class of implementable real-time automata. Theor. Comp. Sci. **253**, 61–93 (2001). https://doi.org/10.1016/S0304-3975(00)00089-X
6. Dierks, H.: Time, Abstraction and Heuristics – Automatic Verification and Planning of Timed Systems using Abstraction and Heuristics, Berichte aus dem Department für Informatik, vol. 01-06. Universität Oldenburg (2006), Habilitationsschrift
7. Dierks, H., Fehnker, A., Mader, A., Vaandrager, F.W.: Operational and logical semantics for polling real-time systems. In: Ravn, A.P., Rischel, H. (eds.) Formal Techniques in Real-Time and Fault-Tolerant Systems, 5th International Symposium, FTRTFT'98, Proceedings. LNCS, vol. 1486, pp. 29–40. Springer (1998). https://doi.org/10.1007/BFB0055334
8. Dierks, H., Kupferschmid, S., Larsen, K.G.: Automatic abstraction refinement for timed automata. In: Raskin, J., Thiagarajan, P.S. (eds.) Formal Modeling and Analysis of Timed Systems, 5th International Conference, FORMATS 2007, Proceedings. LNCS, vol. 4763, pp. 114–129. Springer (2007). https://doi.org/10.1007/978-3-540-75454-1
9. Feo-Arenis, S., Vujinovic, M., Westphal, B.: On implementable timed automata. In: Gotsman, A., Sokolova, A. (eds.) Formal Techniques for Distributed Objects, Components, and Systems, FORTE 2020, Proceedings. LNCS, vol. 12136, pp. 78–95. Springer (2020). https://doi.org/10.1007/978-3-030-50086-3
10. Henzinger, T., Nicollin, X., Sifakis, J., Yovine, S.: Symbolic model checking for real-time systems. Inf. Comput. **111**, 193–244 (1994). https://doi.org/10.1006/INCO.1994.1045
11. Hoenicke, J.: Combination of processes, data, and time. Ph.D. Thesis, Report Nr. 9/2006, University of Oldenburg (2006), https://d-nb.info/981576087
12. IEC International Standard 1131-3, Programmable Controllers, Part 3, Programming Languages (1993)
13. Kiviriga, A., Larsen, K.G., Nyman, U.: Randomized reachability analysis in UPPAAL: fast error detection in timed systems. Int. J. Softw. Tools Technol. Trans. **24**(6), 1025–1042 (2022). https://doi.org/10.1007/S10009-022-00681-Z
14. Koymans, R.: Specifying real-time properties with metric temporal logic. Real-Time Syst. **2**, 255–299 (1990). https://doi.org/10.1007/BF01995674

15. Krieg-Brückner, B., Peleska, J., Olderog, E.R., Baer, A.: The UniForM workbench, a universal development environment for formal methods. In: Wing, J.M., Woodcock, J., Davies, J. (eds.) FM'99 – Formal Methods, World Congress on Formal Methods in the Development of Computing Systems, Proceedings, Vol. II. LNCS, vol. 1709, pp. 1186–1205. Springer (1999).https://doi.org/10.1007/3-540-48118-4
16. Larsen, K.G., Petterson, P., Yi, W.: Uppaal in a nutshell. STTT Int. J. Softw. Tools Technol. Trans. **1**, 134–152 (1997). https://doi.org/10.1007/S100090050010
17. Lewis, R.W.: Programming industrial control systems using IEC 1131-3. The Institution of Electrical Engineers (1998). https://doi.org/10.1049/PBCE050E, Revised Edition
18. Milner, R.: Communication and Concurrency. Prentice-Hall International, Hoboken (1989)
19. Olderog, E.R., Dierks, H.: Real-Time Systems - Formal Specification and Automatic Verification. Cambridge University Press, Cambridge (2008). https://doi.org/10.1017/CBO9780511619953
20. Olderog, E.R., Swaminathan, M.: Structural transformations for data-enriched real-time systems. Formal Aspects Comput. **27**(4), 727–750 (2015). https://doi.org/10.1007/S00165-014-0306-Y
21. Ravn, A.P.: Design of embedded real-time computing systems. Tech. Rep. ID-TR 1995-170, Technical University of Denmark (October 1995), Thesis of the degree of Doctor Technics, ISSN 0902-2821
22. Wulf, M.D., Doyen, L., Raskin, J.F.: Almost ASAP semantics: from timed models to timed implementations. Formal Aspects Comput. **17**, 319–341 (2005). https://doi.org/10.1007/S00165-005-0067-8
23. Zhou, C., Hansen, M.R.: Duration calculus: a formal approach to real-time systems. In: Monographs in Theoretical Computer Science. An EATCS Series, Springer (2004). https://doi.org/10.1007/978-3-662-06784-0
24. Zhou, C., Hansen, M.R., Sestoft, P.: Decidability and undecidability results for duration calculus. In: Enjalbert, P., Finkel, A., Wagner, K. (eds.) Symposium on Theoretical Aspects of Computer Science (STACS 93). LNCS, vol. 665, pp. 58–68. Springer, Cham (1993). https://doi.org/10.1007/3-540-56503-5
25. Zhou, C., Hoare, C.A.R., Ravn, A.P.: A calculus of durations. Inf. Process. Lett. **40**, 269–276 (1991). https://doi.org/10.1016/0020-0190(91)90122-X

Nudging Strategies for User Journeys: Take a Path on the Wild Side

Einar Broch Johnsen$^{(\boxtimes)}$ ⓘD, Paul Kobialka ⓘD, Andrea Pferscher ⓘD,
and Silvia Lizeth Tapia Tarifa ⓘD

Department of Informatics, University of Oslo, Oslo, Norway
{einarj,paulkob,andreapf,sltarifa}@ifi.uio.no

Abstract. With the emergence of service orientation as a major business driver, companies crucially depend on understanding the flow of their services from the user's perspective. Models of these *user journeys* help to create a common understanding, but in practice their availability is limited. Process mining addresses the challenge of creating models that enable processes to be analyzed. Our goal is to mine user journey models. In this paper, we use automata learning algorithms to create behavioral models of stochastic user behavior from a given data set. The initially learned automaton is annotated with time and cost variables to capture aspects of the user experience. In a game scenario, we can model check properties of these enriched automata regarding the user behavior. Using UPPAAL, we can synthesize strategies for nudging users into a different behavior. The approach is illustrated in a case study with a large dataset describing user behavior for a well-known music streaming application. Can we synthesize a strategy that nudges a computer science professor to take a path on the wild side of the usual listening habits?

Keywords: User journeys · Nudging · Process discovery · Passive automata learning · UPPAAL

1 Introduction

The servitization of business [46] results in business models shaped by user demand: user satisfaction is critical to the success of a business, and directly impacts financial rewards [21]. Consequently, businesses invest in improving the user experience they offer to their users. User journeys describe the actual communication and interaction between service provider and user, when engaging in a service, from the user's point of view. Traditionally, user journeys are modeled and analyzed manually, based on, e.g., questionnaires addressing selected users to identify the experienced user journey and the associated user satisfaction (e.g. [23,42]). Although successful, this approach to the modeling and analysis

This work is part of the *Smart Journey Mining* project, funded by the Research Council of Norway (Grant No. 312198).

of user journeys comes with inherent restrictions [24]: it lacks tool support for automated analysis and does not scale beyond a very limited number of users.

The analysis of user journeys can also be achieved by data-driven formal methods. In a series of papers [29–33], we have explored how formal models can be generated from the event logs of digital services and automatically analyzed using existing tool-supported analysis methods. In this line of work, we have used process mining techniques [1] to generate automata from event logs. The extracted automata can be extended into *weighted automata* [11]; the weights can reflect a notion of user experience as aggregated values computed from numerous actual user journeys recorded in the event logs. The generated automata can be analyzed using model-checking tools such as UPPAAL [35]. The automata can be further transformed into *weighted games*, modeling the interactions between the users and the service provider. To capture the underlying stochasticity of these interactions, the weighted games can be further extended into *stochastic weighted games* [30]. Using tools such as UPPAAL STRATEGO [19] and PRISM-games [16], these *user journey games* can be analyzed, e.g., to derive optimal strategies, thus providing strategic recommendations for service providers to guide their users through the service. These strategies can again form the basis for actor-based simulations in tools such as ABS [10,27,28].

In this paper, we review the ideas underlying data-driven formal methods for user journey analysis, starting from a large data set: the event logs of the music streaming service Spotify [12]. We are interested in whether model-checking techniques can be used to derive nudging strategies [45] for selected user groups; for example, can we identify a strategy for the music streaming service that optimizes for changing the musical taste of a computer science professor? The crucial events to analyze are the *skip* actions of a user when streaming music, which suggests dissatisfaction or impatience with the track proposed by the algorithm (e.g., [37]). In this paper, we explore techniques for *passive automata learning* [22] to generate *probabilistic, timed games* from event logs. To this aim, we extend our previous work on stochastic user journey games [30] to account for timing properties. We further extend the resulting user journey games with *user profiles* that identify the initial states of the games we consider. Our objective is to use the resulting probabilistic and timed games to find the optimal strategy for the music streaming service, that nudges the professor to be adventurous and take a path on the wild side through the user journey game.

2   Preliminaries

Let X^* denote the finite, ordered sequences (or traces) $x_0 \cdot x_1 \ldots x_{n-1}$ over a set X, with $x_i \in X$ for $0 \leq i < n$ and $n \in \mathbb{N}$ is the length of the sequence. Let ϵ denote the empty sequence, $s \cdot s'$ the concatenation of sequences s, s', and x the singleton sequence for any $x \in X$. We write $\mathcal{B}(X)$ for the set of multisets over X.

2.1   Event Logs

An *event log* [1] records the behavior of a system as sequences of observed events. The set of observable events A of an event log is called its *alphabet*.

Definition 1 (Event log [1]). *An* event log $\mathcal{T}$ *over an alphabet A is a multiset of traces over A, $\mathcal{T} \in \mathcal{B}(A^*)$.*

2.2   Automata Learning

Automata learning is a technique to automatically generate behavioral models from a sample, which is a set of system traces. The goal of automata learning algorithms is to generate an automaton that models the unknown language of the system under learning (SUL). Depending on the way the sample is generated, we distinguish between two learning paradigms: active and passive learning. Active learning algorithms interact with the SUL to generate the sample, instead passive learning algorithms use a given sample.

We here focus on passive learning from a given event log. Many passive learning algorithms assume that the sample contains *positive* traces that are part of the language of the SUL, as well as *negative* traces that are not part of the language. Angluin [7] showed that by considering specific attributes of the sample, e.g., the distribution of the actions, positive samples are sufficient to learn an accurate model. Alergia [13] has shown that considering certain properties of the sample, e.g. the distribution of events, makes it possible to learn an accurate model only from positive samples. To learn Markov chains, we consider a variant of Alergia that is available in the state-of-the-art machine learning library AALPY [38]. This variant of Alergia starts with the creation of a *frequency prefix tree acceptor* from an event log $\mathcal{T}$:

Definition 2 (Frequency prefix tree acceptor (FPTA)). *An* FPTA *is a tuple $\mathcal{P} = \langle Q, q_0, A, E, F, L \rangle$, where*

- *Q is the finite set of states,*
- *$q_0 \in Q$ is the initial state (or root),*
- *A is the observable universe of events,*
- *$E \subseteq Q \times Q$ is the set of directed transitions between states,*
- *$F: E \to \mathbb{N}$ is a labeling function assigning frequencies to transitions, and*
- *$L: Q \to A$ is a labeling function for states with events from the alphabet A.*

A *path* is a sequence $q_0 \cdot q_1 \ldots q_m$ of states such that there are transitions $q_{i-1} \to q_i$ for all $0 < i \leq m$. Traces $t \in A^*$ can be obtained by applying the event-labeling function L to each element of a path $q_0 \cdot q_1 \ldots q_m$; i.e., $t = L(q_0) \cdot L(q_1) \ldots L(q_m)$.

The FPTA created by Alergia is a concise representation of the underlying event log $\mathcal{T}$, where each path in the FPTA represents a prefix of a trace $t \in \mathcal{T}$ in the event log. To ensure that there is a single initial state, we let all traces start with an identical event. If two traces have equal prefixes, they share the same path for the prefix. A frequency assigned to the transition indicates the cumulative number of traces that share this transition in their path. After the tree construction, Alergia merges the states of the tree to create a Markov chain. The state merging is done from the root (the initial state) to the leaves, coloring the states to indicate possible merge candidates, with suitable merge candidates having the same event labels. Let $q \to q'$ be a transition from state q to state q', with $(q, q') \in E$. The auxiliary function $out(q)$ defines the number of outgoing transitions from a state $q \in Q$, i.e., the number of elements of the set $\{q' | q \to q' \in E\}$. The compatibility check between two states $q, q' \in Q$ is based on the Hoeffding bound [26], which defines that the two states are equal if

$$\left| \frac{F(q \to q_x)}{out(q)} - \frac{F(q' \to q_y)}{out(q')} \right| \leq \sqrt{\frac{1}{2} \log \frac{2}{\alpha}} \left(\frac{1}{\sqrt{out(q)}} + \frac{1}{\sqrt{out(q')}} \right), \quad (1)$$

where $L(q_x) = L(q_y)$. The parameter $\alpha \in (0, 1]$ represents a *confidence parameter* that allows the probability of the merging state to be adjusted based on the assumptions of the underlying event log. Thus, if we assume that the event log adequately represents the underlying distribution of the SUL, we should set α low, otherwise, α should be set higher to account for likely larger differences between the compared states due to missing observations. If two states can be merged, we accumulate the frequencies at outgoing transitions to the same states. If no further states can be merged, the Alergia variant for learning Markov chains updates the accumulated frequencies for the transitions to probabilities such that they fulfill the requirements of the probabilistic state transition function (see Def. 3). Alergia then returns the Markov chain that was finally generated.

2.3   Markov Chains

A *Markov chain* [40] defines the observable random behavior of a system by a finite state machine. On a semantic level, the behavior defined by the Markov chain implements a Markov process, i.e., the future behavior only depends on the current state independent from the history of events. Let $Dist(X)$ be a set of probability distributions over a finite set X, where for each $\mu \in Dist(X)$, $\mu \colon X \to [0, 1]$ and $\sum_{x \in X} \mu(x) = 1$ holds.

Definition 3 (Markov chain). *A Markov chain is a tuple $\mathcal{M} = \langle Q, q_0, A, \delta, L \rangle$, where*

- *Q is a finite set of states,*
- *$q_0 \in Q$ is an initial state,*
- *A is an observable universe of events,*
- *$\delta \colon Q \to Dist(Q)$ is a partial stochastic state transition function, and*
- *$L \colon Q \to A$ is a state labeling function.*

Note that δ is a partial function, hence we do not require for all $q \in Q$ to be defined in δ. Let $Q' \subseteq Q$ be the set for which δ is defined. $\mathcal{M}$ *is* deterministic *iff* $\forall q \in Q', \forall q', q'' \in Q \colon \delta(q)(q') > 0 \land \delta(q)(q'') > 0 \implies q' = q'' \lor L(q') \neq L(q'')$.

2.4   Priced Timed Systems under Stochastic Behavior

Markov chains can be extended by (1) considering the passage of time, (2) extending the state transition function for dedicated actions to determine the distribution of successor states, (3) accounting for journey experience features as costs/weights, and (4) separating controllable from uncontrollable actions.

Stochastic timed automata (STAs) [39] extend Markov chains with timed behavior. STAs account for timed behavior via real-valued clock variables that define invariants *inv* on states and constraints *enab* that enable transitions, and allow for multiple actions each leading to a distribution of successor states (thereby implementing the Markov chain extensions (1) and (2)). Clocks are non-negative, real-valued variables. Let $\mathcal{C}$ denote a (finite) set of *clocks*. The set $\mathcal{G}(\mathcal{C})$ of *clock constraints* consists of Boolean constraints $c \sim x$ over clock variables $c \in \mathcal{C}$, a comparison parameter $\sim \in \{\leq, <, >, \geq\}$ and a constant $x \in \mathbb{N}$. The *clock valuation* function $\nu\colon \mathcal{C} \to \mathbb{R}_{\geq 0}$ maps clocks to their current value. We write $\nu \models g$ if the clock valuation ν fulfills the clock constraint g Let $\nu + x$ express that the value of every clock $c \in \mathcal{C}$ is increased by a constant $x \in \mathbb{R}_{\geq 0}$ and let $\nu[r]$ express that all clocks $c \in r$ are reset to zero, where $r \subseteq \mathcal{C}$.

Definition 4 (Stochastic timed automata (STAs)[39]). *A stochastic timed automaton (STA) is a tuple* $\mathcal{A} = (Q, q_0, A, \mathcal{C}, \Sigma, inv, enab, prob, L)$*, where*

- Q, q_0, A, L *are defined as for Markov chains,*
- $\mathcal{C}$ *is a finite set of clocks,*
- Σ *is a finite set of actions,*
- $inv\colon Q \to \mathcal{G}(\mathcal{C})$ *maps states to their invariants,*
- $enab\colon Q \times \Sigma \to \mathcal{G}(\mathcal{C})$ *is a transition-enabling condition function, and*
- $prob\colon Q \times \Sigma \to Dist(2^{\mathcal{C}} \times Q)$ *is a (partial) stochastic transition function.*

We briefly outline the semantics of STAs (for further details, see Norman *et al.* [39]): States of STAs are pairs $(q, \nu) \in Q \times \mathbb{R}_{\geq 0}^{\mathcal{C}}$ such that all invariants are satisfied, $\nu \models inv(q)$. In each state (q, ν), a time elapse $t \in \mathbb{R}_{\geq 0}$ is possible if the invariants $inv(q)$ are continuously satisfied, resulting in state $(q, \nu + t)$, or an enabled action $a \in \Sigma$ is taken to decide on a stochastic transition from the current state. An action $a \in \Sigma$ is *enabled* in state (q, ν) if $\nu \models enab(q, a)$. A state (q, ν) is *urgent* if no time can elapse in q.

Stochastic priced timed automata (SPTAs). An SPTA is an STA extended with *price variables*. We consider functions $P\colon Q \to \mathbb{R}_{\geq 0}$ that assign a rate for the accumulation of prices while time passes in a state. Price variables are monotonic, real-valued variables that account for resources spent while halting in states. States may utilize an exponential rate of increase for price variables, incurred constantly within a state. For formal definitions of priced timed automata on a semantic level, we refer to Behrman *et al.* [9]. Figure 3 depicts an SPTA including the price variables: `acousticness_c` and `duration_c`.

Stochastic priced timed games (SPTGs). An SPTG divides the set Σ of actions of an SPTA into controllable actions Σ_c and uncontrollable actions Σ_u. In, e.g., the synthesis of a strategy, the controller can only select actions in Σ_c and the analysis is conducted under a worst-case assumption about the actions Σ_u, i.e., without insights into which actions would be chosen by the environment.

Model checking of games. UPPAAL [35] is a tool that allows the modeling, simulation, and verification of timed systems. The tool can be used to synthesize controllers [8] for systems considering timed and stochastic behavior [19]. UPPAAL can also synthesize cost-optimal strategies by considering real-valued cost variables and cost rates [34]. The UPPAAL STRATEGO extension allows game settings, which are by now integrated into the latest UPPAAL version. *Strategies* assign a set of actions to each state that guarantee or optimize a certain outcome. Further details on the computation of strategies can be found in [14,18].

User journey games (UJGs) [33] can be modeled as SPTGs by assigning the controllable actions to the service provider and the uncontrollable actions to the user. Analysis for a UJG is user-centric since it does not constrain the user in its possible actions and it requires the service provider to guide the user through the system. In our previous work, we explored the use of strategies for user journey games [29,31–33], for among others, highlighting changes in the UJG over time, and game theoretic reductions to discover outcome determining interactions. In this paper, we are going to use strategies to nudge users toward exploring other alternative behaviors in the UJG.

3   Method

We now explain our method to generate a UJG for nudging users in terms of a concrete case study. The method allows us to automatically create behavioral models from event logs by learning Markov chains and enriching them to an STA with meta-data in the dataset from which the event log is generated. First, we explain the process of converting the dataset into an event log and extracting features from the dataset to create an STA. We then lift the created STA to an SPTG by separating actions into controllable and uncontrollable, where the controller takes deterministic actions, and the environment performs stochastic actions. All resources and code are published online in the project's repository.[1]

3.1   Case Study: The Music-Streaming User Journey

We consider a case study in which users interact with a music streaming service provider to listen to music. Users listen to tracks in listening sessions. Depending on the context, the service provider suggests or selects tracks for the user. The user responds by deciding whether to listen to or skip each particular track.

---

[1] https://github.com/smartjourneymining/spotify_journey/releases/tag/wang2024

Thus, the user journey consists of back-and-forth interaction between user and service provider. This scenario can be understood as a user journey in which both the service provider and user are interested in maximizing the listening time while minimizing the number of skips. The goal of the case study is to synthesize *nudging strategies*, concretely, to use the inferred user journey game to nudge users toward a different musical taste. Our case study uses the *Music-Streaming Sessions Dataset* (MSSD), provided by Brost *et al.* [12].

Brost *et al.* [12] present six *challenges* targeting techniques to predict the skipping of tracks given a session prefix. Due to a lack of datasets recording rich user interactions within a system, the accompanying MSSD that records user interactions with the listened tracks, has been made available online.[2] The proposed challenges are mainly aimed at research on recommender systems, e.g., recommendations for long-term user satisfaction or proactive recommendations and interventions. However, *Challenge 4* targets the evaluation of "user journeys" under the consideration of "user moods", i.e. the analysis of profiles for musical taste. The method described in our paper is concerned with using the MSSD to nudge users towards a different musical taste profile.

The full dataset contains 160 million listening sessions with 3.7 million unique tracks recorded by the music streaming platform Spotify. Each session contains 10–20 different tracks; shorter sessions are excluded and longer sessions are truncated to 20 tracks to protect user's privacy. Sessions record the listened tracks and additional user interactions, the listening context (e.g., a pre-generated playlist or a personal playlist), whether the track was skipped, and whether the user took a short or long pause before playing the track. Sessions are recorded individually and are not linked to other sessions by the same user. The track dataset is accompanied by metadata about the tracks containing characteristics such as acoustics, danceability, energy, and many more. MSSD further includes a "sample" version, recording 10 000 listening sessions, which we use in the remainder of the paper to demonstrate our method. An excerpt of the dataset is shown in Table 1, the session information is displayed in Table 1a, and the track information in Table 1b.

3.2 Disentangling the Music-Streaming User Journey

To model the user journey, we utilize several aspects of the information recorded in the MSSD. As a first step, we parse the tabular records of the MSSD by grouping tracks by their sessions in the order they were played. Each recorded session is then processed to include a designated *start state* (start session) and a *start profile state* (startprofile) that is computed by averaging track metadata of the first five listened tracks. From there on, the service provider and user engage in a loop of entering a listening context, proposing tracks and reacting to tracks. If the current listening context is controllable, i.e., the *context state* (select context$_i$) corresponds to "radio", "editorial playlists", "charts", or "personalized playlists", the service provider chooses the next track by selecting a *song state*

---

[2] https://www.aicrowd.com/challenges/spotify-sequential-skip-prediction-challenge

Table 1. Excerpt from the Music-Streaming Sessions Dataset (MSSD) [12]. The dataset can split into two tables, where Table Table 1a provides streaming session information and Table Table 1b includes metadata about the individual tracks.

SessionID	Session Position	TrackID	...	Not skipped
2d8ead1e	1	a19d63a	...	TRUE
2d8ead1e	2	s8d42lo	...	FALSE
a9082maw	1	ao8r7n4	...	TRUE
633e57da	1	a19d63a	...	TRUE
⋮	⋮	⋮	...	⋮

(a) Excerpt of music session data.

TrackID	Duration	Acousticness	Danceability	...	Energy
a19d63a	103.74	0.37	0.39	...	0.82
s8d42lo	185.28	0.82	0.48	...	0.17
ao8r7n4	159.59	0.93	0.48	...	0.36
l92bz48	362.63	0.47	0.57	...	0.49
⋮	⋮	⋮	⋮	...	⋮

(b) Excerpt of track metadata.

($song_i$); otherwise the *context state* corresponds to "catalog" or "user collection", and some track is played by randomly selecting a *played state* ($played_i$). (We use *track* when we do not want to differentiate user selection from service selection; in the sequel, a *track state* is either a song state or a played state.) The user responds to the track by either skipping it or listening to it completely. MSSD contains different binary skipping information, called **Skip_1**, **Skip_2**, and **Skip_3**. The different flags indicate when the track has been skipped. For example, **Skip_1** is true if a track is skipped shortly after the start, whereas **Skip_3** would also include very late skips. As suggested in the MSSD challenge, we use the field **Skip_2** from the dataset as ground truth for skipping tracks, thereby ignoring short skips towards the end of a track. Further, the user may take a break from a listening session and return afterward to a context in which a new track is chosen. The *end state* (end) marks the end of a recorded listening session. We constrain sessions to include exactly 20 tracks, the maximum length of sessions in the MSSD, though any other number of tracks could have been chosen. Sessions that are shorter than 20 tracks are not part of the event log. Figure 1 summarizes the overall structure of the considered music-streaming user journey. Solid transitions represent controllable and dashed transitions uncontrollable actions. Circles (○) represent stochastic branching points.

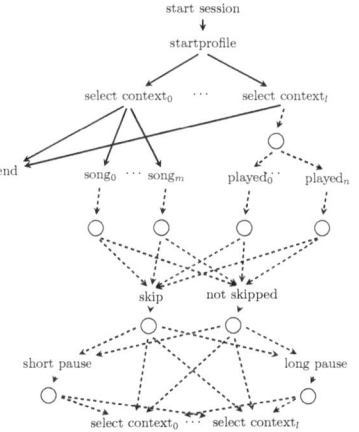

Fig. 1. The basic layout of a music-streaming user journey.

3.3 User Profiles for Musical Taste

A user profile for musical taste can be represented by a vector in which the components reflect the musical

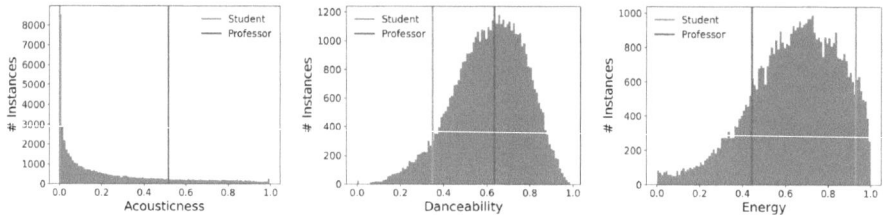

Fig. 2. Histograms over track features in the MSSD. We also indicate the user profiles of the professor and student in the histograms.

user preferences in terms of the features described in the metadata of the tracks, e.g., danceability, energy, etc.

For our case study, we collected two real user profiles: one representing the musical preferences of a professor[3] and the other representing those of a Ph.D. student, both in computer science. The profiles were constructed by querying the Spotify API for the long-term favorite tracks of the subjects in question by a Python script using the *spotipy*[4] library, and averaging quantitative track features. For simplicity, we concentrated on a subset of the available metadata features, including the three features that maximized the difference between the two profiles: *acousticness*, *danceability*, and *energy*. Each track gets an associated a feature vector $\mathbf{f} \in \mathbb{N}_{\geq 0}^3$, constructed by the following structure: $\mathbf{f} := \langle acousticness, danceability, energy \rangle$. Figure 2 shows the two profiles over the histograms of track features in the MSSD. Observe that the user profile of the student tends towards the *"wild side"* with respect to acousticness, danceability and energy (i.e., a musical preference in the direction of heavy metal). Consequently, we use the professor profile as the start profile $\mathbf{s}$ to be nudged, targeting the student's profile $\mathbf{t}$. To unify the representation of all track features, we multiply the track features that are originally in the range $[0,1]$, by 10 and round down, to lift them to the range $[0,10] \cap \mathbb{N}_{\geq 0}$. The start profile then becomes $\mathbf{s} := \langle 5,6,4 \rangle$, and the target profile $\mathbf{t} := \langle 0,3,9 \rangle$.

3.4   Learning the Structure of the Music-Streaming User Journeys

We now describe how session and track information are parsed into sequences of observed events to create an event log. We then explain how this event log is used to learn the stochastic structure of the process, following Sect. 2.2.

From Dataset to Event Log. We preprocess the MSSD according to the structure depicted in Fig. 1 for the creation of an event log. After identifying the individual sessions, we generate the user profile for each session. The user profile is the averaged track metadata of the first five listened tracks.

---

[3] The particular individual is not an author of this paper.
[4] https://github.com/spotipy-dev/spotipy

Applying Abstractions to the Event Log. To reduce the number of included sessions and thereby reduce the learning time, we filtered the sessions in the event log by the start and target user profiles **s** and **t**. Only sessions with a profile **p** with a distance $\leq k$ from **s** and **t** in each profile dimension are retained. Thus, remaining user journeys have a start profile **p** satisfying:

$$\forall_{i \in [0,\ldots,|\mathbf{p}|-1]} \quad \mathbf{p}_i \geq \min(\mathbf{s}_i, \mathbf{t}_i) - k \wedge \mathbf{p}_i \leq \max(\mathbf{s}_i, \mathbf{t}_i) + k. \tag{2}$$

In our experiments, we set $k := 1$, resulting in a total of 8 600 included sessions.

We encode tracks according to the year the track was released, e.g. 1990 or 2010, its key (related to scale, either "major" or "minor"), and the three discretized track features. With this encoding, similar tracks are grouped into the same event. Additionally, different states are introduced for tracks proposed by the service provider, to model the later controllable actions in the UJG, and tracks selected by the user, the later uncontrollable actions, resulting in multiple states for the same track. An example of an event sequence with two tracks is:

start · startprofile$\langle 5, 6, 4 \rangle$ · select_context(radio) · song_2010_minor_$\langle 2, 7, 8 \rangle$
· not_skipped · select_context(user_playlist) · played_1990_major$\langle 4, 7, 3 \rangle$ ...

Discovering the Underlying Behavioral Model. We use the Alergia automata learning algorithm for Markov chains (see Sect. 2.2) to learn the stochastic structure of the underlying user journey. Automata learning allows us to automatically generate stochastic models from large datasets in a reasonable amount of time. In the following, we extend the learned Markov chain to a UJG used to nudge users from their start profile to a target profile.

3.5   Generating Music-Streaming User Journeys

The learned Markov chain describes the stochastic structure of the user journey. We now extend the Markov chain with timed behavior, costs, and controllable and uncontrollable actions to create a UJG, following Sect. 2.4.

When streaming music from a platform, the passage of time is an important characteristic. In our work, we model a user getting used to different track profiles by aggregating the track features over the actual listening times; i.e., the longer a user listens to an energetic track, the more energy is accumulated. Therefore, we extend the learned Markov chain with real-valued clock variables that capture the time spent while listening to tracks, resulting in an STA (see Def. 4). Here, we use the track durations as logged in the MSSD.

Figure 3 depicts a simplified UJG, including two user profiles and three tracks. The UJG defines one clock variable c that is used to model listening and pausing times. The clock progresses only in states where the user actively spends time by either listening to a track or taking a pause; all other states are marked as urgent, meaning that they progress to the next state immediately. For simplicity, we define constants for short and long pauses that determine the duration during which a user can dwell in the paused states. The states where a track is selected are also urgent and lead immediately to the skip or not skipped states while setting a minimum and maximum listening time. The *maximum listening time* is set to be the maximum track duration in minutes over all tracks aggregated in the targeted track state. The *minimum listening time* is set to be the minimum track duration over all aggregated tracks in the targeted track state, if the track is not skipped. Otherwise, when the track is skipped, it is set to be the aggregated minimum minus one, capped to be at least one. For example, the state not_skipped_1 of the UJG in Fig. 3, defines an invariant limiting the dwell time to the maximum listening time, where the earliest possible time to leave is regulated by the minimum listening time.

We extend the STA to an SPTA (Sect. 2.4) by adding *price* variables for duration, acousticness, danceability, and energy. Transitions from song and played states update variables storing update ratios for each price variable, which are set as invariant in the skipped and not skipped states. We use discretized values for the continuous features as ratios; e.g., listening to a long track with high energy accumulates more energy than listening to a short track with high energy or a long track with low energy. Skipping sets each ratio to a constant of one; a basic increase is accumulated but insignificant. Duration is accumulated at the same rate as time passes. For readability, the music-streaming UJG shown in Fig. 3 only considers one feature, acousticness. In the example, the played track played_X has high acousticness, which is considered if the track is not skipped.

In the final step of our transformation, we build a UJG by partitioning the set of actions into *controllable* and *uncontrollable* actions, see Fig. 1. We resolve the stochastic observations in the learned Markov chain that are controlled by the service provider by neglecting the learned probabilities and defining these actions to be deterministic. For these actions, the service provider can deterministically propose a track $song_i$ from the controllable contexts. In Fig. 3 uncontrollable actions are dashed, whereas controllable ones are solid. For example, the state editorial_playlist defines a listening context that is controlled by the service provider, therefore song_Y and song_Z can be selected by the controller. However, skipping a track is, e.g., controlled by the user. To account for the user behavior in the event log, we annotate the uncontrollable transitions with the probabilities in the learned Markov chain. For example, if the controller chooses song_Y, then the environment skips the track with a probability of 0.1.

By controlling the confidence bound in Alergia, we control the sensitivity by which states are considered to be equal and thus merged. Therefore, the confidence parameter α, see Sect. 2.2, allows to influence the structure of resulting music-streaming user journeys. We illustrate the effect of α by a simplified UJG shown in Fig. 4, which includes two tracks song_X and song_Y. In these user journeys, the probabilities of skipping song_X change, if the user previously listened to song_X. Choosing a higher α results in journeys as depicted in Fig. 4, where we can see two states representing song_X.

In the future, we plan to extend the model generation to Markov decision processes, which will allow us to have a precise differentiation between actions that are controllable by the service provider and by the user.

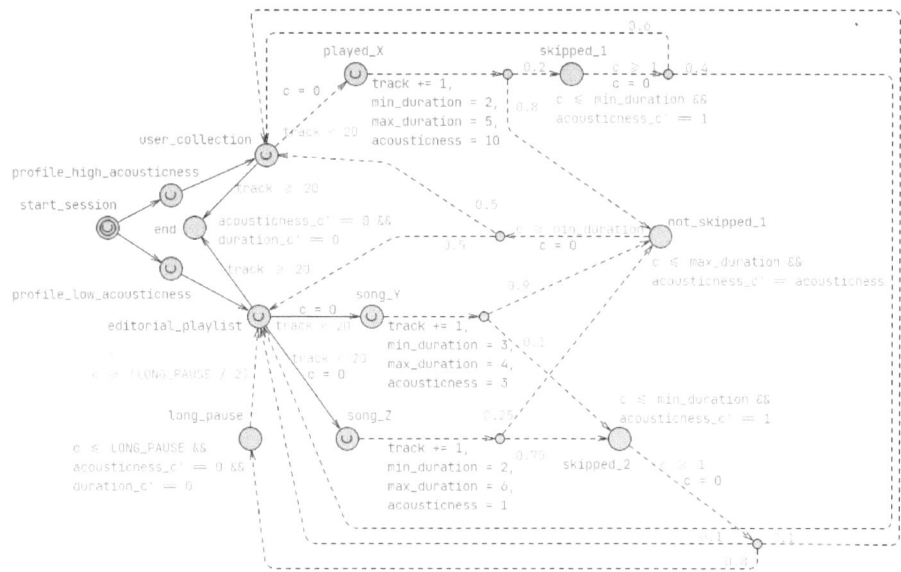

Fig. 3. User journey game modeling music-streaming user journeys that contain some elements of the basic structure shown in Fig. 1. The model considers two user profiles (**profile_high_acousticness**, **profile_low_acousticness**) and three different track categories (**played_X**, **song_Y**, **song_Z**).

3.6   Synthesizing Nudging Strategies

We use UPPAAL to generate service provider strategies to nudge a user from her user profile towards a target profile by synthesizing a strategy that optimizes track features towards the target profile. According to the differences between the concrete start (the professor) and target (the student) profiles (Sect. 3.3), we minimize acousticness and danceability, and maximize energy and duration; visiting the start profile is encoded as a boolean flag. To evaluate the achieved nudging, we compare it to a random strategy, which selects tracks randomly.

UPPAAL synthesizes strategies by optimizing values, including clocks, represented by variables that can be used to define verification queries. For example, to maximize acousticness in the UJG shown in Fig. 4, we could propose song_X from the start, risking many skips. However, by first proposing song_Y and then—unless this track is skipped—proposing song_X, the chances of the user not skipping this track increase, thereby increasing the accumulated acousticness. The strategy synthesized by UPPAAL should comply with this observation. The strategy for nudging a user towards a different user profile is computed by:

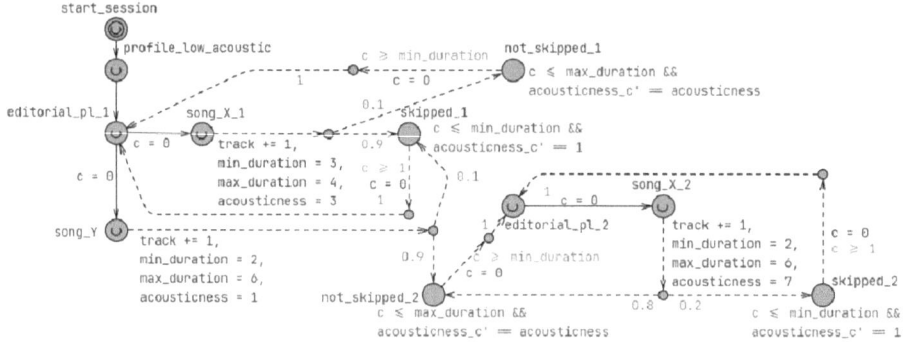

Fig. 4. Concatenated UJG.

```
strategy nudge = maxE(-danceability_c - 3*acousticness_c + energy
    +duration_c) [<= 1000]{MusicJourney.location, visited_start}
      ->{danceability_c, acousticness_c, duration_c, energy_c}:
         <> MusicJourney.end && visited.
```

We introduce the flag visited, which is set to TRUE when the state start-profile for the given start profile s was visited, and a weight of 3 for the acousticness as its expected maximum under a random strategy is only a third of danceability and energy. To facilitate more efficient learning, we consider only MusicJourney.location, visited_start, and the four price clocks to be observable. After generating the nudging strategy, we evaluate the expected achieved maximum for feature

$$f \in \{duration\_c, danceability\_c, acousticness\_c, energy\_c\}$$

under strategy nudge for 10 000 runs:

$$E[<=1000; 10000] \ (max: \ f) \ under \ nudge$$

and compare it to the achieved maximum by a random strategy:

$$E[<=1000; 10000] \ (max: \ f).$$

The exported strategy stores a mapping from states to actions and the reward for each action in each state. We parse the file to gain insights into which actions are recommended and how the nudging traverses the UJG.

4   Evaluation

We generate a UJG from the event log based on the MSSD. We then synthesize a strategy to nudge a person from a given start user profile towards a

Table 2. Comparison of generated nudging strategies and random track selection. The aim is to decrease acousticness and danceability, and increase duration and energy. The presented numbers show improvement of nudging in percentage, averaged over 10 synthesized strategies, for different confidence values α.

α	Feature	random	nudge	α	Feature	random	nudge
0.1	Acousticness	90.35	-42.83%	0.999	Acousticness	89.70	-40.49%
0.1	Danceability	232.15	-2.77%	0.999	Danceability	232.03	-6.98%
0.1	Duration	50.09	+14.82%	0.999	Duration	50.15	+9.84%
0.1	Energy	235.13	+37.34%	0.999	Energy	235.11	+33.56%
0.6	Acousticness	90.54	-37.29%	0.9999	Acousticness	90.09	-40.0%
0.6	Danceability	232.28	-3.63%	0.9999	Danceability	232.00	-2.4%
0.6	Duration	50.10	+13.84%	0.9999	Duration	50.07	+9.5%
0.6	Energy	235.49	+39.62%	0.9999	Energy	235.52	+29.73%
0.9	Acousticness	90.12	-36.46%	0.9999999999999	Acousticness	90.26	-39.5%
0.9	Danceability	232.31	+1.92%	0.9999999999999	Danceability	232.38	-4.33%
0.9	Duration	50.09	+17.35%	0.9999999999999	Duration	50.08	+13.33%
0.9	Energy	235.33	+45.43%	0.9999999999999	Energy	234.93	+39.26%

target user profile. The quantified achieved nudging is measured and collected when analyzing the different UJGs resulting from the different learned automata, when using Alergia with different confidence bounds. As described in Sect. 3.6, we then compare the expected feature values of our synthesized strategy with the expected feature values of a random strategy. Additionally, we investigate the path traversed by executing the nudging strategy and highlight the best tracks for nudging a professor to *"take a path on the wild side"* of musical taste.

All experiments were performed on a laptop with 32 GB memory and an i7-1165G7 Intel processor, and were implemented in Jupyter Notebooks using Python 3.10.6. The resources are published in an online repository.[5] For automata learning, we used AALPY [38], version 1.3.3, and for the synthesis of the strategies, we used UPPAAL 5.0.0.[6]

In Table 2, we collect estimates for all four features under the nudging strategy against the random strategy, entries for nudging are given in percentage of the measured change in comparison to random. Note that our nudging strategy aims to minimize acousticness and danceability while maximizing duration and energy. An experiment (one entry in the table) consists of synthesizing 10 strategies with the default parameters for UPPAAL's Q-learning implementation [47], we then average the calculated estimates. The synthesis of multiple strategies aims to compensate for imprecisions due to the limited exploration budget of the Q-learning setup for the given state space of the underlying UJG. We repeat these experiments for the different confidence values α that were used for learning the behavioral model in Alergia. As explained in Sect. 2.2, the confidence parameter α influences the state merging when learning the behavioral model.

---

[5] https://github.com/smartjourneymining/spotify_journey/releases/tag/wang2024
[6] https://uppaal.org/

For the MSSD and its separation into different user profiles, we assume due to the variety of different listening behaviors that the dataset lacks multiple samples for equal user profiles. Therefore, we aim for higher α values considering that we have less confidence that the MSSD represents each user profile adequately. The number of states of the learned Markov chains varies between 6 734 and 6 851 states. In future work, it would be interesting to evaluate the influence of α by comparing the different learned user journeys from the same event log.

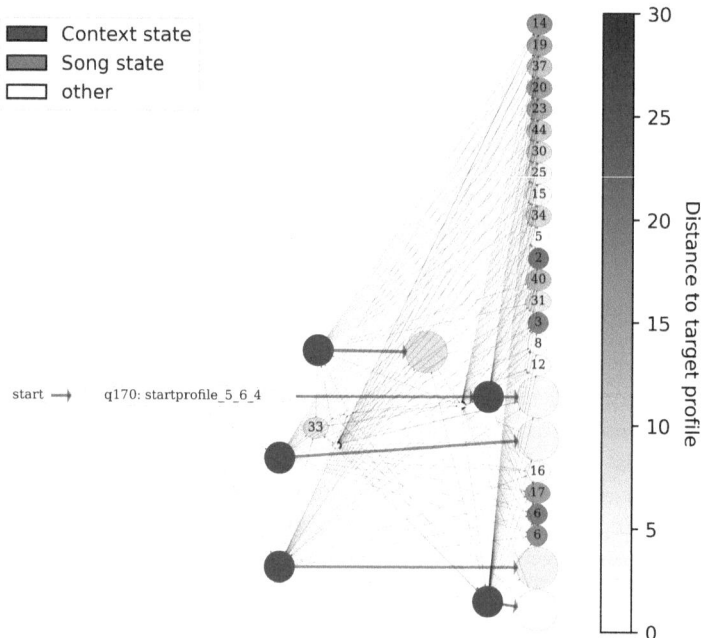

Fig. 5. Partial illustration showing the path in a user journey from the start profile of a professor towards a profile with a *wilder* taste in music.

The results presented in Table 2 show that the nudging strategy has a major influence on the user profile, often outperforming the random strategy, however danceability cannot always be reduced. The nudging strategy effectively influences the user towards the target profile by significantly changing all features except danceability; e.g., energy is increased by up to 45.43%. The results also show that the confidence parameter α has less influence on the synthesis of the nudging strategy, which suggests that we can develop a successful nudging strategy independently of the learned Markov chain.

Figure 5 shows parts of a learned UJG generated with the maximal confidence value used in the experiments (0.9999999999999). The depicted part of the UJG only shows the states explored by the synthesized strategy. For visibility, we removed any transition or state labels and applied a color-encoding for state types. Therefore, Fig. 5 abstracts from the time constraints of the original generated UJG. We color song states in a range of red tones, context states in blue, and other states in white. To calculate the red tones of states, we first encode the distance between track features $\mathbf{f}$ of a track and the target profile $\mathbf{t}$ using the sum of the element-wise distances, i.e. $\sum_i |\mathbf{t}_i - \mathbf{f}_i|$, we then map these results into a range of red tones, where the larger the distance to the target, the darker the color with red tonalities. We highlight the best selection of controllable actions from explored contexts with blue transitions and their corresponding song states are enlarged. Figure 5 also shows transitions to darker red states that could be traversed earlier in the nudging strategy to reach context states with blue transitions. The depicted UJG merges other song states into abstracted song states, aggregating song states with the same track feature distance. The aggregated states are labeled with the number of clustered song states. For example, the uppermost red state aggregates 14 concrete song states, all of which have the same distance to the target profile. The figure shows that most of the explored tracks are closer to the target profile (states with lighter red tonalities), and only a few states with darker red tonalities have a high count number.

Finally, we investigate the best actions in each state by parsing the path generated by the nudging strategy and selecting the actions leading to states with a maximal associated value. When guiding the user from the start profile, the nudging strategy selects, e.g., a track with the feature vector $\langle 1, 3, 5 \rangle$, that lies in between the starting profile $\mathbf{s} := \langle 5, 6, 4 \rangle$ and the target profile $\mathbf{t} := \langle 0, 3, 9 \rangle$. The average feature vector of the five selected songs with the smallest distance to the target is $\langle 1.2, 4.6, 7 \rangle$. One of the five tracks has an aggregated distance of 1 to the target, three tracks have an acousticness of one or smaller, two tracks have a danceability of seven, and four tracks have an energy of seven or above.

5   Related Work

The Music Streaming Sessions Dataset used was proposed by Brost *et al.* [12] in the context of skip prediction, to spur progress for counterfactual analysis. The dataset triggered a wide range of work on skip prediction using, e.g., recurrent neural networks [15,25,49] as well as on recommender systems [41,43]. Brost *et al.* consider several research directions that could be enabled by the published dataset, among others, research challenges related to user journeys. Going in this direction, our work uses the dataset to automatically build a user-centric model of listening behavior to nudge users towards different musical taste.

Spotify. Zhang *et al.* [48] investigate user behavior from Sweden, the United Kingdom, and Spain on a Spotify dataset from 2010–2011. They found statistical patterns in several aspects of the user journey: (1) daily patterns in starting a session, playback arrival, and session length, (2) switching behavior between different devices, (3) the favorite time for using Spotify, and (4) correlations between successive sessions and downtimes. Compared to our work, the authors had access to non-disclosed user information, allowing them to identify consecutive user sessions, and to provide statistical insights also on a global level. In contrast, we learned a model formalizing a music-streaming user journey based only on publicly available data describing finite streaming sessions, which were non-relatable to concrete users. Furthermore, we use model-checking tools to generate strategies optimizing specific aspects of the user journey, e.g., nudging a user towards a different music genre. Anderson *et al.* [6] use a non-public, massive Spotify dataset recorded over a year of sessions, with more than 100 million distinct users and 70 billion listened tracks, to investigate the diversity of listening behavior and churn, and to advocate diversity in recommender systems. Similar to our work, they distinguish between tracks that are selected by the user and by an algorithm. Meggetto *et al.* investigate skip behavior in music recommendations [36], using clustering to propose four different categories of skipping behavior, and propose a deep reinforcement learning model using explainable AI techniques to discover the most relevant features for skip prediction [37].

Automata learning and model checking. Automata learning has previously been used to extract finite state machines (FSM) from event logs. Cook and Wolf [17] propose a tool to learn FSMs of software processes. Similar to our work, they also consider the Markov property to construct FSMs from event logs. However, in contrast to our technique, they neglect the learned probabilities in their created models and require manual post-processing of the learned model. Agostinelli *et al.* [2] studied different automata learning algorithms for learning FSMs from event logs, assuming the availability of traces that are not part of SUL. Esparza *et al.* [20] present an algorithm for learning Petri nets that actively interacts with the SUL to complete the sample. Aichernig *et al.* [3,5] extend existing models by timed values to create STAs. They create the time variables by actively sampling the system using property-based testing techniques. Similar to our work, they then use the generated STAs for statistical model checking. Automata learning has also been used to learn timed behavior directly from a set of timed traces by applying a meta-heuristic search [4,44]. Most closely related to this work is our previous work on learning stochastic multi-player games from event logs [30]. In contrast to [30], we here use automata learning to create Markov chains instead of Markov decision processes, as we assume users to be fully stochastic in their actions and the streaming service to be deterministic.

6   Conclusion

Summary. In this paper, we show how automata learning and statistical model checking can be used to generate nudging strategies for user behavior. The proposed method is demonstrated on a case study of user behavior for a music-streaming service. We show that the method can be used to answer questions such as whether the service can nudge a professor to be adventurous and take a path on the "wild side" through the user journey game. In the case study, We learned Markov chains from the Spotify Music-Streaming Sessions Dataset

(MSSD) [12] and mined user profiles from a professor in computer science and a PhD student. Afterward, we enriched the Markov chain to a user journey game by adding timed behavior, cost variables and (un)controllable actions. The generated nudging strategies noticeably influence the listening behavior when compared to a random strategy on a set of musical features.

Discussion. The automatic generation of user journey games in this paper is based on Markov chains. We justify this approach by assuming that, for the considered case study, user behavior follows a stochastic process that can be described by a finite state structure fulfilling the Markov property. For the generation of the user journey game, we define some actions as controllable, ignoring their probabilities, and make them deterministic. Uncontrollable actions reflect learned stochastic behavior from the underlying dataset. Therefore, the generated user journey games do not have any uncontrollable deterministic actions. Other case studies might require an adaption regarding this modeling technique. The construction of user journey games in this paper approximated time boundaries and constants using averaged values. Other techniques might capture these values more precisely, but would require more in-depth expertise on the given data. Furthermore, we did not study differences between Markov chains learned with different parameters that reflect the confidence in the underlying distribution of the dataset. Our results show that a successful nudging strategy can be synthesized regardless of the parameters. For other analysis techniques, the influence of the confidence parameter might be more critical.

Our work derives user profiles from the MSSD and, based on these profiles, creates a user journey model that defines the listening behavior of users. By constructing UJGs, we also synthesize strategies to nudge a user towards a different musical taste. However, we have not explored how the synthesized strategy actually works when applied to the user. There could be a risk that actual user behavior might not align as planned when a user is actively nudged by the underlying service or application. Indeed, validating the synthesized strategy would be very interesting, but would require advanced access to the music-streaming service to steer the music recommendations based on the features we derived as well as the logging mechanism for the experienced user journey.

Future Work. This paper opens a range of possibilities for future work. In our experiments, the strategies generated with the default Q-learning parameters in UPPAAL explore only a small fraction of the state space leading to possible fluctuations in quality. We plan to investigate techniques to improve the synthesis of strategies by adapting the Q-learning technique. This work only considered the small version of the MSSD. In the future, we will examine the feasibility of automata learning for massive datasets as presented in the challenge.

Another interesting extension of our work would be lifting the synthesized strategies to more easily understandable actions. or our nudging strategy, we could, e.g., suggest specific genres that should be suggested to the users with a certain profile for adapting their taste. In previous work [30], we already worked towards making UJGs easier to understand by illustrating model-checking results using Sankey diagrams that enable the service bottleneck analysis.

Acknowledgments. We thank the providers of user profiles, and Florian Lorber for his help with designing the UPPAAL model.

References

1. van der Aalst, W.M.P.: Process Mining-Data Science in Action. Springer, 2 edn. (2016), https://doi.org/10.1007/978-3-662-49851-4
2. Agostinelli, S., Chiariello, F., Maggi, F.M., Marrella, A., Patrizi, F.: Process mining meets model learning: discovering deterministic finite state automata from event logs for business process analysis. Inf. Syst. **114**, 102180 (2023). https://doi.org/10.1016/j.is.2023.102180
3. Aichernig, B.K., et al.: Learning and statistical model checking of system response times. Softw. Qual. J. **27**(2), 757–795 (2019). https://doi.org/10.1007/s11219-018-9432-8
4. Aichernig, B.K., Pferscher, A., Tappler, M.: From passive to active: learning timed automata efficiently. In: Lee, R., Jha, S., Mavridou, A. (eds.) Proc. 12th International NASA Formal Methods Symposium (NFM 2020). Lecture Notes in Computer Science, vol. 12229, pp. 1–19. Springer (2020), https://doi.org/10.1007/978-3-030-55754-6_1
5. Aichernig, B.K., Schumi, R.: How fast is MQTT? - Statistical model checking and testing of IoT protocols. In: McIver, A., Horváth, A. (eds.) Proc. 15th International Conference on Quantitative Evaluation of Systems (QEST 2018). Lecture Notes in Computer Science, vol. 11024, pp. 36–52. Springer (2018), https://doi.org/10.1007/978-3-319-99154-2_3
6. Anderson, A., Maystre, L., Anderson, I., Mehrotra, R., Lalmas, M.: Algorithmic effects on the diversity of consumption on Spotify. In: Huang, Y., King, I., Liu, T., van Steen, M. (eds.) Proc. The Web Conference 2020 (WWW'20). pp. 2155–2165. ACM / IW3C2 (2020), https://doi.org/10.1145/3366423.3380281
7. Angluin, D.: Identifying languages from stochastic examples. Tech. rep., Yale University (1988), https://cpsc.yale.edu/sites/default/files/files/tr614.pdf
8. Behrmann, G., et al.: UPPAAL-Tiga: time for playing games! In: Damm, W., Hermanns, H. (eds.) Proc. 19th International Conference on Computer Aided Verification (CAV 2007). Lecture Notes in Computer Science, vol. 4590, pp. 121–125. Springer (2007), https://doi.org/10.1007/978-3-540-73368-3_14
9. Behrmann, G., Larsen, K.G., Rasmussen, J.I.: Priced timed automata: algorithms and applications. In: de Boer, F.S., Bonsangue, M.M., Graf, S., de Roever, W.P. (eds.) Proc. Third International Symposium, on Formal Methods for Components and Objects (FMCO 2004). Lecture Notes in Computer Science, vol. 3657, pp. 162–182. Springer (2005), https://doi.org/10.1007/11561163_8
10. Bjørk, J., de Boer, F.S., Johnsen, E.B., Schlatte, R., Tapia Tarifa, S.L.: User-defined schedulers for real-time concurrent objects. Innov. Syst. Softw. Eng. **9**(1), 29–43 (2013). https://doi.org/10.1007/S11334-012-0184-5
11. Bouyer, P., Fahrenberg, U., Larsen, K.G., Markey, N.: Quantitative analysis of real-time systems using priced timed automata. Commun. ACM **54**(9), 78–87 (2011). https://doi.org/10.1145/1995376.1995396

12. Brost, B., Mehrotra, R., Jehan, T.: The music streaming sessions dataset. In: Liu, L., White, R.W., Mantrach, A., Silvestri, F., McAuley, J.J., Baeza-Yates, R., Zia, L. (eds.) Proc. World Wide Web Conference (WWW 2019). pp. 2594–2600. ACM (2019), https://doi.org/10.1145/3308558.3313641

13. Carrasco, R.C., Oncina, J.: Learning stochastic regular grammars by means of a state merging method. In: Carrasco, R.C., Oncina, J. (eds.) Proc. 2nd International Colloquium Grammatical Inference and Applications (ICGI-94). Lecture Notes in Computer Science, vol. 862, pp. 139–152. Springer (1994), https://doi.org/10.1007/3-540-58473-0_144

14. Cassez, F., David, A., Fleury, E., Larsen, K.G., Lime, D.: Efficient on-the-fly algorithms for the analysis of timed games. In: Abadi, M., de Alfaro, L. (eds.) Proc. 16th International Conference on Concurrency Theory (CONCUR 2005), Lecture Notes in Computer Science, vol. 3653, pp. 66–80. Springer (2005), https://doi.org/10.1007/11539452_9

15. Chang, S., Lee, S., Lee, K.: Sequential skip prediction with few-shot in streamed music contents. CoRR **abs/1901.08203** (2019), http://arxiv.org/abs/1901.08203

16. Chen, T., Forejt, V., Kwiatkowska, M.Z., Parker, D., Simaitis, A.: PRISM-games: A model checker for stochastic multi-player games. In: Piterman, N., Smolka, S.A. (eds.) Proc. 19th International Conference on Tools and Algorithms for the Construction and Analysis of Systems (TACAS 2013). Lecture Notes in Computer Science, vol. 7795, pp. 185–191. Springer (2013), https://doi.org/10.1007/978-3-642-36742-7_13

17. Cook, J.E., Wolf, A.L.: Discovering models of software processes from event-based data. ACM Trans. Softw. Eng. Methodol. **7**(3), 215–249 (1998). https://doi.org/10.1145/287000.287001

18. David, A., Jensen, P.G., Larsen, K.G., Legay, A., Lime, D., Sørensen, M.G., Taankvist, J.H.: On time with minimal expected cost! In: Cassez, F., Raskin, J. (eds.) Proc. 12th International Symposium pn Automated Technology for Verification and Analysis (ATVA 2014), Lecture Notes in Computer Science, vol. 8837, pp. 129–145. Springer (2014), https://doi.org/10.1007/978-3-319-11936-6_10

19. David, A., Jensen, P.G., Larsen, K.G., Mikucionis, M., Taankvist, J.H.: UPPAAL Stratego. In: Baier, C., Tinelli, C. (eds.) Proc. 21st International Conference on Tools and Algorithms for the Construction and Analysis of Systems (TACAS 2015). Lecture Notes in Computer Science, vol. 9035, pp. 206–211. Springer (2015), https://doi.org/10.1007/978-3-662-46681-0_16

20. Esparza, J., Leucker, M., Schlund, M.: Learning workflow Petri nets. Fundam. Informaticae **113**(3–4), 205–228 (2011). https://doi.org/10.3233/FI-2011-607

21. Fornell, C., Mithas, S., Morgeson, F.V., Krishnan, M.: Customer satisfaction and stock prices: high returns, low risk. J. Market. **70**(1), 3–14 (2006). https://doi.org/10.1509/jmkg.70.1.003.qxd

22. Gold, E.M.: Language identification in the limit. Inf. Control **10**(5), 447–474 (1967). https://doi.org/10.1016/S0019-9958(67)91165-5

23. Halvorsrud, R., Kvale, K., Følstad, A.: Improving service quality through customer journey analysis. J. Serv. Theory Pract. **26**(6), 840–867 (2016). https://doi.org/10.1108/JSTP-05-2015-0111

24. Halvorsrud, R., Mannhardt, F., Johnsen, E.B., Tapia Tarifa, S.L.: Smart journey mining for improved service quality. In: Carminati, B., Chang, C.K., Daminai, E., Deng, S., Tan, W., Wang, Z., Ward, R., Zhang, J. (eds.) Proc. International Conference on Services Computing (SCC 2021). pp. 367–369. IEEE (2021), https://doi.org/10.1109/SCC53864.2021.00051

25. Hansen, C., Hansen, C., Alstrup, S., Simonsen, J.G., Lioma, C.: Modelling sequential music track skips using a Multi-RNN approach. CoRR **abs/1903.08408** (2019), http://arxiv.org/abs/1903.08408
26. Hoeffding, W.: Probability inequalities for sums of bounded random variables. Journal of the American Statistical Association **58**(301), 13–30 (1963), https://doi.org/10.2307/2282952
27. Johnsen, E.B., Hähnle, R., Schäfer, J., Schlatte, R., Steffen, M.: ABS: A core language for abstract behavioral specification. In: Aichernig, B.K., de Boer, F.S., Bonsangue, M.M. (eds.) Proc. 9th International Symposium on Formal Methods for Components and Objects FMCO 2010. Lecture Notes in Computer Science, vol. 6957, pp. 142–164. Springer (2010), https://doi.org/10.1007/978-3-642-25271-6_8
28. Johnsen, E.B., Schlatte, R., Tapia Tarifa, S.L.: Integrating deployment architectures and resource consumption in timed object-oriented models. J. Log. Algeb. Methods Progr. **84**(1), 67–91 (2015). https://doi.org/10.1016/J.JLAMP.2014.07.001
29. Kobialka, P., Mannhardt, F., Tapia Tarifa, S.L., Johnsen, E.B.: Building user journey games from multi-party event logs. In: Proc. 3rd Intl. Workshop on Event Data and Behavioral Analytics (EdbA 2022). LNBIP, vol. 468. Springer (2022), https://doi.org/10.1007/978-3-031-27815-0_6
30. Kobialka, P., Pferscher, A., Bergersen, G.R., Johnsen, E.B., Tapia Tarifa, S.L.: Stochastic games for user journeys. In: Platzer, A., Pradella, M., Rossi, M., Rozier, K.Y. (eds.) Proc. 26th International Symposium on Formal Methods (FM 2024). Lecture Notes in Computer Science, Springer (2024), to appear
31. Kobialka, P., Schlatte, R., Bergersen, G.R., Johnsen, E.B., Tapia Tarifa, S.L.: Simulating user journeys with active objects. In: de Boer, F.S., Damiani, F., Hähnle, R., Johnsen, E.B., Kamburjan, E. (eds.) Active Object Languages: Current Research Trends, Lecture Notes in Computer Science, vol. 14360, pp. 199–225. Springer (2024), https://doi.org/10.1007/978-3-031-51060-1_8
32. Kobialka, P., Tapia Tarifa, S.L., Bergersen, G.R., Johnsen, E.B.: Weighted games for user journeys. In: Proc. 20th International Conference Software Engineering and Formal Methods (SEFM 2022). Lecture Notes in Computer Science, vol. 13550, pp. 253–270. Springer (2022), https://doi.org/10.1007/978-3-031-17108-6_16
33. Kobialka, P., Tapia Tarifa, S.L., Bergersen, G.R., Johnsen, E.B.: User journey games: automating user-centric analysis. Softw. Syst. Model. **23**(3), 605–624 (2024). https://doi.org/10.1007/s10270-024-01148-2
34. Larsen, K.G., Behrmann, G., Brinksma, E., Fehnker, A., Hune, T., Pettersson, P., Romijn, J.: As cheap as possible: Efficient cost-optimal reachability for priced timed automata. In: Berry, G., Comon, H., Finkel, A. (eds.) Proc. 13th International Conference on Computer Aided Verification (CAV 2001). Lecture Notes in Computer Science, vol. 2102, pp. 493–505. Springer (2001), https://doi.org/10.1007/3-540-44585-4_47
35. Larsen, K.G., Pettersson, P., Yi, W.: UPPAAL in a nutshell. Int. J. Softw. Tools Technol. Transf. **1**(1–2), 134–152 (1997). https://doi.org/10.1007/S100090050010
36. Meggetto, F., Revie, C., Levine, J., Moshfeghi, Y.: On skipping behaviour types in music streaming sessions. In: Demartini, G., Zuccon, G., Culpepper, J.S., Huang, Z., Tong, H. (eds.) Proc. 30th ACM International Conference on Information and Knowledge Management (CIKM'21). pp. 3333–3337. ACM (2021), https://doi.org/10.1145/3459637.3482123

37. Meggetto, F., Revie, C., Levine, J., Moshfeghi, Y.: Why people skip music? On predicting music skips using deep reinforcement learning. In: Gwizdka, J., Rieh, S.Y. (eds.) Proc. Conference on Human Information Interaction and Retrieval (CHIIR 2023). pp. 95–106. ACM (2023), https://doi.org/10.1145/3576840.3578312
38. Muškardin, E., Aichernig, B.K., Pill, I., Pferscher, A., Tappler, M.: AALpy: an active automata learning library. Innov. Syst. Softw. Eng. **18**(3), 417–426 (2022). https://doi.org/10.1007/S11334-022-00449-3
39. Norman, G., Parker, D., Sproston, J.: Model checking for probabilistic timed automata. Formal Methods Syst. Des. **43**(2), 164–190 (2013). https://doi.org/10.1007/S10703-012-0177-X
40. Norris, J.R.: Markov chains. Cambridge series in statistical and probabilistic mathematics, Cambridge University Press (1998)
41. Ricci, F., Rokach, L., Shapira, B. (eds.): Recommender Systems Handbook. Springer (2015), https://doi.org/10.1007/978-1-4899-7637-6
42. Rosenbaum, M.S., Otalora, M.L., Ramírez, G.C.: How to create a realistic customer journey map. Busi. Horiz. **60**(1), 143–150 (2017). https://doi.org/10.1016/j.bushor.2016.09.010
43. Schedl, M., Knees, P., McFee, B., Bogdanov, D.: Music recommendation systems: Techniques, use cases, and challenges. In: Ricci, F., Rokach, L., Shapira, B. (eds.) Recommender Systems Handbook, pp. 927–971. Springer (2022), https://doi.org/10.1007/978-1-0716-2197-4_24
44. Tappler, M., Aichernig, B.K., Larsen, K.G., Lorber, F.: Time to learn - learning timed automata from tests. In: André, É., Stoelinga, M. (eds.) Proc. 17th International Conference on Formal Modeling and Analysis of Timed Systems (FORMATS 2019). Lecture Notes in Computer Science, vol. 11750, pp. 216–235. Springer (2019), https://doi.org/10.1007/978-3-030-29662-9_13
45. Thaler, R.H., Sunstein, C.R.: Nudge: Improving decisions about health, wealth, and happiness. Penguin (2009)
46. Vandermerwe, S., Rada, J.: Servitization of business: Adding value by adding services. Europ. Manag. J. **6**(4), 314–324 (1988). https://doi.org/10.1016/0263-2373(88)90033-3
47. Watkins, C.J.C.H., Dayan, P.: Technical note Q-learning. Mach. Learn. **8**, 279–292 (1992). https://doi.org/10.1007/BF00992698
48. Zhang, B., Kreitz, G., Isaksson, M., Ubillos, J., Urdaneta, G., Pouwelse, J.A., Epema, D.H.J.: Understanding user behavior in Spotify. In: Proc. INFOCOM 2013. pp. 220–224. IEEE (2013), https://doi.org/10.1109/INFCOM.2013.6566767
49. Zhu, L., Chen, Y.: Session-based sequential skip prediction via recurrent neural networks. CoRR **abs/1902.04743** (2019), http://arxiv.org/abs/1902.04743

Adaptive Task Planning and Formal Control Synthesis Using Temporal Logic Trees

Yulong Gao[1(✉)], Can Zhou[1], Alessandro Abate[2], and Karl H. Johansson[3]

[1] Department of Electrical and Electronic Engineering,
Imperial College London, London, UK
`{yulong.gao,c.zhou24}@imperial.ac.uk`
[2] Department of Computer Science, University of Oxford, Oxford, UK
`alessandro.abate@cs.ox.ac.uk`
[3] Division of Decision and Control Systems, KTH Royal Institute of Technology,
and Digital Futures, Stockholm, Sweden
`kallej@kth.se`

Abstract. Temporal logics have garnered significant attention in the control community due to their use for formal control synthesis, namely for the synthesis of control policies with provable correctness guarantees for more complex and interesting properties than traditional control objectives. Formal control under temporal logics is fundamentally challenging though, particularly when dealing with uncertain infinite systems and complex temporal logic specifications for real-time task planing, as the established methods struggle with handling models in high dimensions and with accommodating online deployment. In this article, we propose Temporal Logic Trees (TLT) as a mitigation for these challenges. TLT are constructed from Linear Temporal Logic (LTL) formulae via reachability analysis, offering an abstraction-free design method. Building upon the TLT framework, we present approaches for adaptive task planning and formal control synthesis that are usable on both finite and infinite systems. Furthermore, we demonstrate the applicability of our approach for online control synthesis, particularly in addressing time-varying tasks: namely, our method allows for dynamic online updates of the specifications, which showcases its practical utility and flexibility.

Keywords: Formal control synthesis · Task planning · Linear temporal logic · Temporal logic tree · Real-time systems

1 Introduction

In recent years, temporal logics – such as Linear Temporal Logic (LTL) [16], Computational Tree Logic (CTL) [3], and Signal Temporal Logic (STL) [13] – have captured significant attention within the control community. This interest is due to the capability of these logics to facilitate formal control synthesis for objectives that are richer than traditional control tasks like stability and set invariance, whilst emphasising provable correctness guarantees with the synthesised

© The Author(s), under exclusive license to Springer Nature Switzerland AG 2025
S. Graf et al. (Eds.): Festschrift Wang Yi, LNCS 15230, pp. 64–78, 2025.
https://doi.org/10.1007/978-3-031-73751-0_7

policy. In particular, temporal logics provide a structured framework for expressing and reasoning about complex, temporally-extended properties of dynamical systems, encompassing intricate and interesting aspects, such as safety (nothing bad will ever happen), liveness (something good will eventually happen), and richer combinations of Boolean and temporal requirements [1]. The diverse applications of control synthesis under temporal logic specifications, including single-robot control in dynamic environments [15], multi-robot planning [8], and control of transportation networks [4], further underscore the utility of temporal logics in the area of control.

The prevalent approaches in formal control synthesis under temporal logic specifications for dynamical systems revolve around automata-based methods. These methods typically begin by abstracting a given dynamical process as a finite transition system, under formal guarantees. Subsequently, they convert a given (linear) temporal logic formula into an equivalent automaton. Then, the transition system is synchronised with the automata that is obtained to constructed a "product automaton". This automaton can be converted into a decision problem or, more broadly, a game [11]. By solving this game, a control strategy is derived [5]. However, significant challenges arise when dealing with dynamical systems affected by uncertainty, and inherent limitations also exist within the dominant automata-based methods when addressing complex scenarios.

Firstly, abstraction from infinite systems to finite systems runs into the curse of dimensionality: abstraction techniques typically involve partitioning the state space and constructing transitions through reachability analysis, however computational complexity grows exponentially as system dimensionality increases. Secondly, there is a shortage of solutions for handling general LTL formulae for dynamical systems under uncertainty, such as bounded disturbance or additive noise. Recent advances [9,14] typically only cover fragments of LTL, such as bounded LTL and co-safe LTL. However, when LTL formulae are defined over infinite trajectories, it is difficult to handle uncertainty propagation along such trajectories. Thirdly, current methods often hardly cope with online deployment: instead, in numerous applications, obtaining full a-priori knowledge of a specification is unfeasible. As such, offline automata-based design methods become severely constrained. Lastly, controllers derived from automata-based methods often result in a single control policy, whereas certain applications necessitate *a set* of feasible control inputs to provide more flexibility in actual implementation.

This article moves beyond the above limitations by closely investigating the connection between temporal logic and reachability analysis. We leverage a novel tool "Temporal Logic Trees" (TLT) proposed in [6] and extend the results for jointly adaptive task planning and formal control synthesis for discrete-time uncertain dynamical systems in partly known environments. The new framework systematically integrates a task planner and a formal controller. Different from [6] where the task is time-invariant, the task planner in this article can update a given LTL tasks by incorporating real-time environmental information and observing the system state. Meanwhile, a given LTL task can be transformed to a corresponding TLT via reachability analysis. As shown in [6], the TLT represents an under-approximation of the LTL formula, which ensures the soundness of TLT-based control synthesis. We thus offer a new tool for applications in formal control synthesis for time-varying tasks within real-time systems, thus demonstrating how specifications can be dynamically updated online through our approach and controllers adaptively synthesised with guarantees.

2   Preliminaries and Problem Statement

This section presents preliminaries and problem statement. We first introduce the notion of controlled transition system and recall the concept of reachability analysis.

2.1   Controlled Transition System

Definition 1. *A controlled transition system* CTS *is a tuple* $\mathsf{CTS} = (\mathbb{S}, \mathbb{U}, \rightarrow, \mathbb{S}_0, \mathcal{AP}, L)$ *consisting of*

- *a set* $\mathbb{S}$ *of states;*
- *a set* $\mathbb{U}$ *of control inputs;*
- *a transition relation* $\rightarrow \in \mathbb{S} \times \mathbb{U} \times \mathbb{S}$;
- *a set* $\mathbb{S}_0$ *of initial states;*
- *a set* $\mathcal{AP}$ *of atomic propositions;*
- *a labelling function* $L : \mathbb{S} \rightarrow 2^{\mathcal{AP}}$.

Definition 2. *For* $x \in \mathbb{S}$ *and* $u \in \mathbb{U}$, *the set* $\mathsf{Post}(x, u)$ *of direct successors of* x *under* u *is defined by* $\mathsf{Post}(x, u) = \{x' \in \mathbb{S} \mid x \xrightarrow{u} x'\}$.

Note that the controlled transition system CTS presents nondeterminism which can be explicitly characterised by the post set $\mathsf{Post}(x, u)$: there may exist multiple successors $x' \in \mathbb{S}$ from x under a fixed u.

Definition 3. *For* $x \in \mathbb{S}$, *the set* $\mathbb{U}(x)$ *of admissible control inputs at state* x *is defined by* $\mathbb{U}(x) = \{u \in \mathbb{U} \mid \mathsf{Post}(x, u) \neq \emptyset\}$.

Definition 4. *(Policy) For a controlled transition system* CTS, *a policy* $\boldsymbol{\mu} = u_0 u_1 \ldots u_k \ldots$ *is a sequence of maps* $u_k : \mathbb{S} \rightarrow \mathbb{U}$. *Denote by* $\mathcal{M}$ *the set of all policies.*

Definition 5. *(Trajectory) For a controlled transition system* CTS, *an infinite trajectory* $\boldsymbol{p}$ *starting from* x_0 *under a policy* $\boldsymbol{\mu} = u_0 u_1 \ldots u_k \ldots$ *is a sequence of states* $\boldsymbol{p} = x_0 x_1 \ldots x_k \ldots$ *such that* $\forall k \in \mathbb{N}$, $x_{k+1} \in \mathsf{Post}(x_k, u_k(x_k))$. *Denote by* $\mathsf{Trajs}(x_0, \boldsymbol{\mu})$ *the set of infinite trajectories starting from* x_0 *under* $\boldsymbol{\mu}$.

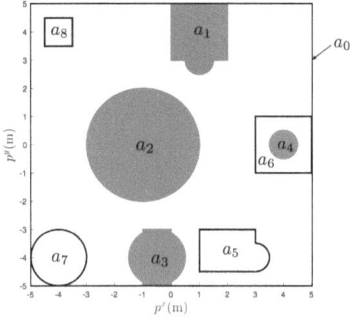

Fig. 1. Motion planning scenario

Example 1. (Motion Planning Example) We consider the motion planning problem for a mobile robot in an environment, as shown in Fig. 1. We describe the dynamics of the robot under disturbance as $x_{k+1} = x_k + f(x_k, u_k, w_k)\Delta$, where

$$f(x, u, w) = \begin{bmatrix} v\cos\theta \\ v\sin\theta \\ \sigma \end{bmatrix} + w,$$

and $x = [p^x, p^y, \theta]^T$ is the vehicle's x position, y position, and heading, respectively. The control input is $u = [v, \sigma]^T$, where v is the vehicle's velocity and σ is the angular velocity. Here, $\Delta = 0.05$s is the sampling period. The working space is $\mathbb{S} = \{z \in \mathbb{R}^3 \mid [-5, -5, -\pi]^T \leq z \leq [-5, 5, \pi]^T\}$, the control set is $\mathbb{U} = \{z \in \mathbb{R}^2 \mid [-0.5, -\pi/5]^T \leq z \leq [0.5, \pi/5,]^T\}$, and the disturbance set is $\mathbb{W} = \{z \in \mathbb{R}^3 \mid [-0.1, -0.1, -0.1]^T \leq z \leq [0.1, 0.1, 0.1]^T\}$. The atomic propositions are labels over the working space, and are denoted by a_i corresponding to the sets shown in Fig. 1. In particular, a_0 is the working space, a_i, $i = 1, 2, 3, 4$, represent obstacles, and a_i, $i = 5, 6, 7, 8$, represent target sets. Denote by $\mathbb{O}$ the union of the obstacles.

2.2 Reachability Analysis

Let us review the reachability analysis for a controlled transition system CTS.

Definition 6. *Consider a controlled transition system* CTS *and two sets* $\Omega_1, \Omega_2 \subseteq \mathbb{S}$. *The k-step reachable set from* Ω_1 *to* Ω_2 *is defined as*

$$\mathcal{R}(\Omega_1, \Omega_2, k) = \Big\{x_0 \in \mathbb{S} \mid \exists \boldsymbol{\mu} \in \mathcal{M} \text{ s.t., } \forall \boldsymbol{p} \in \mathsf{Trajs}(x_0, \boldsymbol{\mu}),$$

$$\boldsymbol{p}[..k] = x_0 \ldots x_k, \forall i \in \mathbb{N}_{[0,k-1]}, x_i \in \Omega_1, x_k \in \Omega_2 \Big\}.$$

The reachable set from Ω_1 *to* Ω_2 *is defined as*

$$\mathcal{R}(\Omega_1, \Omega_2) = \bigcup_{k \in \mathbb{N}} \mathcal{R}(\Omega_1, \Omega_2, k).$$

Definition 7. *A set $\Omega_f \subseteq \mathbb{S}$ is said to be a robust controlled invariant set (RCIS) of a transition system TS if for any $x \in \Omega_f$, there exists $u \in \mathbb{U}(x)$ such that $\mathsf{Post}(x, u) \subseteq \Omega_f$. A set $\mathcal{RCI}(\Omega) \subseteq \mathbb{S}$ is said to be the largest RCIS in Ω if each RCIS $\Omega_f \subseteq \Omega$ satisfies $\Omega_f \subseteq \mathcal{RCI}(\Omega)$.*

Many algorithms have been proposed to compute the reachable set $\mathcal{R}(\Omega_1, \Omega_2)$ and the largest RCIS $\mathcal{RCI}(\Omega)$, see [2,12]. As we shall see, reachable sets and RCISs provide us a way to transfer the LTL formulae to the TLT framework, and to synthesize formal controllers. In the following, we treat the maps $\mathcal{R} : 2^{\mathbb{S}} \times 2^{\mathbb{S}} \to 2^{\mathbb{S}}$ and $\mathcal{RCI} : 2^{\mathbb{S}} \to 2^{\mathbb{S}}$ as the reachability operators.

2.3 LTL

An LTL formula is defined over a finite set of atomic propositions $\mathcal{AP}$ (in particular those relevant to a given dynamical system), and depends on propositional and temporal operators. The syntax of LTL in weak-until positive normal form is:

$$\varphi ::= \text{true} \mid \text{false} \mid a \mid \neg a \mid \varphi_1 \wedge \varphi_2 \mid \varphi_1 \vee \varphi_2 \mid \bigcirc\varphi \mid \varphi_1 \mathsf{U}\varphi_2 \mid \varphi_1 \mathsf{W}\varphi_2. \quad (1)$$

Here $\bigcirc$, U, and W denote the "next", "until", and "weak-until" operators, respectively. Recall that $\varphi_1 \mathsf{W}\varphi_2 = \varphi_1 \mathsf{U}\varphi_2 \vee \square\varphi_1$, where $\square$ is the always operator. By employing the until operator, we can define its dual, known as "eventually," as: $\Diamond\varphi = \text{true} \mathsf{U} \varphi$.

Definition 8. *(LTL semantics) For an LTL formula φ and a trajectory $\boldsymbol{p}$, the satisfaction relation $\boldsymbol{p} \vDash \varphi$ is defined as*

$$\boldsymbol{p} \vDash p \Leftrightarrow p \in L(x_0); \quad \boldsymbol{p} \vDash \neg p \Leftrightarrow p \notin L(x_0),$$

$$\boldsymbol{p} \vDash \varphi_1 \wedge \varphi_2 \Leftrightarrow \boldsymbol{p} \vDash \varphi_1 \wedge \boldsymbol{p} \vDash \varphi_2; \quad \boldsymbol{p} \vDash \varphi_1 \vee \varphi_2 \Leftrightarrow \boldsymbol{p} \vDash \varphi_1 \vee \boldsymbol{p} \vDash \varphi_2,$$

$$\boldsymbol{p} \vDash \bigcirc\varphi \Leftrightarrow \boldsymbol{p}[1..] \vDash \varphi; \quad \boldsymbol{p} \vDash \varphi_1 \mathsf{U}\varphi_2 \Leftrightarrow \exists j \in \mathbb{N} \; s.t. \begin{cases} \boldsymbol{p}[j..] \vDash \varphi_2, \\ \forall i \in \mathbb{N}_{[0,j-1]}, \boldsymbol{p}[i..] \vDash \varphi_1, \end{cases}$$

$$\boldsymbol{p} \vDash \Diamond\varphi \Leftrightarrow \exists j \in \mathbb{N}, \; s.t. \; \boldsymbol{p}[j..] \vDash \varphi; \quad \boldsymbol{p} \vDash \square\varphi \Leftrightarrow \forall j \in \mathbb{N}, \; s.t. \; \boldsymbol{p}[j..] \vDash \varphi,$$

$$\boldsymbol{p} \vDash \varphi_1 \mathsf{W}\varphi_2 \Leftrightarrow \begin{cases} \forall j \in \mathbb{N}, \boldsymbol{p}[j..] \vDash \varphi_1, \; or \\ \exists j \in \mathbb{N} \; s.t. \begin{cases} \boldsymbol{p}[j..] \vDash \varphi_2, \\ \forall i \in \mathbb{N}_{[0,j-1]}, \boldsymbol{p}[i..] \vDash \varphi_1. \end{cases} \end{cases}$$

Example 2. Let us continue considering Example 1. The motion planning task of interest is expressed by $\varphi = \phi_1 \wedge (\phi_2 \vee \phi_3) \wedge \phi_4 \wedge \phi_5$, where

$$\phi_1 = \square \left(a_0 \wedge \neg (a_1 \vee a_2 \vee a_3 \vee a_4) \right), \phi_2 = (a_0 \wedge \neg a_5) \mathsf{U} a_6,$$
$$\phi_3 = (a_0 \wedge \neg a_5) \mathsf{U} a_7, \phi_4 = \Diamond a_5, \phi_5 = \Diamond\square a_8.$$

The formula φ specifies that the mobile robot is expected to first visit the region a_5 or a_6, then visit a_7, and finally stay in a_8 upon visiting it, while always avoiding the obstacles a_i, $i = 1, 2, 3, 4$.

2.4   Temporal Logic Trees

A TLT is a tree that simulates a hierarchical structure with set of linked nodes and of operator nodes. TLTs are proposed in [6] as an alternative tool for model checking and control synthesis over dynamical systems. The intuition underpinning a TLT is that it collects a sequence of sets of states (from its root node to the leaf nodes), indicating how a state trajectory of the model ought to evolve in order to satisfy the corresponding temporal logic specification.

Definition 9. *A TLT is a tree, for which the next properties hold:*

- *each node either represents a set, namely a subset of $\mathbb{S}$, or is an operator node from $\{\wedge, \vee, \bigcirc, \mathsf{U}, \square\}$;*
- *the root node and the leaf nodes are set nodes;*
- *if a set node is not a leaf node, its unique child is an operator node;*
- *the children of any operator node are set nodes.*

Definition 10. *A complete path of a TLT is a sequence of nodes and edges from the root node to a leaf node. Any subsequence of a complete path is called a fragment of the complete path.*

Theorem 1 ([6]). *For a controlled transition system* CTS *and given any LTL formula φ, the following holds:*

- *(i) a TLT can be constructed from the formula φ through the reachability operators $\mathcal{R}$ and $\mathcal{RCI}$;*
- *(ii) given an initial state x_0, if there exists a policy $\boldsymbol{\mu}$ such that $\boldsymbol{p}$ satisfies the constructed TLT, $\forall \boldsymbol{p} \in \mathsf{Trajs}(x_0, \boldsymbol{\mu})$, then $\boldsymbol{p} \models \varphi$, $\forall \boldsymbol{p} \in \mathsf{Trajs}(x_0, \boldsymbol{\mu})$.*

Example 3. Let us continue to consider Example 2 and detail how to perform reachability analysis for constructing a TLT from the given LTL formula $\varphi = \phi_1 \wedge (\phi_2 \vee \phi_3) \wedge \phi_4 \wedge \phi_5$, cf. Fig. 2(a). We begin with $\phi_1 = \square\,(a_0 \wedge \neg\,(a_1 \vee a_2 \vee a_3 \vee a_4))$. Note that the set $\mathbb{S}\backslash\mathbb{O}$ corresponds to $a_0 \wedge \neg\,(a_1 \vee a_2 \vee a_3 \vee a_4)$. Since the formula ϕ_1 is a safety property, we use the robust invariance operator to compute $\mathbb{Y}_1 = \mathcal{RCI}(\mathbb{S} \setminus \mathbb{O})$. Then, the fragment $\mathbb{Y}_1 \square (\mathbb{S} \setminus \mathbb{O})$ in Fig. 2(a). corresponds to the subformula ϕ_1. For $\phi_2 = (a_0 \wedge \neg a_5)\,\mathsf{U}a_6$ and $\phi_3 = (a_0 \wedge \neg a_5)\,\mathsf{U}a_7$, we define $\mathbb{Y}_2 = \mathcal{R}(\mathbb{S} \backslash L^{-1}(a_5), L^{-1}(a_6))$ and $\mathbb{Y}_3 = \mathcal{R}(\mathbb{S} \backslash L^{-1}(a_5), L^{-1}(a_7))$. Then, the fragments $\mathbb{Y}_2 \mathsf{U}L^{-1}(a_6)$ and $\mathbb{Y}_3 \mathsf{U}L^{-1}(a_7)$ in Fig. 2(a) correspond to the subformulae ϕ_2 and ϕ_3, respectively and they are connected by the disjunction operator. For $\varphi_4 = \lozenge a_5$, let $\mathbb{Y}_4 = \mathcal{R}(\mathbb{S}, L^{-1}(a_5))$. Then, the fragment $\mathbb{Y}_4 \mathsf{U}L^{-1}(a_5)$ in Fig. 2(a) corresponds to the subformula ϕ_4. Finally, we consider $\phi_5 = \lozenge\square a_8$, which is a safety property. Let $\mathbb{Y}_6 = \mathcal{RCI}(L^{-1}(a_8))$ and $\mathbb{Y}_5 = \mathcal{R}(\mathbb{S}, \mathbb{Y}_6)$. Then, the fragment $\mathbb{Y}_5 \mathsf{U}\mathbb{Y}_6 \square L^{-1}(a_8)$ in Fig. 2(a) corresponds to the subformula ϕ_5. According to the logical connection among these formulae, we connect these fragment and finally construct the TLT, as shown in Fig. 2(a).

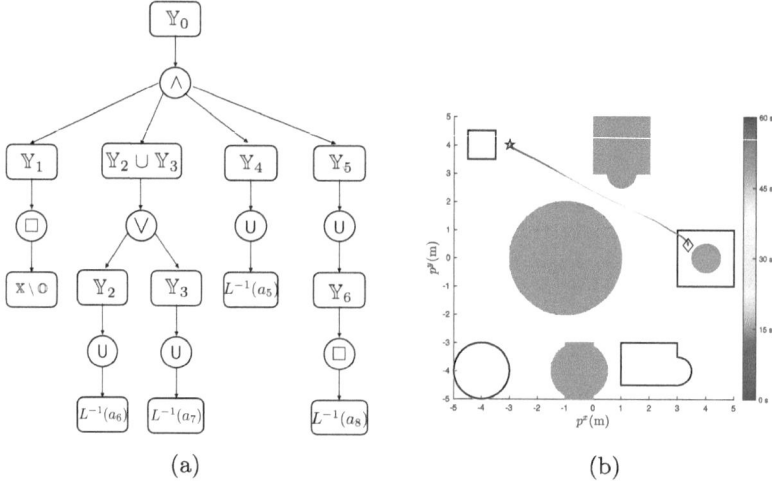

(a)   (b)

Fig. 2. (a) The controlled TLT for the LTL formula $\varphi = \phi_1 \wedge (\phi_2 \vee \phi_3) \wedge \phi_4 \wedge \phi_5$ in Example 3. (b) A state trajectory that fulfills the sub-formula ϕ_2 in Example 4.

2.5   Problem Statement

In this work, we consider the following task planing and control synthesis problem for a dynamical system.

Problem 1. Consider a controlled transition system CTS. At each time step k, (1) plan a time-varying LTL task φ_k and (2) synthesise a formal controller $\boldsymbol{\mu}_k$ such that φ_k is fulfilled.

We remark that in Problem 1, we focus on the dynamical system CTS which is fully observable, not partially observable. In comparison with a more standard control problem under a fixed LTL formula, the studied time-varying LTL planning provides much more flexibility. Firstly, it allows to consider time-varying (e.g., partially observable) environments: that is, the task φ_k can be updated from new features of the surrounding environment. For instance, when new obstacles are present (or equivalently detected in our fully observable setup), the LTL formula φ_k can naturally incorporate such new safety or collision-avoidance requirement. In addition, the formula φ_k can also be updated under the supervision of a human operator: for example, in a shared control scenario, a human operators is authorised to plan around the task and make decisions. Last but not least, our task planning allows for online deployment, hence enabling to monitor task completion and to decompose complex tasks into simple and easily solvable tasks in real time.

3   Adaptive Task Planner and Formal Control Synthesis

In order to solve the Problem 1, in this section, we propose a new TLT-based framework, as displayed in Fig. 3. The task planner adaptively updates the LTL

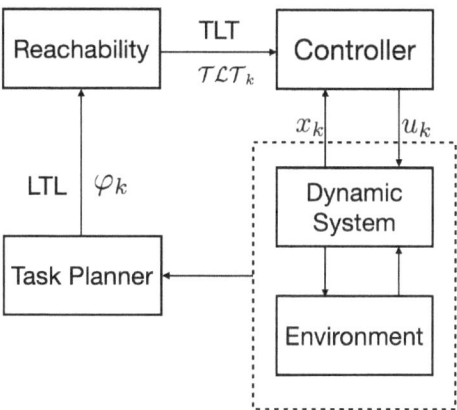

Fig. 3. A framework that integrates adaptive task planner and formal controller.

formula φ_k based on system information and environment knowledge. The task φ_k is then transformed into the corresponding TLT, denoted by $\mathcal{TLT}_k$, via reachability analysis (as presented above). Note that the TLT construction can be performed by pruning/modifying a previous TLT, which can be more efficient. An formal controller is then automatically synthesised using $\mathcal{TLT}_k$ and deployed online. In the following, we will detail how the functional blocks in Fig. 3 work and how they are systematically integrated.

3.1   Adaptive Task Planner

In general, the task planner is a function of the environment information and the system state, and it incrementally updates a given task. That is, at each time $k + 1$, the new task φ_{k+1} can be written as a function g,

$$\varphi_{k+1} = g(\mathrm{Env}_k, \varphi_k, x_k)$$

where Env_k is the environment state, φ_k is the previous task, and x_k is the system state. The function g depends the context, for example:

- The function g can serve as a task monitor. When a sub-formula ϕ_k of the task φ_k is fulfilled at time x_k, then such a sub-formula can be removed to obtain a simplified task φ_{k+1}. Please see Example 4 for more information.
- The function g can be part of the environment exploration: the planner is only aware of partial environment information at the initial stage. Real-time perception/observations enable to learn the environment and to update the task φ_k by adding new sub-tasks. For example, a new safety requirement should be incorporated when unknown obstacles are detected. Please see Sect. 4 for more details.
- The function g can also depend on the supervision from human operators. The task can be accordingly updated when the human operator intervenes

and provides new requirements. This may occur in remote control scenarios. Please refer to [7,10] for an example on remote car parking.

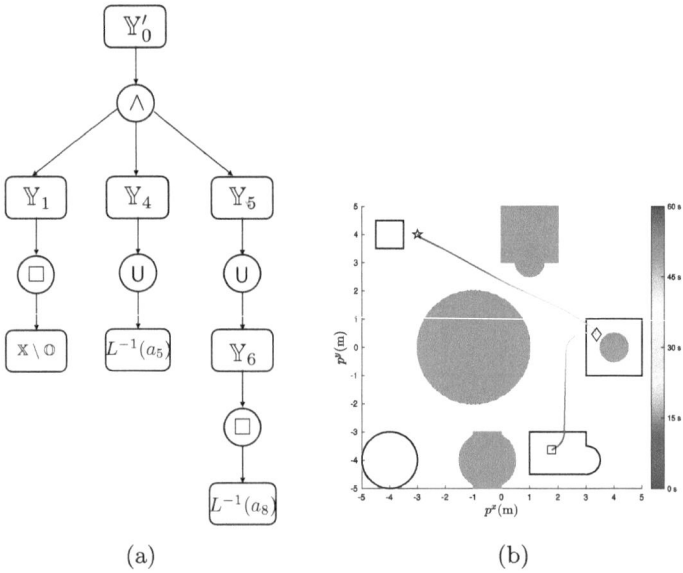

(a)   (b)

Fig. 4. (a) The TLT for the simplified LTL formula $\varphi_k = \phi_1 \wedge \phi_4 \wedge \phi_5$. (b) The state trajectory that fulfills the subformula $\phi_2 \wedge \phi_4$.

3.2   TLT-based Formal Control Synthesis

Given the current state x_k, the control synthesis algorithm is structured as follows: (1) construct the controlled TLT by replacing each state-set node in the TLT $\mathcal{TLT}_k$ with a corresponding control set: if x_k belongs to a state-set node in the TLT, collect all the control inputs such that the next states is feasible under the connected operators; (2) compress this controlled TLT by taking union of the control sets over the fragments without logic operators: the compressed tree only has the control-set nodes and logic operator nodes; (3) backtrack a single control set $\mathbb{U}(x_k) \subseteq \mathbb{U}$ by taking union and intersection through a bottom-up traversal. Note, this control set $\mathbb{U}(x_k)$ collects all the feasible control inputs, such that the LTL specification φ_k is recursively feasible. That is, the controller is able to utilize the $\mathcal{TLT}_k$ to synthesize least-restrictive control sets that ensures the recursive feasibility and task satisfiability from x_k for each φ_k. In addition, we remark that the control set $\mathbb{U}(x_k)$ is least-restrictive in the sense that it permits any control inputs that do not violate φ_k. This control set thus provides more freedom to select the control input $u_k \in \mathbb{U}(x_k)$ to be deployed. For more details, we refer the readers to [6].

Example 4. Let us continue to consider Example 3. Let the initial task $\varphi_0 = \phi_1 \wedge (\phi_2 \vee \phi_3) \wedge \phi_4 \wedge \phi_5$. Before reaching the regions associated with a_6 or a_7 (that is, the subformlae ϕ_2 or ϕ_3 are fulfilled), the task φ_k will be the same as φ_0. Using the TLT shown in Fig. 2(a), the synthesised control set is $\mathbb{U}(x_k) = \mathbb{U}_1(x_k) \cap (\mathbb{U}_2(x_k) \cup \mathbb{U}_3(x_k))$, where $\mathbb{U}_1(x_k) = \{u \in \mathbb{U} \mid \mathsf{Post}(x_k, u) \subseteq \mathbb{Y}_1\}$, $\mathbb{U}_2(x_k) = \{u \in \mathbb{U} \mid \mathsf{Post}(x_k, u) \subseteq \mathbb{Y}_2\}$, and $\mathbb{U}_3(x_k) = \{u \in \mathbb{U} \mid \mathsf{Post}(x_k, u) \subseteq \mathbb{Y}_3\}$. The controller can freely select any $u_k \in \mathbb{U}(x_k)$ for implementation. In this example, we select the control input $u_k \in \mathbb{U}(x_k)$ in a time-optimal manner. That is, we minimise the task completion time of ϕ_2 or ϕ_3 subject to $u_k \in \mathbb{U}(x_k)$. A resulting state trajectory is shown in Fig. 2(b), which fulfills the sub-formula ϕ_2.

To this end, the task planner can remove the sub-formulae ϕ_2 and ϕ_3, and obtain a simplified formula $\varphi_k = \phi_1 \wedge \phi_4 \wedge \phi_5$. The corresponding TLT $\mathcal{TLT}_k$ can be easily obtained by pruning the TLT in Fig. 2(a), that is, removing two complete paths of the TLT associated with ϕ_2 and ϕ_3. The new TLT is shown in Fig. 4(a). The corresponding TLT-based control set is $\mathbb{U}(x_k) = \mathbb{U}_1(x_k) \cap \mathbb{U}_4(x_k)$, where $\mathbb{U}_4(x_k) = \{u \in \mathbb{U} \mid \mathsf{Post}(x_k, u) \subseteq \mathbb{Y}_4\}$. An extended state trajectory is shown in Fig. 4(b), which fulfills the sub-formula $\phi_2 \wedge \phi_4$.

Now the task planner can further remove the sub-formula ϕ_4 and obtain a simplified formula $\varphi_k = \phi_1 \wedge \phi_5$. The corresponding TLT $\mathcal{TLT}_k$ can be easily obtained by removing the complete path associated with ϕ_4 in the TLT of Fig. 4(a). The new TLT is shown in Fig. 5(a). The corresponding TLT-based control set is $\mathbb{U}(x_k) = \mathbb{U}_1(x_k) \cap \mathbb{U}_5(x_k)$, where $\mathbb{U}_5(x_k) = \{u \in \mathbb{U} \mid \mathsf{Post}(x_k, u) \subseteq \mathbb{Y}_5\}$. An extended state trajectory is shown in Fig. 5(b), which fulfills the subformula $\phi_2 \wedge \phi_4 \wedge \Diamond \mathbb{Y}_6$.

As long as the state enters the set $\mathbb{Y}_6$, the task planner can update the task to be $\varphi_k = \Box a_8$, whose TLT is shown in Fig. 6(a). The control set is $\mathbb{U}(x_k) = \{u \in \mathbb{U} \mid \mathsf{Post}(x_k, u) \subseteq \mathbb{Y}_6\}$, from which any control input u_k can keep the state in the region a_8. A resulting state trajectory satisfying φ_0 is shown in Fig. 6(b).

4   Application: Planning in Partially Known Environment

In this section, we provide another case study where the environment is only partially known and the task is time-varying. As shown in Fig. 7, we consider a scenario where an automated vehicle plans to move to a target set $\mathbb{T}$ but with some obstacles on the road that ought to be avoided. We assume that the sensing region of the vehicle is limited, hence the obstacles are only found on the way to the target. We use a single integrator model with a sample period of 1 second to describe the dynamics of the vehicle:

$$x_{k+1} = \begin{bmatrix} 1 & 0 \\ 0 & 1 \end{bmatrix} x_k + \begin{bmatrix} 1 & 0 \\ 0 & 1 \end{bmatrix} u_k + w_k. \tag{3}$$

The working space is $\mathbb{X} = \{z \in \mathbb{R}^2 \mid [0, -5]^T \leq z \leq [150, 5]^T\}$, the control set is $\mathbb{U} = \{z \in \mathbb{R}^2 \mid [-2, -0.5]^T \leq z \leq [2, 0.5]^T\}$, the disturbance set is $\mathbb{W} = \{z \in$

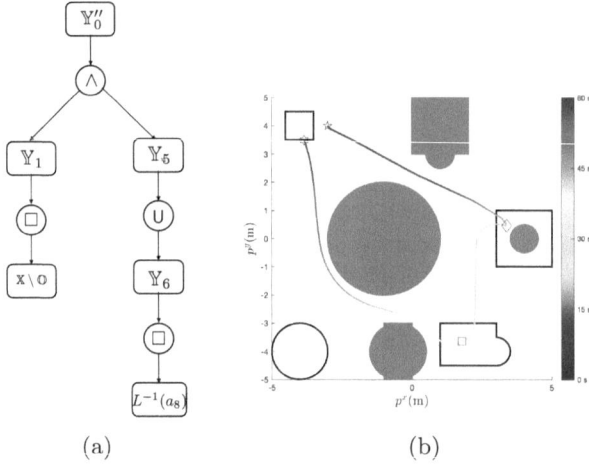

(a)   (b)

Fig. 5. (a) The TLT for the simplified LTL formula $\varphi_k = \phi_1 \wedge \phi_5$. (b) The state trajectory that fulfills the subformula $\phi_2 \wedge \phi_4 \wedge \Diamond \mathbb{Y}_6$.

$\mathbb{R}^2 \mid [-0.1, -0.1]^T \leq z \leq [0.1, 0.1]^T\}$, and the target region is $\mathbb{T} = \{z \in \mathbb{R}^2 \mid [145, -5]^T \leq z \leq [150, 0]^T\}$. We assume that $\mathbb{X}$, $\mathbb{U}$, and $\mathbb{W}$ are known *a priori* to the vehicle and the vehicle should move along the lane in the right direction unless a lane change is necessary to avoid broken vehicles. In Fig. 7, the two broken vehicles are encompassed by the sets $\mathbb{O}_1 = \{z \in \mathbb{R}^2 \mid [40, -5]^T \leq z \leq [45, 0]^T\}$ and $\mathbb{O}_2 = \{z \in \mathbb{R}^2 \mid [100, 0]^T \leq z \leq [105, 5]^T\}$. We assume that $\mathbb{O}_1$ and $\mathbb{O}_2$ are unknown to the vehicle at the beginning, but as soon as the vehicle can sense them, they become known to it.

Let the initial state be $x_0 = [0.5, -2.5]^T$ and the sensing range is 15 [m]. At time step $k = 0$, the set of atomic propositions is $\mathcal{AP} = \{a_1, a_2\}$ and if $x \in \mathbb{X}$, we

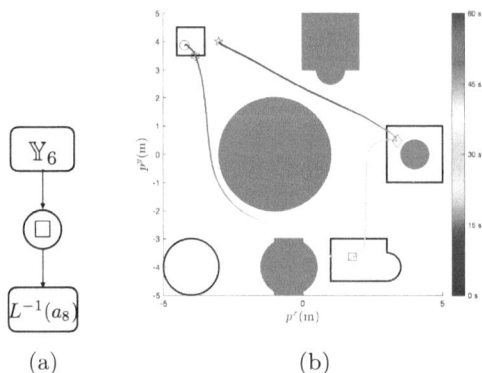

(a)   (b)

Fig. 6. (a) The TLT for the simplified LTL formula $\varphi_k = \Box a_8$. (b) The state trajectory that fulfills the formula φ_0.

define the labelling function as follows: if $x \in \mathbb{X} \cap \mathbb{T}$, $L(x) = \{a_1, a_2\}$; otherwise, $L(x) = \{a_1\}$. The initial specification can be expressed as an LTL $\varphi = a_1 \mathsf{U} a_2$. By constructing the controlled TLT of φ shown in Fig. 8 and implementing the TLT-based control synthesis algorithm, we obtain one realization as shown in Fig. 9. We can see that the vehicle keeps moving straightforward until it senses the obstacle $\mathbb{O}_1$ at $[25.46 - 2.53]^T$.

When the vehicle can sense $\mathbb{O}_1$, a new observation a_3 with $a_3 \neq a_1$ and $a_3 \neq a_2$ is added to the set of atomic propositions $\mathcal{AP}$, which becomes $\mathcal{AP} = \{a_1, a_2, a_3\}$. If $x \in \mathbb{X}$, we update the labelling function as follow: if $x \in \mathbb{X} \cap \mathbb{T}$, $L(x) = \{a_1, a_2\}$; if $x \in \mathbb{X} \cap \mathbb{O}_1$, $L(x) = \{a_1, a_3\}$; otherwise, $L(x) = \{a_1\}$. To avoid $\mathbb{O}_1$, the task planner update the task φ to be $\varphi' = \varphi \wedge (\Box \neg a_3)$. We can

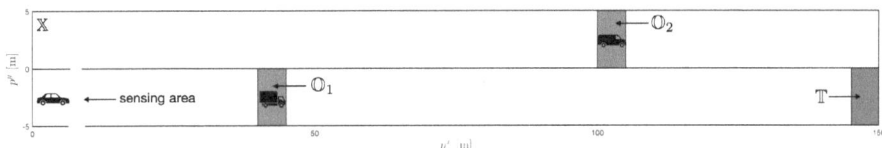

Fig. 7. Illustration of planning scenario for Example 2: an automated vehicle aims to reach a target set $\mathbb{T}$, however there are some unknown (broken) vehicles on the road to be avoided.

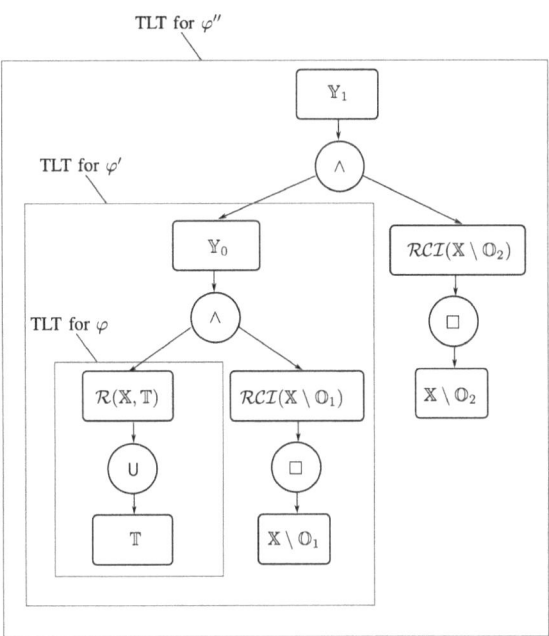

Fig. 8. The controlled TLT for the LTL formulae in Example 2, where $\varphi = a_1 \mathsf{U} a_2$, $\varphi' = \varphi \wedge (\Box \neg a_3)$, $\varphi'' = \varphi' \wedge (\Box \neg a_4)$, $\mathbb{Y}_0 = \mathcal{R}(\mathbb{X}, \mathbb{T}) \cap \mathcal{RCI}(\mathbb{X} \setminus \mathbb{O}_1)$, and $\mathbb{Y}_1 = \mathcal{R}(\mathbb{X}, \mathbb{T}) \cap \mathcal{RCI}(\mathbb{X} \setminus \mathbb{O}_1) \cap \mathcal{RCI}(\mathbb{X} \setminus \mathbb{O}_2)$.

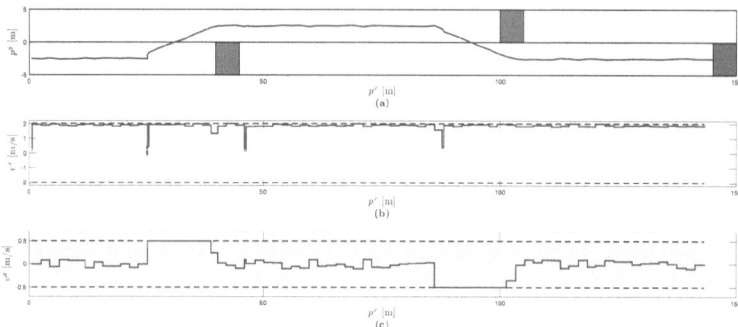

Fig. 9. Trajectories for one realization of disturbance trajectories: (a) state trajectories; (b) control trajectories of x-axis; (c) control trajectories of y-axis.

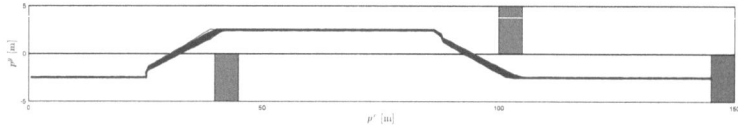

Fig. 10. State trajectories for 100 realizations of disturbance trajectories.

construct the TLT of φ' based on that of φ, which is shown in Fig. 8, and then continue to implement the TLT-based control synthesis algorithm. We can see that the vehicle changes lane from $[25.5, -2.4]$ and keeps moving forward. The trajectories are shown in Fig. 9. The vehicle is under the control obtained under φ' until it can sense $\mathbb{O}_2$ at $[86.11 \ 2.58]^T$.

Similarly, when the vehicle can sense $\mathbb{O}_2$, we update the set $\mathcal{AP} = \{a_1, a_2, a_3, a_4\}$ and the labelling function as follows: if $x \in \mathbb{X} \cap \mathbb{T}$, $L(x) = \{a_1, a_2\}$; if $x \in \mathbb{X} \cap \mathbb{O}_1$, $g(x) = \{a_1, a_3\}$; if $x \in \mathbb{X} \cap \mathbb{O}_2$, $L(x) = \{a_1, a_4\}$; otherwise, $L(x) = \{a_1\}$. To avoid $\mathbb{O}_2$, the task planner update the task φ' to be $\varphi'' = \varphi' \wedge (\square \neg a_4)$. We can construct the TLT of φ'' based on that of φ', which is shown in Fig. 8. Under the TLT-based control, we can see that the vehicle merges back from $[86.11 \ 2.58]^T$. Under the control with respect to φ'', the vehicle finally reaches the target set $\mathbb{T}$. Figure 9 (a) shows the state trajectories, from which we can appreciate that the entire specification is attained. Figure 9 (b)–(c) show the corresponding control inputs, where the dashed lines denote the control bounds. The cyan regions represent the synthesized control sets and the blue lines are the control trajectories. We repeat the above process for 100 realizations of the disturbance trajectories: the state trajectories for such 100 realizations are shown in Fig. 10.

5   Conclusion

In this article, we have introduced a TLT-based solution for integrating adaptive task planning and formal control synthesis. Unlike automaton-based methods, the TLT is constructed from LTL via reachability analysis, offering an abstraction-free method for control synthesis. By leveraging the controlled TLTs, we have presented techniques for adaptive task planning and formal control synthesis that are suitable to both finite- and infinite models under LTL specifications. We have showcased the effectiveness of our approach in a real-time problem, particularly in managing time-varying tasks and adaptively synthesising controllers accordingly. Future endeavors will focus on extending TLTs to accommodate broader temporal specification frameworks, such as CTL, along with comprehensive experimental validation and applications of our approach.

Acknowledgements. This work is supported in part by Knut and Alice Wallenberg Foundation Wallenberg Scholar Grant and Swedish Research Council Distinguished Professor Grant 2017-01078.

References

1. Baier, C., Katoen, J.P.: Principles of Model Checking. MIT Press, Cambridge (2008)
2. Blanchini, F., Miani, S., et al.: Set-Theoretic Methods in Control, vol. 78. Springer, Cham (2008). https://doi.org/10.1007/978-3-319-17933-9
3. Clarke, E.M., Emerson, E.A.: Design and synthesis of synchronization skeletons using branching time temporal logic. In: Workshop on logic of programs, pp. 52–71. Springer, Cham (1981). https://doi.org/10.1007/bfb0025774
4. Coogan, S., Gol, E.A., Arcak, M., Belta, C.: Traffic network control from temporal logic specifications. IEEE Trans. Control Netw. Syst. **2**(3), 162–171 (2016)
5. Emerson, E.A.: Automata, tableaux, and temporal logics. In: Proceedings of Workshop on Logic of Programs, pp. 79–88 (1985)
6. Gao, Y., Abate, A., Jiang, F.J., Giacobbe, M., Xie, L., Johansson, K.H.: Temporal logic trees for model checking and control synthesis of uncertain discrete-time systems. IEEE Trans. Autom. Control **67**(10), 5071–5086 (2022)
7. Gao, Y., Jiang, F.J., Ren, X., Xie, L., Johansson, K.H.: Reachability-based human-in-the-loop control with uncertain specifications. IFAC-Papers Online **53**(2), 1880–1887 (2020)
8. Guo, M., Tumová, J., Dimarogonas, D.V.: Communication-free multi-agent control under local temporal tasks and relative-distance constraints. IEEE Trans. Autom. Control **12**(61), 3948–3962 (2016)
9. Hashimoto, K., Dimarogonas, D.V.: Resource-aware networked control systems under temporal logic specifications. Discret. Event Dyn. Syst. **29**, 473 (2019)
10. Jiang, F.J., Gao, Y., Xie, L., Johansson, K.H.: Human-centered design for safe teleoperation of connected vehicles. IFAC-PapersOnLine **53**(5), 224–231 (2020)
11. Rabin, M.O.: Decidability of second-order theories and automata on infinite trees. Trans. Am. Math. Soc. **141**, 1–35 (1969)
12. Rakovic, S.V., Kerrigan, E.C., Mayne, D.Q., Lygeros, J.: Reachability analysis of discrete-time systems with disturbances. IEEE Trans. Autom. Control **51**(4), 546–561 (2006)
13. Raman, V., Donzé, A., Maasoumy, M., Murray, R.M., Sangiovanni-Vincentelli, A., Seshia, S.A.: Model predictive control with signal temporal logic specifications. In: 53rd IEEE Conference on Decision and Control, pp. 81–87. IEEE (2014)

14. Sessa, P.G., Frick, D., Wood, T.A., Kamgarpour, M.: From uncertainty data to robust policies for temporal logic planning. In: Proceedings of ACM International Conference on Hybrid Systems: Computation and Control, pp. 157–166 (2018)
15. Ulusoy, A., Belta, C.: Receding horizon temporal logic control in dynamic environments. Int. J. Robot. Res. **12**(33), 1593–1607 (2014)
16. Vardi, M.Y.: An automata-theoretic approach to linear temporal logic. In: Moller, F., Birtwistle, G. (eds.) Logics for Concurrency, pp. 238–266. Springer (1996)

Trading Space for Simplicity in Stateless Model Checking

Parosh Aziz Abdulla[1]([✉])[iD], Mohamed Faouzi Atig[1][iD], Sarbojit Das[1][iD],
Bengt Jonsson[1][iD], and Konstantinos Sagonas[1,2][iD]

[1] Uppsala University, Uppsala, Sweden
parosh@it.uu.se
[2] National Technical University of Athens, Athens, Greece

Abstract. Stateless model checking is a fully automatic verification technique for concurrent programs. which checks for safety violations by exploring all possible thread schedulings. It becomes effective when coupled with Dynamic Partial Order Reduction (DPOR), which introduces an equivalence on schedulings and reduces the amount of exploration. DPOR algorithms that are *optimal* are particularly effective in that they guarantee to explore *exactly* one execution from each equivalence class. Recently, the authors of this paper presented Parsimonious-OPtimal (POP) DPOR, an optimal DPOR algorithm for analyzing multi-threaded programs under sequential consistency, whose space consumption is polynomial in the worst case. This space consumption bound was realized due to a carefully crafted encoding of so-called sleep sets, a mechanism for preventing redundant exploration. This encoding brings some conceptual complexity to POP, which achieves good worst-case performance at the possible expense of worse average-case performance. In this paper, we present a simpler technique for managing sleep sets, which has exponential worst-case space consumption but better average-case performance. We experimentally compare these two sleep set management schemes on a range of benchmarks. The experimental results confirm that a simpler sleep set is a better choice when designing DPOR algorithms as they are faster and have similar memory consumption for average programs.

1 Introduction

Model checking is one of the success stories of formal methods. While the first incarnations of model checking algorithms targeted small models or programs, through the development of increasingly efficient techniques and implementations, model checking is now standardly applied in industry in numerous applications. One prominent branch of model checking is the analysis of timed systems, where a central problem has been the analysis of (variations of) timed automata. An important reason for the success of model checking for timed systems is the UPPAAL tool [25] by Wang Yi, Kim Larsen, Paul Pettersson, and colleagues,

S. Graf et al. (Eds.): Festschrift Wang Yi, LNCS 15230, pp. 79–97, 2025.
https://doi.org/10.1007/978-3-031-73751-0_8

which won the CAV award in 2013 for being the "foremost tool suite for the automated analysis and verification of real-time systems".[1]

The problem of checking control state reachability in a timed automaton is known to be PSPACE complete [7]. However, model checking tools such as UPPAAL do not implement an algorithm in PSPACE, but most often an algorithm based on enumerating reachable zones [24]. This is a very natural algorithm, which turns out to scale well in practice, but its worst-case space consumption is, in theory, doubly exponential. This observation illustrates the (common?) property that the best, or most natural, algorithm in practice is not always the one that provides the best theoretical worst-case guarantees.

In this paper, we consider a loosely related choice of algorithm in the area of *stateless model checking* (SMC) [11] for multithreaded programs. When supplied with a terminating program and fixed input data, SMC explores the set of all thread schedulings that are possible during program execution, driven by a dedicated runtime scheduler. Given sufficient resources, the exploration covers all possible executions and detects any program crashes and assertion violations. The technique is entirely automatic, has no false positives, and can reproduce the concurrency bugs it detects. It can be implemented in a memory-efficient way, since it only needs to maintain the current state of a program execution, together with information to support (say) a backtracking depth-first exploration of all program executions. For non-pathological programs, this can be done using space that is linear in the size of the analyzed program. SMC has been implemented in many tools (e.g., VeriSoft [12], CHESS [28], Concuerror [8], NIDHUGG [2], and GENMC [22]), and successfully applied to realistic programs (e.g., by Godefroid *et al.* [13] and Kokologiannakis and Sagonas [21]).

To reduce the number of explored executions generated by combinatorial explosion, SMC tools employ *dynamic partial order reduction* (DPOR) [1,9,17]. DPOR defines an equivalence relation on executions, typically Mazurkiewicz trace equivalence [27], which preserves important correctness properties, such as reachability of local states, and explores at least one execution in each equivalence class. The reduction in number of executions comes at a modest overhead, which in the original DPOR algorithm of Flanagan and Godefroid [9] could consume space quadratic in the length of the longest program execution (or the size of the program after unrolling loops). Over the years, DPOR has been adapted and refined to a number of programming models [4,14,16,26,29,31]; to be efficient in the presence of parallel programming constructs [15,20], and has been adapted for weak concurrency memory models [2,17,19,33].

An important improvement has been the development of *optimal* DPOR algorithms [1], which are efficient in that they guarantee to explore *exactly* one execution from each equivalence class and can achieve exponential reduction compared to non-optimal ones. This reduction improvement comes at the cost of increased memory consumption, which for most programs is modest [3], but in the worst case can be exponential in the length of the longest execution. This worst-case bound was improved by optimal algorithms with polynomial

---

[1] https://i-cav.org/cav-award/.

space complexity, one (called TruSt, for Truly Stateless) for a graph-based representation of executions [18], and one (called POP, for Parsimonious-OPtimal) for sequence-based representation of executions [6], which is the most natural representation when the analysis done for a sequentially consistent model of concurrency.

The POP DPOR algorithm for analyzing multi-threaded programs under sequential consistency (SC) is designed for programs in which threads interact by atomic reads, writes, and read-modify-writes (RMWs) to shared variables. It presents several novel algorithmic techniques:

- A *parsimonious race reversal* technique which avoids to reverse (almost) all races that will not lead to previously unexplored executions. In contrast, most existing DPOR algorithms reverse races indiscriminately, only to thereafter discard redundant reversals (e.g., by sleep sets or similar mechanisms).
- An *eager race reversal* strategy (inspired from TruSt [18]), which starts exploration of the new execution immediately following a race reversal. This prevents accumulation of a potentially exponential number of execution fragments generated by race reversals.
- A *parsimonious characterization* of sleep sets, stemming from the fact that POP accumulates sleep sets, which in the worst case can be exponentially many. Therefore, POP employs a (compact) parsimonious characterization of sleep sets, which uses at most polynomial space.

The POP algorithm achieves its space complexity by means of the two last features, where in particular the parsimonious characterization of sleep sets is somewhat complex, causing the pseudocode to be somewhat nontrivial (cf. [6]). However, by accepting an exponential worst-case memory consumption, relying only on the parsimonious race reversal technique, and possibly also the eager race reversal strategy, we derive a version of POP, which is conceptually simpler to explain and implement. We refer to such a simpler version of pop as *Dynamic POP (DPOP)*, for the reason that it generates new elements of sleep sets in a dynamic fashion by accumulating elements of sleep sets one-by-one throughout the exploration process, in contrast to the originally presented POP, in which the sleep set associated with a schedule is generated from the information in the race that induced this schedule.

In this paper, we present DPOP, and experimentally compare its performance to the original POP algorithm. We will actually consider two versions of DPOP, without or with the eager race reversal strategy, called *Lazy DPOP* (LPOP in short) and *Eager DPOP* (EPOP in short), respectively.

2   Illustration

In this section, we informally present the core principles of our approach. We introduce the algorithmic techniques of parsimonious race reversal and eager race reversal, along with how they relate to previous sequence-based DPOR algorithms, on a simple example, shown in Fig. 1. In this code, four threads

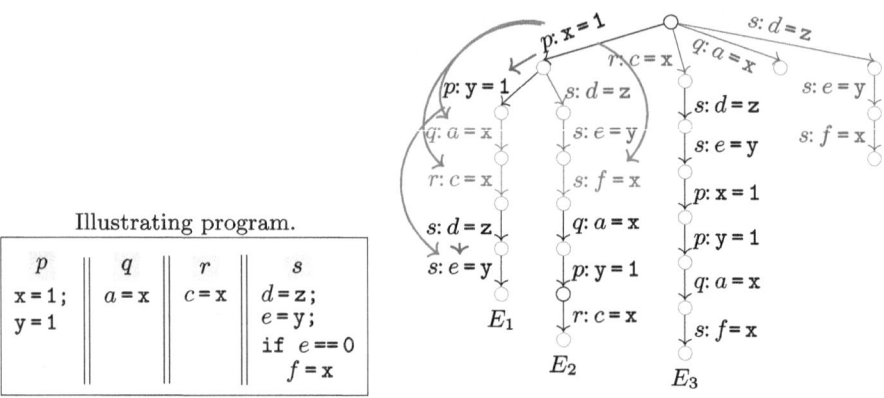

Illustrating program.

p	q	r	s
x = 1;	a = x	c = x	d = z;
y = 1			e = y;
			if e == 0
			f = x

Fig. 1. A program and part of its execution tree with three executions (E_1–E_3) that POP will explore plus two schedules that will be the start of subsequent exploration. In E_1 and E_2, the blue arrows are program order, and red arcs show races that will be reversed. The three fresh reads on x are shown in teal, and the four schedules that POP will construct are shown in purple. (Color figure online)

(p, q, r, and s) access three shared variables (x, y, and z), using five thread-local registers (a, c, d, e, and f).[2] DPOR algorithms typically first explore an arbitrary execution, which is then inspected to detect races. Assume that the first execution is E_1 (cf. the tree in Fig. 1). To detect races in an execution E, one must first compute its happens-before order, denoted $\xrightarrow{\text{hb}}_E$, which is the smallest transitive relation that orders two events that are (i) in the same thread, or (ii) access a common shared variable and at least one of them is a write. A *race* consists of two events in different threads that are adjacent in the $\xrightarrow{\text{hb}}_E$ order. The execution E_1 contains three races (the red arcs left of E_1 in Fig. 1). Let us first consider the race on y, in which the first event is p: y = 1 and the second is s: e = y. For each race, a DPOR algorithm constructs an initial fragment of an alternative execution, which reverses the race and branches off from the explored execution just before the race. In early DPOR algorithms, including the "Classic" DPOR algorithm by Flanagan and Godefroid [9] and the Source DPOR algorithm of Abdulla *et al.* [1], this initial fragment consists of just one event which can initiate an execution which reverses the race. For this race, these algorithms would store s: d = z as an alternative to p: y = 1, since s: d = z must be performed before the racing access to y (i.e., s: e = y). Storing only the first event of an alternative execution has the advantage that it does not consume much space, but has the problem that the execution after that event (s: d = z in our case) is not controlled, and may deviate from the path towards the racing event (s: e = y in our case), potentially leading to redundant exploration. Some DPOR algorithms, including Optimal DPOR and POP, address this problem by constructing the

---

[2] Throughout this paper, we assume that threads are spawned by a `main` thread, and that all shared variables get initialized to 0, also by the main thread.

initial fragment as a *sequence* of events that lead to the second event, $s: e = y$ in this case. POP DPOR constructs a minimal such sequence (called a *schedule*) consisting of the events that happen before (in the $\xrightarrow{\text{hb}}_{E_1}$ order) the second event of the race while omitting the first event of the race. The schedule in this case is $s: d = z; s: e = y$, which is inserted as an alternative continuation after $p: x = 1$, marked purple in Fig. 1. This continuation can be extended to a maximal execution E_2.

Let us next consider the races on x in E_1; their first event is $p: x = 1$. For the race whose second event is $r: c = x$, POP constructs the schedule $r: c = x$ (there are no additional events happening before $r: c = x$), which is inserted as an initial fragment of an alternative execution, which can later be extended to E_3 (cf. Fig. 1). For the race whose second event is $q: a = x$, POP constructs the schedule $q: a = x$, which is also inserted as an initial fragment of an alternative execution.

Parsimonious Race Reversals: To illustrate POP's mechanism for reversing each race only once, let us next consider the races in execution E_2. There is one race on y, between $s: e = y$ and $p: y = 1$. However, this race should not be reversed since it would give back the event order in E_1. POP avoids this redundant exploration by forbidding to consider races whose first event (in this case $s: e = y$) is in some schedule: reversing a race whose first event is in a schedule yields a fragment that was already explored in some previous execution. The execution E_2 also exhibits three races on x, all including $p: x = 1$. The race with $s: f = x$ is new, but the two other races have already occurred in E_1. These two races should therefore not be considered by POP, since the schedules they would generate have already been generated from the corresponding races in E_1. POP achieves this by forbidding to consider races whose second event is not *fresh*. Intuitively, a fresh event is an event which did not occur with the same $\xrightarrow{\text{hb}}$ predecessors in a previously explored execution (and whose reversal will therefore generate a schedule that did not appear before). More precisely, a second event of a race is fresh if it happens after (in the $\xrightarrow{\text{hb}}$ order) the last event of each schedule that occurs between the two racing events in the execution; to check this the exploration algorithm remembers whether events in occur in a schedule or not. Returning to the three races on x in E_2, the only second event which is fresh is $s: f = x$. Therefore, only this race is considered; it generates the schedule $s: d = z; s: e = y; s: f = x$, which is inserted as the start of an alternative exploration (top right in Fig. 1). Note that the second event $q: a = x$ is *not* fresh, since it does not happen after the last event of the schedule $s: d = z; s: e = y$. for the same reason the second event $r: c = x$ is not fresh.

Eager Race Reversal Strategy: POP as described so far can be implemented so that the schedules constructed as alternative continuations of an event are all collected before they are explored. We refer to this realization of POP as *lazy POP* (with lazy race reversal strategy), and more specifically as *lazy dynamic POP* (with dynamic sleep set) or LPOP in short. However, such a lazy strategy can in the worst case consume memory that is exponential in the program size.

The reason is that for some programs, the number of schedules that branch off at a particular point in an execution may become exponential in the size of the program; this was first observed by Abdulla *et al.* [3, Sect. 9]; an illustrating shared-variable program is given in [18, Sect. 2.3]. POP DPOR avoids this problem by *exploring schedules eagerly*: immediately after the creation of a schedule, exploration switches to continuations of that schedule. We then obtain *eager DPOP* (EPOP for short). This policy can be realized by an algorithm that calls a recursive function to initiate exploration of a new schedule. EPOP still has worst-case exponential memory consumption, since the exponential size of sleep sets cannot be avoided. We establish, in the CAV 2024 POP DPOR paper [6], that the recursion depth of such an algorithm is at most $n(n-1)/2$, where n is the length longest execution of the analyzed program.

Sleep Sets: Even though the parsimonious race reversal strategy guarantees that the initial fragments of alternative executions are inequivalent, one must prevent that their continuations become equivalent. To illustrate this problem, let us return to the reversal of races on x in Fig. 1 (in both E_1 and E_2). The top leftmost event $p: x = 1$ races with three fresh reads on x: two in E_1 and one in E_2, shown in teal color. From these races, three schedules are constructed as initial fragments of alternative explorations: $r: c = x$ and $q: a = x$ from E_1 and $s: d = z$; $s: e = y$; $s: f = x$ from E_2. At this point, the algorithm needs to be careful: these schedules are not conflicting (i.e., both can be performed in the same execution sequence), since they all read from their common shared variable x. There is then a danger that the first schedule will be continued using the second, and the second will be continued using the first; the DROR algorithm would then explore two equivalent executions, consisting of these two schedules in either order. The standard DPOR technique for avoiding such redundant exploration is *sleep sets* [10]. In its standard form, a sleep set is a set of events that should not be performed before some conflicting event. Since POP uses schedules as beginnings of alternative explorations, the appropriate adaptation would be to let a sleep set be a set of schedules that should not be performed unless some conflicting event is performed before that. In Fig. 1, this would mean that after exploring the continuations of $r: c = x$, this schedule is added to the sleep set when starting to explore the continuations of $q: a = x$, which is thereafter also added to the sleep set when starting exploration from $s: d = z$; $s: e = y$; $s: f = x$ from E_2. This mechanism is simple to combine with eager exploration of schedules, resulting in the EPOP algorithm.

Unfortunately, there are programs where the number of schedules that conflict with a write event is exponential, whence the memory consumption may become exponential in the size of the program, because of large sleep sets. POP DPOR [6] avoids this problem by a *parsimonious characterization of sleep sets*, which consumes memory that is polynomial in the size of the program. This characterization is conceptually somewhat complex, therefore in this paper we investigate the effects of using a conceptually simpler handling of sleep sets (in DPOP).

3   Programs, Executions, and Equivalence

We consider programs consisting of a finite set of *threads* that share a finite set of *(shared) variables*. Each thread has a finite set of local registers and runs a deterministic code, built in a standard way from expressions (over local registers) and atomic commands, using standard control flow constructs (sequential composition, selection, and bounded loop constructs). Atomic commands either write the value of an expression to a shared variable, assign the value of a shared variable to a register, or atomically both read and modify a shared variable. Conditional control flow constructs can branch on the value of an expression. From here on, we use t to range over threads, and x, y, z to range over shared variables. The local state of a thread is defined as usual by its program counter and the contents of its registers. The global state of a program consists of the local state of each thread together with the valuation of the shared variables. The program has a unique initial state, in which shared variables have predefined initial values. We assume that memory is sequentially consistent [23].

The execution of a program statement is an *event*, which affects or is affected by the global state of the program. An event is represented by a tuple $\langle t, i, \mathrm{T}, x \rangle$, where t is the thread performing the event, i is a positive integer, denoting that the event results from the i-th execution step in thread t. T is the type of the event (either R for read or W for write and read-modify-write), and x is the accessed variable. If e is the event $\langle t, i, \mathrm{T}, x \rangle$, we write $e.th$ for t, $e.\mathrm{T}$ for T, and $e.var$ for x. We say that two events e and e' are *dependent* if they access the same variable and at least one of them writes to it.

An *execution sequence* (or just *execution*) E is a finite sequence of events, starting from the initial state of the program. We let $\mathtt{enabled}(E)$ denote the set of events that can be performed in the state to which E leads. An execution E is *maximal* if $\mathtt{enabled}(E) = \emptyset$. We let $\mathtt{dom}(E)$ denote the set of events in E; we also write $e \in E$ to denote $e \in \mathtt{dom}(E)$. We use u and w, possibly with superscripts, to range over sequences of events (not necessarily starting from the initial state), $\langle \rangle$ to denote the empty sequence, and $\langle e \rangle$ to denote the sequence with only the event e. We let $w \cdot w'$ denote the concatenation of sequences w and w', and let $w \backslash e$ denote the sequence w with the first occurrence of e (if any) removed. For a sequence $u = e_1 \cdot e_2 \cdot \ldots \cdot e_m$, we let $w \backslash u$ denote $(\cdots ((w \backslash e_1) \backslash e_2) \backslash \cdots) \backslash e_m$.

The basis for a DPOR algorithm is an equivalence relation on the set of execution sequences, which is based on a happens-before relation on the events of each execution sequence. Given an execution sequence E, define the *happens-before relation* on E, denoted $\xrightarrow{\mathrm{hb}}_E$, as the smallest irreflexive partial order on $\mathtt{dom}(E)$ such that $e \xrightarrow{\mathrm{hb}}_E e'$ if e occurs before e' in E, and either (i) $e.th = e.th'$, or (ii) e and e' are dependent. The hb-*trace* (or *trace* for short) of E is the directed graph $(\mathtt{dom}(E), \xrightarrow{\mathrm{hb}}_E)$. Two execution sequences E and E' are *equivalent*, denoted $E \simeq E'$, if they have the same hb-trace. We let $[E]_\simeq$ denote the equivalence class of E.

The equivalence relation $\simeq$ partitions the set of execution sequences into equivalence classes, paving the way for an optimal DPOR algorithm which explores precisely one execution in each equivalence class.

4   The Dynamic POP Algorithm

In this section, we explain the design of Dynamic POP (DPOP), which is optimal in the sense that it explores precisely one execution in each equivalence class. We will also show the two variants LPOP and EPOP. We first need some auxiliary definitions.

For two execution sequences $E \cdot w$ and $E \cdot w'$,

- the sequences w and w' are called *compatible*, denoted $w \sim w'$, iff there are sequences w'' and w''' such that $E \cdot w \cdot w'' \simeq E \cdot w' \cdot w'''$,
- the sequence w is called a *happens-before prefix* of w', denoted $w \sqsubseteq w'$, iff there is a sequence w'' such that $E \cdot w \cdot w'' \simeq E \cdot w'$.

We illustrate these concepts on the program in Fig. 1. Let w be the sequence of events in $s\colon d = z; s\colon e = y$, and w' be the sequence $q\colon a = x; r\colon c = x; s\colon d = z; s\colon e = y$. Then $w \sqsubseteq w'$ since $E \cdot w \cdot w'' \simeq E \cdot w'$ where w'' is the sequence $q\colon a = x; r\colon c = x$ and E is some preceding execution. Let next u be the sequence $s\colon d = z; s\colon e = y; s\colon f = x$, and u' be the sequence $p\colon y = 1; q\colon a = x$, then $u \not\sim u'$, since u and u''s first accesses to y are in conflict.

A sequence of events σ is called a *schedule* if all its events (except the last one) happen-before its last one, i.e., $e' \xrightarrow{\text{hb}} e$ where e is its last event, and e' is any other event in σ. The last event e of a schedule σ is called the *head* of σ, sometimes denoted $hd(\sigma)$. We sometimes call σ a *read schedule* if $hd(\sigma)$ is a read event. For an execution sequence $E \cdot w$ and event $e \in w$, define the schedule $e \downarrow^w$ to be the subsequence w' of w such that: (i) $e \in w'$ and (ii) for each $e' \in w$ it holds that $e' \in w'$ iff $e' \xrightarrow{\text{hb}}_{E \cdot w} e$.

4.1   Parsimonious Race Reversals

A central mechanism of many DPOR algorithms is to detect and reverse races. Intuitively, a race is a conflict between two consecutive accesses to a shared variable, where at least one access writes to the variable (i.e., it is a write or a read-modify-write).

Definition 1 (Race). *Let E be an execution sequence. Two events e and e' in E are* racing in E *if (i) e and e' are performed by different threads, (i) $e \xrightarrow{\text{hb}}_E e'$, and (iii) there is no event e'' with $e \xrightarrow{\text{hb}}_E e'' \xrightarrow{\text{hb}}_E e'$.*

Intuitively, a race arises when two different threads perform dependent accesses to a shared variable, which are adjacent in the $\xrightarrow{\text{hb}}_E$ order. If e and e' are racing in E, then to reverse the race, E is decomposed as $E = E_1 \cdot e \cdot E_2$ with

e' in E_2, thereafter the schedule $\sigma = e' \downarrow^{E_2}$ is formed as the initial fragment of an alternative execution, which extends E_1.

The key idea of parsimonious race reversal is to reverse a race *only if* such a reversal generates an execution that has not been explored before. To be able to do so, POP remembers whenever an event in a new execution is in a schedule, and whether it is a schedule head. This can be done, e.g., by marking events in schedules, and specifically marking the schedule head. From now on, we consider such markings to be included in the events of executions.

For an execution $E \cdot w \cdot e \cdot w'$, the event e is called *fresh in* $w \cdot e \cdot w'$ *after* E if (i) if e is in a schedule, then it is the head of that schedule, and (ii) for each head e_h of a schedule in w it is the case that $e_h \xrightarrow{\text{hb}}_{E \cdot w \cdot e} e$.

Definition 2 (Parsimonious race). *Let E be an execution sequence. Two events e and e' in E are in a* parsimonious race, *denoted $e \lesssim_E e'$ if (i) e and e' are racing in E, (ii) e is not in a schedule in E, and (iii) e' is fresh in $w \cdot e'$ after E_1, where $E = E_1 \cdot e \cdot w \cdot e' \cdot w'$.*

Conditions (ii) and (iii) are the additional conditions for a race to be parsimonious. They filter out races, whose reversals would lead to previously explored executions. Let us provide the intuition behind these two conditions. (ii) If e is in a schedule, then that schedule, call it σ, was generated by a race in an earlier explored execution E'. Hence σ was contained in E'. Moreover e' would race with the head of σ also in E'; if e' appeared after σ, the resulting new schedule would havw been generated already in E'; if e' appeared before σ, then we would only undo the previous race reversal. This is illustrated in Fig. 1 by the race on y, between $s\!:e = \mathsf{y}$ and $p\!:\mathsf{y} = 1$ in E_2. (iii) If e' is not fresh, then e' appeared with the same happens-before predecessors in an earlier explored execution E', where it was in a race that would generate the same schedule as in E. This is illustrated in Fig. 1 by the race on x between $p\!:\mathsf{x} = 1$ and $r\!:c = \mathsf{x}$ in E_2, which was already considered in E_1.

4.2 Sleep Sets

As described in Sect. 2, POP needs a sleep set mechanism to avoid redundant exploration of read schedules. Such a mechanism is needed whenever POP explores reversals of races with a write event e_W that appears after an execution E_1. Then each parsimonious race $e_W \lesssim_{E'} e_R$ between e_W and a read event e_R results in a schedule σ, which will be explored as a continuation of E_1. For any two such schedules, σ and σ', POP must ensure that *either* the exploration starting with σ does not continue in a way that includes σ', *or* (vice versa) that the exploration starting with σ' does not continue in a way that includes σ. Dynamic POP achieves this by remembering in a data structure $sleep[E]$, for each execution E, all read schedules that have been explored as continuations of E. A *sleep set*, denoted $sleep[E]$, is a set of read schedules that must not be performed during subsequent exploration from E; more precisely, the algorithm must not explore an execution $E.w'''$ such that $s \sqsubseteq w'''$ for some $s \in sleep[E]$.

Algorithm 1: Dynamic POP with Lazy Race Reversal (LPOP)

---

1 $sleep[\langle\rangle] = \emptyset$

2 ExploreLazy($\langle\rangle$)

3 ExploreLazy(E)

4 | $schedules[E] = \emptyset$

5 | **foreach** e *s.t.* $e \lesssim_E \text{last}(E)$ **do**

6 | | **let** $E = E_1 \cdot e \cdot E_2$

7 | | **let** $\sigma = \text{last}(E) {\downarrow}^{E_2}$

8 | | **if** $\nexists s \in sleep[E_1] : s \sqsubseteq \sigma$ **then**

9 | | | $schedules[E_1] \cup= \sigma$

10 | **if** $\exists e \in \text{enabled}(E)$ *s.t.* $\langle e \rangle \notin sleep[E]$ **then**

11 | | $sleep[E \cdot e] = \{s \backslash e \mid s \in sleep[E] \wedge s \sim e\}$

12 | | ExploreLazy($E \cdot e$)

13 | | **foreach** σ *in* $schedules[E]$ **do**

14 | | | $sleep[E \cdot \sigma] = \{s \backslash \sigma \mid s \in sleep[E] \wedge s \sim \sigma\}$

15 | | | ExploreLazy($E \cdot \sigma$)

16 | | | **if** $\text{last}(\sigma).T = R$ **then** $sleep[E] \cup= \sigma$

The sleep set is updated during exploration, as follows: on each explored event e, we obtain $sleep[E \cdot e]$ from $sleep[E]$ by:

$$sleep[E \cdot e] = \{s \backslash e \mid s \in sleep[E] \wedge s \sim e\}$$

That is, the sleep set $sleep[E]$ is updated by removing e from those sequences that are compatible with e and completely discarding the other sequences. It follows that an extension of E by an event e should be blocked if $\langle e \rangle \in sleep(E)$.

As described in Sect. 2, the number of schedules in the sleep set may in the worst case be exponential in the size of the program. Motivated by this observation, the version of POP described in the CAV 2024 paper [6] is equipped with a *parsimonious sleep set characterization*, in which each explored execution E is equipped with a characterization of the sleep set which needs at most polynomial memory. The caveat is that POP's encoding of sleep sets is rather complex, hence we will present two variants of a conceptually simpler algorithm in this paper, which we refer to as Dynamic POP, in which sleep sets are represented explicitly.

4.3   The Dynamic POP Algorithm (Lazy Version)

The Dynamic POP algorithm, shown as Algorithm 1, takes an input program and explores its executions by repeated calls to the procedure ExploreLazy. For each prefix E' of execution under exploration, the algorithm maintains a set $schedules[E']$ of schedules that will be explored, and a sleep set $sleep[E']$ as described in Sect. 4.2 to prevent redundant exploration of read schedules. The algorithm starts with an initialization of the sleep set for empty sequence $\langle\rangle$ to the empty set and a call ExploreLazy($\langle\rangle$). Each call to ExploreLazy(E) first

---

Algorithm 2: Dynamic POP with Eager Race Reversal (EPOP)

---

1 $sleep[\langle\rangle] = \emptyset$

2 ExploreEager($\langle\rangle$)

3 ExploreEager(E)

4 | **if** $\exists e \in$ **enabled** (E) *s.t.* $\langle e \rangle \notin sleep[E]$ **then**

5 | | $sleep[E \cdot e] = \{s\backslash e \mid s \in sleep[E] \wedge s \sim e\}$

6 | | ExploreEager($E \cdot e$)

7 | **else**

8 | | **for** $i = 0$ *to* $|E|$ **do**

9 | | | **foreach** *race* $e \lesssim_E e'$ *where* $e = E[i]$ **do**

10 | | | | **let** $E = E_1 \cdot e \cdot E_2$

11 | | | | **let** $\sigma = e' \downarrow^{E_2}$

12 | | | | **if** $\nexists s \in sleep[E_1] : s \sqsubseteq \sigma$ **then**

13 | | | | | $sleep[E_1 \cdot \sigma] = \{s\backslash\sigma \mid s \in sleep[E_1] \wedge s \sim \sigma\}$

14 | | | | | ExploreEager($E_1 \cdot \sigma$)

15 | | | | | **if** **last** $(E).\text{T} = \text{R}$ **then** $sleep[E_1] \mathrel{\cup}= \sigma$

---

initializes the set of schedules, whereafter, it consists of a race reversal phase (lines 5 to 9) and an exploration phase (lines 10 to 16). In the race reversal phase, it considers all parsimonious races between an event e in E and the last event **last** (E) of E (line 5). For each such race of form $e \lesssim_E$ **last** (E), it decomposes E as $E_1 \cdot e \cdot E_2$ (line 6), and forms the schedule σ that reverses the race as **last** $(E) \downarrow^{E_2}$ (line 7). It then intends to insert σ into the set of schedules, but before that, it needs to check that exploring $E_1 \cdot \sigma$ will not be redundant, and also initialize $sleep[E_1 \cdot \sigma]$. To check that exploring $E_1 \cdot \sigma$ will not be redundant, the algorithm checks that the schedule does not include a schedule from the current sleep set $sleep[E_1]$ of E_1 (line 8). If this check succeeds, σ is added to the schedules after E_1 (line 9). In the exploration phase, ExploreLazy first picks an event e that is enabled for execution and not blocked by the sleep set (line 10). It computes $sleep[E_1 \cdot e]$ (line 11) that is used for continuing exploration through the call ExploreLazy($E \cdot e$) (line 12). After its return, each schedule σ in $schedules[E]$ that has been accumulated during the call ExploreLazy($E \cdot e$) is explored through a call ExploreLazy($E \cdot \sigma$) (line 15). Before each of these calls, $sleep[E \cdot \sigma]$ is computed from $sleep[E]$ (line 14). If the schedule is a read schedule, it is added to the sleep set after the call (line 16).

4.4 The Dynamic POP Algorithm (Eager Version)

Algorithm 1 suffers from the potential problem that the number of schedules in $schedules[E]$ may become exponential for some programs (an example is provided in Sect. 5). To avoid this problem, we can adopt an idea from the TruSt algorithm [18] and explore schedules *eagerly*: immediately after the creation of a schedule, exploration switches to continuations of that schedule. This policy can be realized by an algorithm that calls a recursive function to initiate the exploration of a new schedule. A realization of this policy appears in Algorithm 2, referred to as EPOP. Since this algorithm does not accumulate schedules, there is not need for the data structure *schedules*[E].

The EPOP algorithm features a combination of parsimonious race reversal and eager race reversal. In its exploration phase, ExploreEager first picks an event e that is enabled for execution and not blocked by the sleep set (line 4). The algorithm computes the sleep set *sleep*[$E \cdot e$] (line 5) and extends E by adding e at the end (line 6). In the race reversal phase, the algorithm picks event $e = E[i]$ at each position i from the beginning to the end of the execution E. It detects parsimonious races $e \lesssim_E e'$ (line 9) and constructs schedules (line 11). In contrast to LPOP, newly constructed schedules (line 11) are not added to a set *schedules*[E_1], but instead, the algorithm directly performs a recursive call ExploreEager($E_1 \cdot \sigma$) (line 14), after checking that the schedule is not blocked by the sleep set at E_1 (line 12) and calculating the updated sleep set (line 13). If the schedule is a read schedule, it is added to the sleep set after the call (line 15).

4.5 Correctness and Optimality

Correctness and optimality for LPOP and EPOP can be proven in a similar manner as for the POP algorithm (see [5]). In the CAV 2024 paper [6], it is established that the recursion depth of EPOP is at most $n(n-1)/2$, where n is the length of the longest execution of the analyzed program. Algorithm 2 avoids the accumulation of schedules but may, for some programs, suffer from having to maintain exponential-size sleep sets. We show an example in Sect. 5. The POP algorithm [6] avoids this problem by a compact characterization of potentially exponential-size sleep sets at the cost of a conceptually more complex algorithm.

5 Example Program with Exponential Space Complexity

In this section, we show a program, which is parametric on the number of threads spawned, that leads to storing an exponential number of schedules in LPOP, and to storing sleep sets of exponential size in both the LPOP and EPOP algorithms.

The code of the program (Fig. 2(left)), consists of a thread p doing a write on x, a thread q that spawns n threads, $q_1, \ldots, q_n$, each doing a write on y, followed by thread q performing a read from x to a local register a after all the children threads have been joined. Both LPOP and EPOP explore $2n!$ executions, shown in the exploration tree in the right part of Fig. 2. LPOP's depth-first exploration strategy first explores $n!$ executions $E_1, \cdots E_{n!}$ as a result of the reversal of races involving n write events on y ($n!$ permutations of n write events). In each execution E_i, the algorithm reverses the race (in red arrow) between the events x = 1 and a = x, and stores the produced schedule σ_i. Eventually, LPOP stores $n!$ schedules. In contrast, EPOP's eager race reversal strategy eliminates this problem by exploring each σ_i immediately after production and redundancy check.

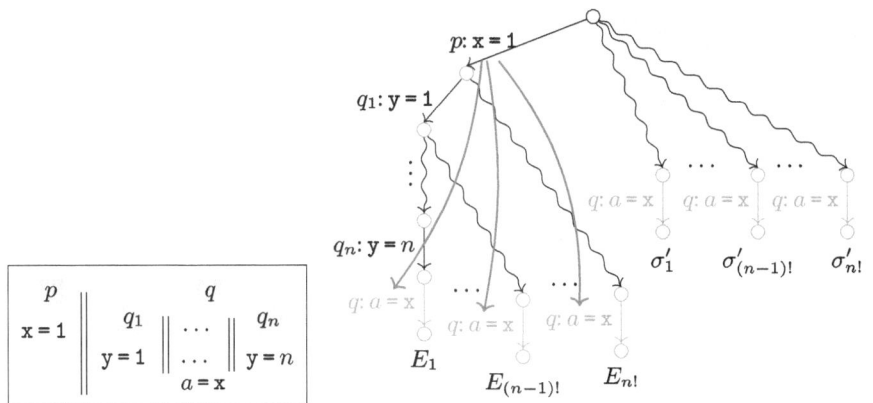

Fig. 2. The exp-mem3 program (left) and its incomplete exploration tree (right). (Color figure online)

However, there is also another problem: both algorithms store an exponential number of schedules in the sleep set $sleep[\langle\rangle]$. This happens because after finishing the exploration of each σ_i, both LPOP and EPOP put the schedule into the sleep set $sleep[\langle\rangle]$. When the last schedule σ_{last} is produced, $sleep[\langle\rangle]$ contains all the $(n! - 1)$ previously explored σ_i's. POP's parsimonious sleep set representation [6] solves this problem by representing sleep sets by polynomial size expressions. POP not only solves the problem with exponential space, but also makes the redundancy check much faster in this case, as it does not have to compare against an exponential number of schedules in the sleep set. The experimental results we present in the next section (benchmark exp-mem3 of Table 1) show exactly that.

6   Implementation and Evaluation

We have implemented the two algorithms in a fork of NIDHUGG. NIDHUGG is a state-of-the-art stateless model checker for C/C++ programs with Pthreads, which operates at the level of LLVM Intermediate Representation. The tool comes with a selection of DPOR algorithms. One of them is Optimal DPOR [1] which was recently enhanced with Partial Loop Purity elimination and support for `await` statements [15]. In our NIDHUGG fork, besides the POP algorithm [6], we have added the LPOP and EPOP algorithms to the selection. The LPOP's implementation uses the same structure as the Optimal DPOR's implementation with an updated race detection procedure conforming to the parsimonious race definition. To improve performance, a simple and efficient data structure implemented to store the execution currently being explored and the schedules. For EPOP's implementation, we used a different data structure to store the execution currently being explored that enables the algorithm to follow the next schedule to explore and backtrack to the previous execution when there are no

Table 1. Time and memory performance of four sequence-based optimal DPOR algorithms on nine benchmark programs which are parametric in the number of threads.

Benchmark	Executions	Time (secs)				Memory (MB)			
		Optimal	LPOP	EPOP	POP	Optimal	LPOP	EPOP	POP
circular-buffer(7)	3432	0.45	0.39	0.43	0.43	84	84	84	84
circular-buffer(8)	12870	1.79	1.51	1.56	1.66	84	84	84	84
circular-buffer(9)	48620	7.21	6.07	6.38	6.67	84	84	84	84
fib-bench(4)	19605	1.93	1.46	1.69	1.82	84	84	84	84
fib-bench(5)	218243	24.66	18.41	21.29	24.10	84	84	84	84
fib-bench(6)	2364418	301.30	227.46	258.68	297.40	84	84	84	84
linuxrwlocks(6)	99442	13.71	11.68	12.32	12.88	91	91	91	91
linuxrwlocks(7)	829168	127.66	110.30	112.76	121.17	91	91	91	91
linuxrwlocks(8)	6984234	1176.13	1023.78	1096.76	1119.23	91	91	91	91
filesystem(22)	512	0.62	0.32	0.32	0.34	84	84	84	84
filesystem(24)	2048	2.97	1.29	1.31	1.32	187	84	84	84
filesystem(26)	8192	15.71	5.40	5.43	5.66	622	84	84	84
indexer(15)	4096	8.58	5.40	5.45	5.65	116	90	90	90
indexer(16)	32768	80.37	46.28	46.63	46.46	464	90	90	90
indexer(17)	262144	827.02	388.24	394.87	399.87	3030	90	90	90
lastzero(10)	3328	0.34	0.26	0.28	0.27	84	84	84	84
lastzero(15)	147456	24.46	13.53	14.73	15.09	276	84	84	84
lastzero(20)	6029312	1828.92	711.81	759.50	786.19	8883	84	84	84
dispatcher(4)	6854	1.75	1.40	1.45	1.47	90	90	90	90
dispatcher(5)	151032	55.07	39.50	41.06	42.76	407	266	90	90
dispatcher(6)	4057388	2333.51	1515.66	1396.23	1424.57	9097	5989	90	90
poke(10)	135944	96.30	60.32	60.20	63.45	791	376	90	90
poke(15)	728559	891.26	514.00	468.69	479.03	5527	2352	90	90
poke(20)	2366924	4356.59	2344.25	1955.71	2008.92	22383	9576	90	90
exp-mem3(7)	10080	0.67	0.52	0.56	0.54	104	91	85	85
exp-mem3(8)	80640	6.15	4.29	4.74	4.61	506	371	311	85
exp-mem3(9)	725760	73.68	41.94	45.66	44.83	4489	2951	2405	85
exp-mem3(10)	7257600	922.94	463.41	500.45	502.50	47884	29241	23801	85

further races to reverse. We also implemented the following simple optimization. Instead of computing and storing sleep set for each prefix of executions as the pseudocode of LPOP and EPOP describes, the implementation computes and stores sleep sets when needed for race reversal. This improves the performance of the implementations of LPOP and EPOP for the exp-mem3 program by avoiding the manipulation of exponential sleep set as much as possible.

In this section, we evaluate the performance of both LPOP's and EPOP's implementation and compare it, in terms of time and memory, against the implementations of Optimal DPOR in NIDHUGG commit 5805d77 and POP in our fork commit 5e89549. All tools employed LLVM 14.0.6, and the numbers we present are measured on a desktop with a Ryzen 7950X CPU running Debian 12.6.

Table 1 presents the results of our experiments. The benchmarks are those used also in our CAV 2024 paper, and originate from various papers of the DPOR literature. They are all parametric on the number of threads they use, which are shown in parentheses after the benchmark's name. Since these four algorithms are optimal w.r.t. the Mazurkiewicz trace equivalence, they all explore the same number of executions (second column) in all benchmarks. We will analyze the results in four groups (cf. Table 1).

The first group consists of three programs: circular-buffer, fib-bench, and lin-uxrwlocks. In these programs, all algorithms consume memory that stays constant as the size of the program and the number of executions explored increase. In terms of time performance, we notice that all four algorithms scale similarly, with LPOP being the fastest implementation, EPOP coming second, followed by POP in third and with Optimal DPOR in the last place. We attribute LPOP's faster execution to the simplicity of its implementation, most notably to its streamlined race reversal phase, which detects all the races, produces schedules, and checks redundancy in a simple way. On the other hand, EPOP's eager race reversal strategy performs some extra work going forward to explore a new execution and backtracking after finishing exploration. Still, this extra work is less than that which is needed by POP's quite complex parsimonious sleep set characterization.

The second group consists also of three programs: filesystem, indexer, and lastzero. These are programs for which Optimal DPOR's memory consumption grows considerably with the size of the program, while the memory consumption of the other three algorithms stays constant. In terms of time performance, we notice a picture similar to that for the programs of the first group: LPOP's implementation is slightly faster than EPOP's and POP's. However, the implementation of all three of these algorithms are now two to three times faster than Optimal DPOR's, which suffers from its increased space consumption.

The third group comprises two programs: dispatcher and poke. For these programs, LPOP's space consumption increases with the size of the program. This also affects the runtime performance of LPOP, which is not the fastest implementation anymore. In contrast, EPOP's and POP's space consumption stays constant. Between these two implementations, EPOP is slightly faster.

Finally, let us examine the performance of the synthetic exp-mem3 program that was presented in Sect. 5. As expected, POP exhibits constant space consumption for this program, while the memory consumption of both LPOP and EPOP increase with the size of the program. Still, this increase is less than that of the Optimal DPOR's implementation. Time-wise, the memory increase does not seem to affect much the implementation of the two DPOP algorithms; in fact, LPOP's implementation is the fastest one.

We can summarize our evaluation with the following conclusions:

i. In most programs, both LPOP's and EPOP's simpler implementations are able to achieve a slight performance advantage in terms of time, often also combined with good memory consumption.

ii. However, there also exist programs for which LPOP's (mainly) and EPOP's (to a lesser extent) performance suffers due to increased memory consumption. For those programs, an algorithm like POP, which comes with space performance guarantees is superior.

7   Conclusion

This paper presents two Dynamic POP algorithms (LPOP and EPOP), which are optimal for analyzing multi-threaded programs under SC. Both algorithms are variants of POP DPOR [6] and attain simplicity at the expense of exponential worst-case memory consumption. Our experiments show that LPOP's and EPOP's implementation are quite often slightly more performant than POP's. In particular, in many cases, LPOP's implementation is the fastest because of its simple and streamlined race reversal phase. However, unlike POP, the exploration process of Dynamic POP is inherently non-concurrent, making it difficult to parallelize.

As future work, it would be interesting to investigate how DPOP's simple yet novel algorithmic techniques on DPOR algorithms are helpful for different computational models and programs under weak concurrency memory models such as TSO and PSO. It is also relevant to extend the techniques to complete (rather than stateless) model checking similarly to the classical early works [10,30,32]. A challenge is to complement notions such as *persistent*, *ample*, and *stubborn* sets that were used in these works to design more efficient verification algorithms.

Acknowledgments. We thank the anonymous reviewers for helpful comments. This research was partially funded by research grants from the Swedish Research Council (Vetenskapsrådet) and from the Swedish Foundation for Strategic Research through project aSSIsT.

Data Availibility Statement. We provide an artifact with the implementations of LPOP and EPOP and all benchmarks we have used for our evaluation in the following URL: https://doi.org/10.5281/zenodo.13225258.

References

1. Abdulla, P., Aronis, S., Jonsson, B., Sagonas, K.: Optimal dynamic partial order reduction. In: Symposium on Principles of Programming Languages, POPL 2014, pp. 373–384. ACM, New York (2014). https://doi.org/10.1145/2535838.2535845
2. Abdulla, P.A., Aronis, S., Atig, M.F., Jonsson, B., Leonardsson, C., Sagonas, K.: Stateless model checking for TSO and PSO. In: Baier, C., Tinelli, C. (eds.) TACAS 2015. LNCS, vol. 9035, pp. 353–367. Springer, Heidelberg (2015). https://doi.org/10.1007/978-3-662-46681-0_28
3. Abdulla, P.A., Aronis, S., Jonsson, B., Sagonas, K.: Source sets: a foundation for optimal dynamic partial order reduction. J. ACM **64**(4), 25:1–25:49 (2017). https://doi.org/10.1145/3073408

4. Abdulla, P.A., et al.: Tailoring stateless model checking for event-driven multi-threaded programs. In: André, É., Sun, J. (eds.) ATVA 2023, Part II. LNCS, vol. 14216, pp. 176–198. Springer, Cham (2023). https://doi.org/10.1007/978-3-031-45332-8_9

5. Abdulla, P.A., Atig, M.F., Das, S., Jonsson, B., Sagonas, K.: Parsimonious optimal dynamic partial order reduction. CoRR abs/2405.11128 (2024). https://doi.org/10.48550/ARXIV.2405.11128

6. Abdulla, P.A., Atig, M.F., Das, S., Jonsson, B., Sagonas, K.: Parsimonious optimal dynamic partial order reduction. In: Gurfinkel, A., Ganesh, V. (eds.) CAV 2024, Part II. LNCS, vol. 14682, pp. 19–43. Springer, Cham (2024). https://doi.org/10.1007/978-3-031-65630-9_2

7. Alur, R., Dill, D.L.: A theory of timed automata. Theor. Comput. Sci. **126**(2), 183–235 (1994). https://doi.org/10.1016/0304-3975(94)90010-8

8. Christakis, M., Gotovos, A., Sagonas, K.: Systematic testing for detecting concurrency errors in Erlang programs. In: Sixth IEEE International Conference on Software Testing, Verification and Validation, ICST 2013, Los Alamitos, CA, USA, pp. 154–163. IEEE (2013). https://doi.org/10.1109/ICST.2013.50

9. Flanagan, C., Godefroid, P.: Dynamic partial-order reduction for model checking software. In: Principles of Programming Languages (POPL), pp. 110–121. ACM, New York (2005). https://doi.org/10.1145/1040305.1040315

10. Godefroid, P.: Partial-order methods for the verification of concurrent systems: an approach to the state-explosion problem. Ph.D. thesis, University of Liège (1996). https://doi.org/10.1007/3-540-60761-7. http://www.springer.com/gp/book/9783540607618, also, volume 1032 of LNCS, Springer

11. Godefroid, P.: Model checking for programming languages using VeriSoft. In: Principles of Programming Languages (POPL), pp. 174–186. ACM Press, New York (1997). https://doi.org/10.1145/263699.263717

12. Godefroid, P.: Software model checking: the VeriSoft approach. Formal Methods Syst. Des. **26**(2), 77–101 (2005). https://doi.org/10.1007/s10703-005-1489-x

13. Godefroid, P., Hanmer, R.S., Jagadeesan, L.: Model checking without a model: an analysis of the heart-beat monitor of a telephone switch using VeriSoft. In: Proceedings of the ACM SIGSOFT International Symposium on Software Testing and Analysis, ISSTA, pp. 124–133. ACM, New York (1998). https://doi.org/10.1145/271771.271800

14. Jensen, C.S., Møller, A., Raychev, V., Dimitrov, D., Vechev, M.T.: Stateless model checking of event-driven applications. In: Proceedings of the 2015 ACM SIGPLAN International Conference on Object-Oriented Programming, Systems, Languages, and Applications, OOPSLA 2015, pp. 57–73. ACM, New York (2015). https://doi.org/10.1145/2814270.2814282

15. Jonsson, B., Lång, M., Sagonas, K.: Awaiting for Godot: stateless model checking that avoids executions where nothing happens. In: Griggio, A., Rungta, N. (eds.) 22nd Formal Methods in Computer-Aided Design, FMCAD 2022, pp. 284–293. IEEE (2022). https://doi.org/10.34727/2022/ISBN.978-3-85448-053-2_35

16. Kastenberg, H., Rensink, A.: Dynamic partial order reduction using probe sets. In: van Breugel, F., Chechik, M. (eds.) CONCUR 2008. LNCS, vol. 5201, pp. 233–247. Springer, Heidelberg (2008). https://doi.org/10.1007/978-3-540-85361-9_21

17. Kokologiannakis, M., Lahav, O., Sagonas, K., Vafeiadis, V.: Effective stateless model checking for C/C++ concurrency. Proc. ACM Program. Lang. **2**(POPL), 17:1–17:32 (2018). https://doi.org/10.1145/3158105

18. Kokologiannakis, M., Marmanis, I., Gladstein, V., Vafeiadis, V.: Truly stateless, optimal dynamic partial order reduction. Proc. ACM Program. Lang. **6**(POPL), 1–28 (2022). https://doi.org/10.1145/3498711
19. Kokologiannakis, M., Raad, A., Vafeiadis, V.: Model checking for weakly consistent libraries. In: Proceedings of the 40th ACM SIGPLAN Conference on Programming Language Design and Implementation, PLDI 2019, pp. 96–110. ACM, New York (2019). https://doi.org/10.1145/3314221.3314609
20. Kokologiannakis, M., Ren, X., Vafeiadis, V.: Dynamic partial order reductions for spinloops. In: Formal Methods in Computer Aided Design, FMCAD 2021, pp. 163–172. IEEE (2021). https://doi.org/10.34727/2021/isbn.978-3-85448-046-4_25
21. Kokologiannakis, M., Sagonas, K.: Stateless model checking of the Linux kernel's read–copy update (RCU). Softw. Tools Technol. Transf. **21**(3), 287–306 (2019). https://doi.org/10.1007/s10009-019-00514-6
22. Kokologiannakis, M., Vafeiadis, V.: GENMC: a model checker for weak memory models. In: Silva, A., Leino, K.R.M. (eds.) CAV 2021, Part I. LNCS, vol. 12759, pp. 427–440. Springer, Cham (2021). https://doi.org/10.1007/978-3-030-81685-8_20
23. Lamport, L.: How to make a multiprocessor computer that correctly executes multiprocess programs. IEEE Trans. Comput. **28**(9), 690–691 (1979). https://doi.org/10.1109/TC.1979.1675439
24. Larsen, K.G., Larsson, F., Pettersson, P., Yi, W.: Compact data structures and statespace reduction for model-checking real-time systems. Real Time Syst. **25**(2–3), 255–275 (2003). https://doi.org/10.1023/A:1025132427497
25. Larsen, K.G., Pettersson, P., Yi, W.: UPPAAL in a nutshell. Softw. Tools Technol. Transf. **1**(1–2), 134–152 (1997). https://doi.org/10.1007/S100090050010
26. Maiya, P., Gupta, R., Kanade, A., Majumdar, R.: Partial order reduction for event-driven multi-threaded programs. In: Chechik, M., Raskin, J.-F. (eds.) TACAS 2016. LNCS, vol. 9636, pp. 680–697. Springer, Heidelberg (2016). https://doi.org/10.1007/978-3-662-49674-9_44
27. Mazurkiewicz, A.: Trace theory. In: Brauer, W., Reisig, W., Rozenberg, G. (eds.) ACPN 1986. LNCS, vol. 255, pp. 278–324. Springer, Heidelberg (1987). https://doi.org/10.1007/3-540-17906-2_30
28. Musuvathi, M., Qadeer, S., Ball, T., Basler, G., Nainar, P.A., Neamtiu, I.: Finding and reproducing heisenbugs in concurrent programs. In: Proceedings of the 8th USENIX Symposium on Operating Systems Design and Implementation, OSDI 2008, pp. 267–280. USENIX Association, Berkeley (2008). http://dl.acm.org/citation.cfm?id=1855741.1855760
29. Palmer, R., Gopalakrishnan, G., Kirby, R.M.: Semantics driven dynamic partial-order reduction of MPI-based parallel programs. In: Ur, S., Farchi, E. (eds.) Proceedings of the 5th Workshop on Parallel and Distributed Systems: Testing, Analysis, and Debugging, PADTAD 2007, pp. 43–53. ACM (2007). https://doi.org/10.1145/1273647.1273657
30. Peled, D.: Partial order reduction: model-checking using representatives. In: Penczek, W., Szałas, A. (eds.) MFCS 1996. LNCS, vol. 1113, pp. 93–112. Springer, Heidelberg (1996). https://doi.org/10.1007/3-540-61550-4_141
31. Tasharofi, S., Karmani, R.K., Lauterburg, S., Legay, A., Marinov, D., Agha, G.: TransDPOR: a novel dynamic partial-order reduction technique for testing actor programs. In: Giese, H., Rosu, G. (eds.) FMOODS/FORTE -2012. LNCS, vol. 7273, pp. 219–234. Springer, Heidelberg (2012). https://doi.org/10.1007/978-3-642-30793-5_14

32. Valmari, A.: Stubborn set methods for process algebras. In: Peled, D.A., Pratt, V.R., Holzmann, G.J. (eds.) Partial Order Methods in Verification, Proceedings of a DIMACS Workshop. DIMACS Series in Discrete Mathematics and Theoretical Computer Science, vol. 29, pp. 213–231. DIMACS/AMS (1996). https://doi.org/10.1090/DIMACS/029/12
33. Zhang, N., Kusano, M., Wang, C.: Dynamic partial order reduction for relaxed memory models. In: Programming Language Design and Implementation (PLDI), pp. 250–259. ACM, New York (2015). https://doi.org/10.1145/2737924.2737956

Performance Analysis of Stochastic Digraph Real-Time Task Model

Martin Kristjansen$^{(\boxtimes)}$⬤ and Kim Guldstrand Larsen⬤

Aalborg University, Selma Lagerløfs Vej 300, 9220 Aalborg Øst, Denmark
{mk,kgl}@cs.aau.dk

Abstract. Different models are available when scheduling tasks on real-time systems depending on the need for expressiveness and the properties of the system. The Digraph Real-Time (DRT) Task Model is one of the most expressive models, where the feasibility for hard real-time scheduling is computable in pseudo-polynomial time. We expand the DRT task model to the Stochastic Digraph Real-Time (SDRT) Task Model, which contains the stochastic behavior and not just worst-case values or minimum separations. We present the operational semantics of DRT task systems and expand those to fit SDRT task systems with soft deadlines. We implement these semantics using UPPAAL SMC, which we use to simulate a set of SDRT tasks. The simulations are used in performance analysis to obtain metrics such as utilization and the ratio between missed deadlines and the number of released jobs. We show how the increase in size of the task set affects these different metrics of a scheduling system.

Keywords: Digraph Real-Time Task Model · Performance Analysis · Soft Real-Time Scheduling · Statistical Model Checking · UPPAAL SMC

1 Introduction

When modeling real-time task systems, different abstract models of varying expressiveness are available. One of the earliest and most well-known abstractions is the Liu and Layland task model [14], which only considers the execution time and period of the task activation. Much research has been done on that model and its extensions, but the formalism is restrictive. Dependencies between tasks and non-periodic timing behavior are needed to describe many realistic real-time systems.

For more than three decades, Wang Yi has made several significant contributions towards extended modeling formalisms for real-time systems while allowing for efficient analysis of their timing properties. In 1995 – together with the second author of this paper, Paul Pettersson and others – Wang Yi founded the award-winning real-time verification tool UPPAAL allowing for symbolic analysis of interacting networks of timed automata. In particular, UPPAAL enabled modeling and verification of a wide variety of real-time schedulability problems, e.g., [4,9,12,15].

© The Author(s), under exclusive license to Springer Nature Switzerland AG 2025
S. Graf et al. (Eds.): Festschrift Wang Yi, LNCS 15230, pp. 98–119, 2025.
https://doi.org/10.1007/978-3-031-73751-0_9

Unfortunately, the high expressive power of timed automata comes with the price of PSPACE-completeness of reachability. Therefore, approximately 10 years after the introduction of UPPAAL [3], Wang Yi and his group in Uppsala introduced the tool TIMES [1] specialized to schedulability analysis, and later the notion of task automata [11]. Though an improvement over the PSPACE-completeness complexity for timed automata, the feasibility checking of a task set turns out to be strongly (co)NP-complete, which still does not allow for scaling to realistic task set sizes.

Most recently, Wang Yi and his collaborators have introduced the Digraph Real-Time (DRT) task model [16] as an abstraction still offering high expressiveness, while feasibility analysis is decidable in pseudo-polynomial time. In this formalism, graphs represent tasks, where nodes are the jobs to be released, and edges dictate the sequence in which jobs can be released and the timing restrictions between releases. In [16], Wang Yi and collaborators investigate the feasibility of such systems, meaning no jobs are allowed to miss a deadline.

In this paper, we extend the DRT task model by adding stochastic distributions on the release and execution times and relative weights on edges to specify which jobs are more likely to be released than others. Defining the stochastic behavior of such systems allows us to simulate the system under scheduling to evaluate different performance metrics. We present the semantics of the DRT task system (Sect. 2) and the Stochastic DRT (SDRT) task system (Sect. 3). We use the statistical model-checker UPPAAL SMC [7], an extension of the symbolic model-checker UPPAAL [3], in our modeling of SDRT systems (Sect. 4). The UPPAAL SMC models are used to make feasibility and performance analysis under hard real-time settings (Sect. 5) and performance analysis of larger systems under soft real-time settings (Sect. 6).

2   Digraph Real-Time Task Model

The introduction of the Digraph Real-Time (DRT) task model allowed one to express the cyclic behaviors of real-time systems abstractly. Earlier abstractions for defining tasks and their behavior, such as non-cyclic Recurrent Real-Time (RRT) task model [2], use a Directed Acyclic Graph (DAG) where each node is a job to be released. For non-cyclic RRT, the DAG has dedicated source and sink nodes, restricting to one starting job and a set of sink jobs with no outgoing edges. Such a model is tractable in the sense that feasibility is decidable in pseudo-polynomial time.

The DRT task model allows cycles within a task and specifies no dedicated source and sink nodes while still being tractable. Informally, a DRT task is a graph where nodes are the jobs that are released, and the edges dictate the order in which jobs can be released and the timing bounds between them. Throughout the paper, we use a running example of a DRT task to explain the semantics of a DRT task system and the extensions we present.

Wang Yi and collaborators [16] presented an example of a DRT task shown in Fig. 1, which consists of 5 jobs where edges represent dependencies between

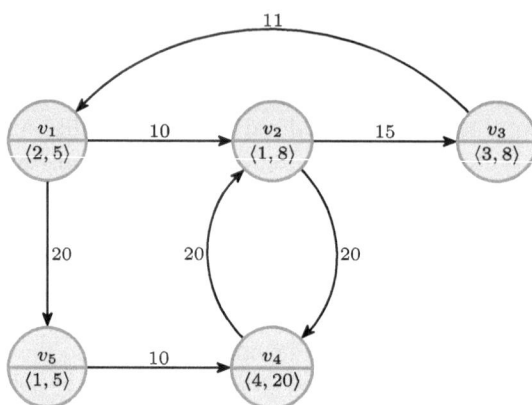

Fig. 1. Example of a single Digraph Real-Time task consisting of 5 jobs. Each job is annotated with its execution demand and relative deadline. Each edge is annotated with the minimum separation of jobs. [16]

jobs. In classical scheduling theory, a sporadic task has an execution demand e, a relative deadline d, and a minimum separation time p. Whenever a job is released in such a setting, it can be released again when a delay respecting the minimum separation has occurred. For a DRT task, the next released job must be the destination of an outgoing edge of the task's latest released job. The next job's execution demand and relative deadline are then defined by that given job in the task.

For example, if the DRT task illustrated in the Fig. 1 released task v_2 at time t, it must be executed for 1 time unit before the global clock exceeds $t + 8$. The following job must either be v_3 or v_4, each with its own minimum separation from v_2's release. In this case, v_3 can be released at $t + 20$ and beyond while v_4 can be released at $t + 15$ and later. The timings are based on the absolute time v_2 was released and the minimum separation value of the edge taken.

The example shown in Fig. 1 only contains a single task. However, a system may consist of multiple different tasks, each consisting of one or more jobs with arbitrary dependencies, where the task can be an arbitrary digraph. A formal definition of a DRT task system is as follows:

Definition 1 (Digraph Real-Time Task Systems). *A Digraph Real-Time (DRT) Task System is a set $\mathcal{T} = \{\tau_1, \ldots, \tau_N\}$, where each $\tau \in \mathcal{T}$ is a DRT task. A DRT task τ is a directed graph $G = (V, E)$, where*

- *V is a set of nodes $\{v_0, \ldots, v_n\}$ each representing a job,*
- *$E \subseteq V \times V$ is a set of directed edges,*
- *each node $v \in V$ is annotated by a ordered pair $\langle e, d \rangle$ where:*
  - *e is the execution demand, and*
  - *d is the relative deadline*
- *each edge $(v, u) \in E$ is annotated by $\langle p \rangle$, which is the minimum separation time between two jobs.*

As a shorthand, when given a task τ, we access its set of edges and vertices by writing E_τ and V_τ, respectively. Likewise, when given a job v, we write e_v and d_v for the job's execution time and relative deadline, respectively. Lastly, we write $p_{(u,v)}$ for the minimum separation time of edge (v, u). We assume that all tasks of task set $\mathcal{T}$ are disjoint, meaning that for all tasks $\tau, \tau' \in \mathcal{T}$, it holds that if $\tau \neq \tau'$ then $V_\tau \cap V_{\tau'} = \emptyset$. For the set of all jobs in a task set $\mathcal{T}$, we write $V_\mathcal{T} = \bigcup_{\tau \in \mathcal{T}} V_\tau$.

As mentioned, a single DRT task consists of a set of jobs with restrictions on which jobs can follow after another and the timing behavior between releases. The definition of a DRT task has no source or sink nodes, so there are no restrictions on which job is the first to be released, and there is no specific "final" job. Even when there is no restriction on which job to release first, all subsequent jobs must respect the task's dependencies. The timing difference in the release of two jobs must be at least the minimum separation time indicated by an edge. However, there is no upper limit for releasing, resulting in sporadic behavior. If a job has two outgoing edges, only one can be used. For a job to be completed, it must be processed for a time duration matching its execution demand before it exceeds its absolute deadline. This leads us to a general definition of feasibility:

Definition 2 (Feasibility). *Given a task set $\mathcal{T}$ of DRT tasks, the task set is feasible on a preemptive uniprocessor if and only if all possible combinations of job releases can be processed in a way such that all jobs respect their deadlines.*

To conclude on a task set's feasibility, Wang Yi and collaborators [16] compute the *demand-bound function* (*dbf*) up to a time-bound, which also can be computed by the given task set. Informally, the function $dbf : \mathbb{R}_{\geq 0} \to \mathbb{R}_{\geq 0}$ expresses the maximum accumulated demand a task set can put on the processor in an interval of a given length. If the demand is strictly greater than the interval length, the task set is not feasible under Earliest Deadline First (EDF), which is known to be optimal on preemptive uniprocessors [10]. Wang Yi and collaborators provide an algorithm that computes $dbf(t)$ up to a given t_{max} in pseudo-polynomial time and proves it is sufficient to compute the dbf for all values between 0 and t_{max}. These results hold for any task set of DRT tasks.

In our work, we want to make a performance analysis of a task set, and we need well-defined semantics that can be easily expanded later with stochastic behavior. First, we define a DRT system's behavior using operational semantics. In order to do so, we first define the states of a system of DRT tasks under scheduling:

Definition 3 (State of DRT Task System under Scheduling). *Let the set of all states of a DRT task System of task set $\mathcal{T}$ be $\mathbb{S} = \mathcal{R} \times \mathcal{L} \times \mathcal{P} \times \mathcal{C}$, where:*

- $\mathcal{R} = \mathbb{P}(V_\mathcal{T} \times \mathbb{R}_{\geq 0} \times \mathbb{R}_{\geq 0})$ *is a powerset of tuples indicating ready jobs by their releasing node, how much it has been processed, and its absolute deadline, respectively,*
- $\mathcal{L} = \mathbb{P}(V_\mathcal{T} \times \mathbb{R}_{\geq 0})$ *is a powerset indicating the latest released job of any task by its node and absolute release time,*

- $\mathcal{P} = (V_{\mathcal{T}} \times \mathbb{R}_{\geq 0} \times \mathbb{R}_{\geq 0}) \cup \{\texttt{idle}, \texttt{miss}\}$ *indicating which ready job is running, if the processor is idle, or a deadline is missed, and*
- $\mathcal{C} = \mathbb{R}_{\geq 0}$, *which is a clock indicating the global time.*

Then let a state of a system of DRT Tasks $\mathcal{T}$ be $\mathcal{S} = (r, l, p, c) \in \mathbb{S}$ where $r \in \mathcal{R}$, $l \in \mathcal{L}$, $p \in \mathcal{P}$, and $c \in \mathcal{C}$.

The first element r of a DRT task system state $\mathcal{S} = (r, l, p, c)$ is the set of tuples indicating the ready (or released) jobs that have yet to be completed. These tuples contain the specific node of the job, the amount of time it has been processing (in case of preemption), and the absolute deadline of the job. More than one job from each task can be present as the minimum separation time for the next job can be shorter than the deadline of previously released jobs. The element l represents which job was the latest released of a task since this restricts which jobs can be released next. The element p is either a ready job from r, the symbol $\texttt{idle}$, indicating that no job is processing, or the symbol $\texttt{miss}$, indicating a missed deadline. Lastly, c is simply a global timer. In totality, these four elements are sufficient to track the state of jobs, what jobs can be released next and when, and the state of processing the individual jobs.

2.1   Operational Semantics of DRT Task System

In the operational semantics, we do not restrict ourselves to a specific scheduler (such as EDF) but assume that preemption can only happen when a new job is released. Additionally, the processor is greedy in the sense that if there are ready jobs, one job will be processed. Given these two assumptions on the scheduler's structure, the scheduler decides which job to execute when either a job has finished its execution or when a job is released. We define the initial state as $\mathcal{S}_0 = (\emptyset, \emptyset, \texttt{idle}, 0)$ since there are no released jobs, no task has a latest job yet, the processor is idle, and the timer starts at 0.

We present 3 groups of transitions: a process transition, two release transitions, and a deadline miss transition. The transitions are on the form $\mathcal{S} \xrightarrow{\alpha}_{\delta, \mathcal{T}} \mathcal{S}'$, where α is the taken action, $\delta \in \mathbb{R}_{\geq 0}$ is the delay before the action takes place, $\mathcal{T}$ is the system's task set, and $\mathcal{S}$ and $\mathcal{S}$' are the system states before and after the transition, respectively. Since a delay is possible in every transition, there is no dedicated delay transition. Please note that the transition delay can be 0 as long as all side conditions are met.

The four transitions of a DRT task system under scheduling are shown in Eqs. (1) to (4) shown in Table 1. Again, ' made with a particular scheduler in mind but are generic since any job can be chosen for execution.

The simplest transitions are the process and deadline miss transitions as shown in Eqs. (1) and (2). Those transitions have a delay δ matching the time left of processing the current job or the time remaining for a job to reach its deadline, respectively. For the processing transition, none of the ready jobs exceeds a deadline, and the completed job is removed from the set of ready jobs. The next running job is chosen from the remaining jobs, if any. For the deadline miss,

Table 1. Semantic rules for DRT task system under scheduling

$(r, l, p, c) \xrightarrow{process}_{\delta, \mathcal{T}} (r', l, p', c')$ if

$\quad p = (v, w, d) \in r$ and

$\quad \delta = e_v - w$ and

$\quad c' = c + \delta$ and

$\quad \forall (\_, \_, d') \in r. \, d' \geq c'$ and   (1)

$\quad r' = r \setminus \{p\}$ and

$\quad p' = \begin{cases} \text{idle} & \text{if } r' = \emptyset \\ (v', w', d') & \text{where } (v', w', d') \in r' \end{cases}$

$(r, l, p, c) \xrightarrow{deadline \; miss}_{\delta, \mathcal{T}} (r', l, \text{miss}, c')$ if

$\quad p = (v, w, d) \in r$ and

$\quad \min_{(\_, \_, d') \in r} (d') = c'$ and

$\quad r' = r \setminus p \cup \{(v, w + \delta, d)\}$ and   (2)

$\quad c' = c + \delta$ and

$\quad e_v > w + \delta$

$(\emptyset, l, \text{idle}, c) \xrightarrow{release_{\mathcal{T}}}_{\delta, \mathcal{T}} (r, l', p, c')$ if

$\quad v \in V_{\mathcal{T}}$ and

$\quad r = \{(v, 0, c' + d_v)\}$ and

$\quad l' = \begin{cases} l \cup \{(v, c')\} & \text{if } \not\exists u \in V_{\mathcal{T}}. \, (u, \_) \in l \\ (l \setminus \{(u, c'')\}) \cup \{(v, c')\} & \text{where } u \in V_{\mathcal{T}} \text{ and } c' - c'' \geq p_{(u,v)} \text{ and} \\ & (u, c'') \in l \end{cases}$ (3)

$\quad p = (v, 0, c' + d_v)$ and

$\quad c' = c + \delta$

$(r, l, p, c) \xrightarrow{release_{\mathcal{T}}}_{\delta, \mathcal{T}} (r', l', p', c')$ if

$\quad p = (v, w, d) \in r$ and

$\quad r'' = (r \setminus \{p\}) \cup \{(v, w + \delta, d)\}$ and

$\quad r' = r'' \cup \{(v', 0, c' + d_{v'})\}$ and

$\quad e_v > w + \delta$ and

$\quad v' \in V_{\mathcal{T}}$ and   (4)

$\quad l' = \begin{cases} l \cup \{(v', c')\} & \text{if } \not\exists u \in V_{\mathcal{T}}. \, (u, \_) \in l \\ (l \setminus \{(u, c'')\}) \cup \{(v', c')\} & \text{where } u \in V_{\mathcal{T}} \text{ and } c' - c'' \geq p_{(u,v')} \text{ and} \\ & (u, c'') \in l \end{cases}$

$\quad p' \in r'$ and

$\quad c' = c + \delta$ and

$\quad \forall (\_, \_, d'') \in r. \, d'' > c'$

one of the ready jobs reaches its deadline while the running job does not reach its execution demand. Here, the set of ready jobs is updated by removing the information about the running job's old state and adding the information about its new state, which ensures that the running job's working time is updated. For both transitions, the global time is advanced by time δ.

For releasing a job, we define two transitions: One for when the processor is idle and another when a job executes on the processor, as shown in Eqs. (3) and (4), respectively. Like the process and deadline miss transitions, a delay δ occurs before releasing a job from task τ. For both release transitions, the release must respect the minimum separation time if the task has released any job earlier. The set of latest releases might include a job for that task; if it does, the new job must follow the latest job. In that case, the set of latest releases is modified by removing the old latest release and adding the new one. If the processor were idle, the new job would also be the running job and the only one in the ready set. If another job was running, the delay must not conclude its execution, the job's working time must be updated in the ready set, and no deadlines must be reached.

With these semantic rules, a task set $\mathcal{T}$ is feasible if and only if the deadline miss transition cannot be taken from the initial state $\mathcal{S}_0 = (\emptyset, \emptyset, \texttt{idle}, 0)$ when the scheduling policy used is EDF.

2.2   Example Use of Operational Rules

Let $\mathcal{T} = \{\tau\}$ be a task set consisting of a single DRT task, where the task has the structure presented in the running example of Fig. 1. An example run of $\mathcal{T}$ with initial state $\mathcal{S}_0 = (\emptyset, \emptyset, \texttt{idle}, 0)$ is as follows:

$$(\emptyset, \emptyset, \texttt{idle}, 0) \xrightarrow{release_\tau}_{10, \mathcal{T}} (\{(v_3, 0, 18)\}, \{(v_3, 10)\}, (v_3, 0, 18), 10) \tag{5}$$

$$\xrightarrow{process}_{3, \mathcal{T}} (\emptyset, \{(v_3, 10)\}, \texttt{idle}, 13) \tag{6}$$

$$\xrightarrow{release_\tau}_{8, \mathcal{T}} (\{(v_1, 0, 26)\}, \{(v_1, 21)\}, (v_1, 0, 26), 21) \tag{7}$$

$$\xrightarrow{process}_{2, \mathcal{T}} (\emptyset, \{(v_1, 21)\}, \texttt{idle}, 23) \tag{8}$$

Here, in Eq. (5), the first job released is v_3 at time 10. The set of ready jobs is updated with v_3, a working time of 0, and an absolute deadline of 18. The set of latest releases is updated by the job and its release time, and, finally, the released job is put on the processor.

In Eq. (6), the transition must be a processing transition with delay 3, as the next job only can be released from time 21 and beyond, since v_3 released at 10 and the minimum separation time is 11. Therefore, the task is processed, and the processor is idle.

After the job is processed, the next job is released as early as it can. The released job in Eq. (7) must be v_1 since v_3 only has an outgoing edge to v_1. Notice that the set of latest is updated to only contain the v_1 job and its release time.

Finally, in Eq. (8), v_1 is processed with a delay of 2, and the processor is yet again idle. From there, the next job is either v_2, which can be released from time 31 and beyond, or v_5, which can be released from time 41 and beyond.

3   Stochastic Digraph Real-Time Task Model

In the previous section, we provided the semantics of a DRT task system under scheduling. The definition of a DRT task system contains exact values for execution time and minimum values for separation, which Wang Yi and collaborators use to calculate the $dfb(t)$ up to a limit t_{max}. They answer the question of whether or not a given task set $\mathcal{T}$ is feasible. Here, we extend their model into a stochastic version in order for us to perform a performance analysis of a given task set.

To obtain results on the expected behavior such as utilization and response times (and not just the upper bounds), we add density distributions to the timing behavior. Moreover, we add relative weights to each job and edge, dictating the likelihood of the first release and the job to follow. We start by updating the running example into a Stochastic Digraph Real-Time (SDRT) task to give an informal description of such a system. Afterward, we give the general definition of systems consisting of stochastic versions of DRT tasks.

3.1   SDRT Task Systems

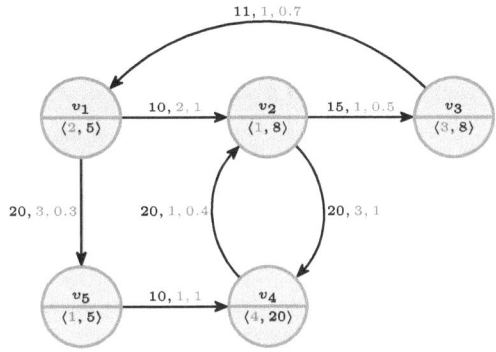

Table 2. Relative weights and exponential rates for the first job release.

Job	Rate	Weight
v_1	0.5	1
v_2	0.7	2
v_3	1.2	5
v_4	0.7	1
v_5	1	3

Fig. 2. Running example as an SDRT Task. Each edge has a relative weight and an exponential rate. The green numbers are use as parameter for uniform or exponential distributions.(Color figure online)

The running example is updated to an SDRT task in Fig. 2, where each edge and job is given a weight. Each value colored green is used as a parameter for a density distribution. Every edge now has 3 values: the minimum separation, the relative weight, and the rate of the exponential. The relative weight is how likely that edge is taken relative to the other outgoing edges of that job. The rate is used in an exponential distribution for the delay before releasing the job, but the minimum separation p must still be respected. To accommodate a minimum separation time p, the exponential distribution for the delay between jobs is slightly modified as follows:

$$f(x; \lambda, p) = \begin{cases} \lambda e^{-\lambda(x-p)} & \text{if } x \geq p \\ 0 & \text{otherwise} \end{cases} \tag{9}$$

where λ is the rate and p is the minimum separation time. The resulting distribution is an exponential distribution with an offset of p, and it holds that $\int_p^\infty f(x; \lambda, p)\, dx = 1$ where λ is positive and p is non-negative. The jobs are now annotated by a maximum executed demand e and a relative deadline d. For the execution time, we use a uniform distribution in the range $[e/2, e]$.

In Table 2, the relative weights and rates of exponential of the individual jobs are shown. These relative weights are used to determine the first job the task releases while the exponential rate determines the delay of the release. E.g., job v_3 is the most likely to be the first released of this task but it has the highest rate.

Now, we formally expand the notion of DRT tasks into a Stochastic Digraph Real-Time (SDRT) Task model:

Definition 4 (Stochastic Digraph Real-Time Task System). *A Stochastic Digraph Real-Time (SDRT) Task System is a set $\mathcal{T} = \{\tau_1, \ldots, \tau_N\}$, where each $\tau \in \mathcal{T}$ is an SDRT task. An SDRT task τ is directed graph $G = (V, E, \Delta, \mathcal{W}, \Delta^{init})$, where*

- *V is a set of nodes $\{v_0, \ldots, v_n\}$ each representing a job,*
- *$E \subseteq V \times V$ is a set of directed edges,*
- *each node $v \in V$ is annotated by a ordered pair $\langle e, d \rangle$ where:*
  - *e is the worst-case execution demand, and*
  - *d is the relative deadline*
- *each edge $(v, u) \in E$ is annotated by $\langle p \rangle$, which is the minimum separation time between two jobs.*
- *$\Delta : V \cup E \to (\mathbb{R}_{\geq 0} \to \mathbb{R}_{\geq 0})$ denotes a probability density function for the execution demand of a node and the separation of jobs .st.*
  - *For all $v \in V$, it holds that $\int_0^{e_v} \Delta(v)(t)\, dt = 1$, such that there is an upper bound equal worst-case execution demand e, and*
  - *For all $(u, v) \in E$, it holds that $\int_{p_{(u,v)}}^\infty \Delta((u, v))(t)\, dt = 1$, such that there is a minimum separation time p between jobs of u and v.*
- *$\mathcal{W} : V \cup E \to \mathbb{R}^+$ denotes a relative weight for every job and every edge.*
- *$\Delta^{init} : V \to (\mathbb{R}_{\geq 0} \to \mathbb{R}_{\geq 0})$ denotes a probability density function for the delay of the task's first job .st. for all $v \in V$, it holds that $\int_0^\infty \Delta(v)(t)\, dt = 1$*

Expanding the shorthand introduced for DRT tasks, we write Δ_τ for the density function of task τ. Likewise, we write $\mathcal{W}_\tau$ and Δ_τ^{init} for the weight function and the first jobs' delay density function of task τ, respectively. Given a job v of task τ, we have the accumulated weight of outgoing edges defined as $\mathcal{W}_\tau^\Sigma(v) = \sum_{(v,u) \in E_\tau} \mathcal{W}((v, u))$. For the accumulated weight of the initial jobs, we write $\mathcal{W}^{init}(\tau) = \sum_{v \in V_\tau} \mathcal{W}(v)$.

The additions to the task definition are two kinds of probability density functions and a weight function. The weight function $\mathcal{W}$ defines the relative weight of edges and jobs. Weights associated with a job are used to determine the likelihood of which job will be released first. Likewise, weights associated with edges determine the likelihood of which job follows a given job. The first probability density function $\varDelta$ denotes the delay distributions of edges and the execution demand distributions of jobs. The execution demand distributions have a given upper bound, while the delay has a given lower bound. The last probability density function $\varDelta^{init}$ denotes the possible delays for a given job if it is the first job to be released of the task.

Now that we have a definition of SDRT tasks and updated the running example, it makes sense to define the state of such a system. Nonetheless, the state of an SDRT system is equivalent to that of a DRT system:

Definition 5 (State of SDRT Task System under Scheduling). *Let the set of all states of a SDRT task System of task set $\mathcal{T}$ be $\mathbb{S} = \mathcal{R} \times \mathcal{L} \times \mathcal{P} \times \mathcal{C}$, where each element is identical to the definition of the DRT task System. Then let a state of a system of SDRT Tasks $\mathcal{T}$ be $\mathcal{S} = (r, l, p, c) \in \mathbb{S}$ where $r \in \mathcal{R}$, $l \in \mathcal{L}$, $p \in \mathcal{P}$, and $c \in \mathcal{C}$.*

We extend the operational semantics to the SDRT task system, but before that, we define a set of helper functions to determine the density of transitions. In that way, it is possible to determine if some transitions are more likely than others, which, in turn, allows us to simulate the system to determine different performance properties.

3.2   Density Helper Functions

The operational semantics for an SDRT system is on the form $\mathcal{S} \xrightarrow{\alpha}_{D,\delta,\mathcal{T}} \mathcal{S}'$, where, as for the DRT system, α is the action taken, $\delta \in \mathbb{R}_{\geq 0}$ is the delay before the action takes place, $\mathcal{T}$ is the system's task set, and $\mathcal{S}$ and $\mathcal{S}'$ are the system states before and after the transition, respectively. The one addition is the density D of the transition, which computation uses the amount of time the processing job has worked, the delay δ of the transition, and the possibility that no other transition occurs before δ time has passed.

To help us in those computations, we introduce three shorthand notations for conditional density and probability. Let $D : \mathbb{R}_{\geq 0} \to \mathbb{R}_{\geq 0}$ be a density and $d, \epsilon \in \mathbb{R}_{\geq 0}$. Then, $D(d \mid \epsilon)$ denotes the conditional density of delaying additionally d assuming a delay of at least ϵ already occurred, which is defined as follows:

$$D(d \mid \epsilon) = \frac{D(d + \epsilon)}{\int_{\epsilon}^{\infty} D(t)\, dt} \tag{10}$$

This allows us to define the $D(\geq d \mid \epsilon)$ and $D(> d \mid \epsilon)$ shorthands. The former denotes the probability of delaying additionally d or more, assuming a delay of at least ϵ already occurred. The latter denotes the probability of delaying additionally more than d, assuming a delay of at least ϵ already occurred. The shorthands are defined as follows:

$$D(\geq d\,|\,\epsilon) = \int_d^\infty D(t\,|\,\epsilon)\,dt \tag{11}$$

$$D(> d\,|\,\epsilon) = \int_{>d}^\infty D(t\,|\,\epsilon)\,dt \tag{12}$$

The difference between the Eqs. (11) and (12) is whether or not the value d is included in the interval of the integration. The two equations compute the probability that a delay either greater-or-equal or greater can occur given that another delay has already occurred, respectively.

The density of a transition can be determined by several factors. What is the probability that the running task finished its execution before the given delay? What is the probability that another job from another task will be released? To help answer these questions, we define several helper functions to calculate those probabilities.

Given a state $\mathcal{S} = (r, l, p, c)$ where $p = (v, w, d)$ and a delay $\delta \in \mathbb{R}_{\geq 0}$, we define the probability that the running job completes after a δ time delay as:

$$D_{\mathcal{S},\delta}^{processing} = \Delta_v(> \delta\,|\,w) \tag{13}$$

Then, the density function of the execution demand density Δ_v and the time w of which the job has already been processed is used to determine the probability that a delay greater than δ can occur.

Before defining any more probability helper functions, we define a helper function that contains all the tasks that have not yet releases a task:

$$inactive(\mathcal{T}, l) = \{\tau \in \mathcal{T}\,|\,\forall (v, \_) \in l.\,v \notin V_\tau\} \tag{14}$$

Then, all tasks in the resulting set do not have a job present in the latest set l, meaning that a job of that task has never been released.

The next density helper function is the probability that all tasks do not release before a delay δ. Here, we are given a $\mathcal{S} = (r, l, p, c)$ and a task set $\mathcal{T}$:

$$D_{\mathcal{T},\mathcal{S},\delta}^{release_{any}} = \prod_{\substack{(u,c') \in l \wedge \\ \tau \in \mathcal{T} \wedge \\ (u,v) \in E_\tau}} \Delta_\tau((u,v))(\geq \delta\,|\,c - c') \cdot \frac{\mathcal{W}_\tau((u,v))}{\mathcal{W}_\tau^\Sigma(u)}$$

$$\cdot \prod_{\tau \in inactive(\mathcal{T},l)} \cdot \prod_{v \in V_\tau} \Delta_\tau^{init}(v)(\geq \delta\,|\,c) \cdot \frac{\mathcal{W}_\tau(v)}{\mathcal{W}^{init}(\tau)} \tag{15}$$

The first product is the probability that a task that previously has released a job will release another job after a delay δ or later. That probability is based on when the previous job was released, the time passed since the release, and the weight of that edge in relation to the other outgoing edges of the previous job. The second and third products are for the tasks that yet have to release a job.

There, the the probability is based on the global time and the job's weight in relation to the other jobs of the task.

We also need den density of releasing a specific task after delay δ. For this, we have v of task τ, such that the density for that specific job and with delay δ in state $\mathcal{S} = (r, l, p, c)$:

$$D^{release_v}_{\mathcal{S},\delta} = \begin{cases} \Delta_\tau((u,v))(\delta \mid c - c') & \text{where } (u, c') \in l \\ \Delta_\tau(v)(\delta \mid c) & \text{otherwise} \end{cases} \tag{16}$$

Then, the density for that job is defined by whether or not the task has released any job previously but does not consider the other tasks' releases. To obtain the probability that no other jobs than a given τ are released before a delay δ in state $\mathcal{S} = (r, l, p, c)$, we have the following:

$$D^{release\_others_\tau}_{\mathcal{T},\mathcal{S},\delta} = \prod_{\substack{(u,c')\in l \wedge \\ \tau' \in \mathcal{T}\setminus\{\tau\} \wedge \\ (u,v)\in E_{\tau'}}} \Delta_{\tau'}((u,v))(\geq \delta \mid c - c') \cdot \frac{\mathcal{W}_{\tau'}((u,v))}{\mathcal{W}^\Sigma_{\tau'}(u)}$$

$$\cdot \prod_{\tau' \in inactive(\mathcal{T},l)\setminus\{\tau\}} \cdot \prod_{v \in V_{\tau'}} \Delta^{init}_{\tau'}(v)(\geq \delta \mid c) \cdot \frac{\mathcal{W}_{\tau'}(v)}{\mathcal{W}^{init}(\tau')}$$

$$\tag{17}$$

Here, the products are identical with those in Eq. (15), except that the releasing task τ is excluded from the sets that the products iterate through. The result is the probability that all tasks other than τ release a job after a delay δ or later. We use all these helper functions to define the semantics of an SDRT task system.

3.3   Operational Semantics of SDRT Task System

The operational semantics for the DRT system are under hard real-time scheduling, where all deadlines must be met, but we define the SDRT semantics under soft real-time scheduling. Under soft real-time scheduling, jobs are allowed to miss deadlines [13]. We can still investigate whether or not a system is feasible by checking if a deadline miss transition is possible. Nonetheless, by defining the rules under soft real-time scheduling, we open up the possibility of analyzing both hard and soft real-time systems.

The transitions for an SDRT system are on the form $\mathcal{S} \xrightarrow{\alpha}_{D,\delta,\mathcal{T}} \mathcal{S}'$, where α is the action taken, D is the density of the transition, δ is the delay before the action is taken, $\mathcal{T}$ is the system's task set, and $\mathcal{S}$ and $\mathcal{S}'$ are the system states. For a transition to be enabled, all the side conditions to be true and the density is greater than zero. The resulting transitions are shown in Eqs. (18) to (21) shown in Table 3. All transitions make use of the helper density functions from the previous section.

The process transition in Eq. (18) is almost identical to the non-stochastic version. The density of the transition is the density $\Delta_\tau(v)(\delta \mid w)$ that the running

Table 3. Semantic rules for SDRT task system under scheduling

$(r, l, p, c) \xrightarrow{process}_{D,\delta,T} (r', l, p', c + \delta)$ if

  $\delta > 0$ and

  $p = (v, w, d) \in r$ and

  $v \in V_\tau$ and

  $D = \Delta_\tau(v)(\delta \mid w) \cdot D_{T,S,\delta}^{releaseany}$ and   (18)

  $\forall(\_, \_, d) \in r. d \geq c + \delta$ and

  $r' = r \setminus \{p\}$ and

  $p' = \begin{cases} \texttt{idle} & \text{if } r' = \emptyset \\ (v', w', d') & \text{where } (v', w', d') \in r' \end{cases}$

$(r, l, p, c) \xrightarrow{deadline\ miss}_{D,\delta,T} (r', l, p', c + \delta)$ if

  $D = D_{T,S,\delta}^{releaseany} \cdot D_{S,\delta}^{processing}$ and

  $p = (v, w, d) \in r$ and

  $\min\limits_{(\_, \_, d') \in r} (d') = c + \delta$ and   (19)

  $\arg\min\limits_{(v', w', d') \in r} (d') = p''$ and

  $r' = \begin{cases} r \setminus \{p\} & \text{if } p = p'' \\ (r \setminus \{p, p''\}) \cup \{(v, w + \delta, d)\} & \text{otherwise} \end{cases}$

  $p' \in r'$ and

$(\emptyset, l, \texttt{idle}, c) \xrightarrow{release_\tau}_{D,\delta,T} (r, l', p, c + \delta)$ if

  $v \in V_\tau$ and

  $D = D_{S,\delta}^{release_v} \cdot D_{T,S,\delta}^{release\_others_\tau}$ and

  $r = \{(v, 0, c + \delta + d_v)\}$ and   (20)

  $l' = \begin{cases} l \cup \{(v, c + \delta)\} & \text{if } \nexists u \in V_\tau. (u, \_) \in l \\ (l \setminus \{(u, c'')\}) \cup \{(v, c + \delta)\} & \text{where } u \in V_\tau \text{ and } (u, c'') \in l \end{cases}$

  $p = (v, 0, c + \delta + d)$

$(r, l, p, c) \xrightarrow{release_\tau}_{D,\delta,T} (r', l', p', c')$ if

  $v \in V_\tau$ and

  $D = D_{S,\delta}^{release_v} \cdot D_{T,S,\delta}^{release\_others_\tau} \cdot D_{S,\delta}^{processing}$ and

  $p = (y, w, d) \in r$ and

  $r' = r'' \cup \{(v, 0, c' + d_v)\}$ and

  $r'' = (r \setminus \{p\}) \cup \{(y, w + \delta, d)\}$ and   (21)

  $l' = \begin{cases} l \cup \{(v, c')\} & \text{if } \nexists u \in V_\tau. (u, \_) \in l \\ (l \setminus \{(u, c'')\}) \cup \{(v, c')\} & \text{where } u \in V_\tau \text{ and } (u, c'') \in l \end{cases}$

  $p' \in r'$ and

  $c' = c + \delta$ and

  $\forall(\_, \_, d'') \in r. d'' > c'$

job finishes after delaying time δ when already have worked w time multiplied by the probability $D_{T,S,\delta}^{releaseany}$ that all tasks do not release any jobs before the delay has elapsed.

Regarding the deadline miss transition, we define it in a soft real-time scheduling setting. There are several ways the system can behave in soft real-time systems, such as when it is observed that a job misses its deadline and what to do with the job when a miss is observed. Here, we observe a deadline miss when the absolute deadline is reached, but the job is not completed. Secondly, when the job has missed its deadline, it is aborted. The deadline miss transition Eq. (19) is, therefore, bigger as the failed job is removed from the ready set and a new job is placed on the processor. Here, the density is based on the probability that no jobs are released before the delay δ and the probability that the running job can finish with a delay longer than δ. Depending on whether or not the running job is missing a deadline, the set of ready jobs is updated accordingly.

Like the other stochastic transitions, the two release transitions in Eqs. (20) and (21) are almost identical to the non-stochastic versions. The main differences are the densities, where both versions use the density $D_{S,\delta}^{release_v}$ of releasing exactly that job after a delay δ and the probability $D_{T,S,\delta}^{release\_others_\tau}$ that no other task releases a job before delay δ. For the second release transition, the probability $D_{S,\delta}^{processing}$ that the current job finished on a delay greater than δ is included. The check of the minimum separation has been removed from the updates of the latest set, as it is included in the density calculation. If the minimum separation is not respected, the density is zero, and the edge will not be enabled.

With the semantics in place, we are ready to investigate how to make a model of an SDRT task system and how the system performs.

4   Modeling Using UPPAAL SMC

To implement the semantics of an SDRT task system, we use the statistical model-checker UPPAAL SMC [7]. This tool extends the symbolic model-checker UPPAAL [3], where one can make models of networks of Timed Automata (TAs) that synchronize over channels. A C-like language is part of the tool to define variables and helper functions supporting these TAs. Where UPPAAL uses symbolic verification, UPPAAL SMC runs simulations of systems to obtain statistical properties in the system. For the feasibility of a scheduling system, UPPAAL has been used in several cases to analyze different scheduling systems [5,6]. As the complexity of scheduling systems increases, using UPPAAL SMC gives statistical properties when the question of feasibility is intractable [12] or can be used to conduct a performance analysis [4] of the system. In our work, we make use of both symbolic and statistical model-checking.

As we model a scheduling system with preemption, clocks measuring the time spent processing can be paused, which can be achieved using StopWatch Automata [8]. Just as with Wang Yi and collaborators [16], the system has a single processor. The scheduling policy used is EDF, even though the operational semantics do not specify precisely how tasks are chosen.

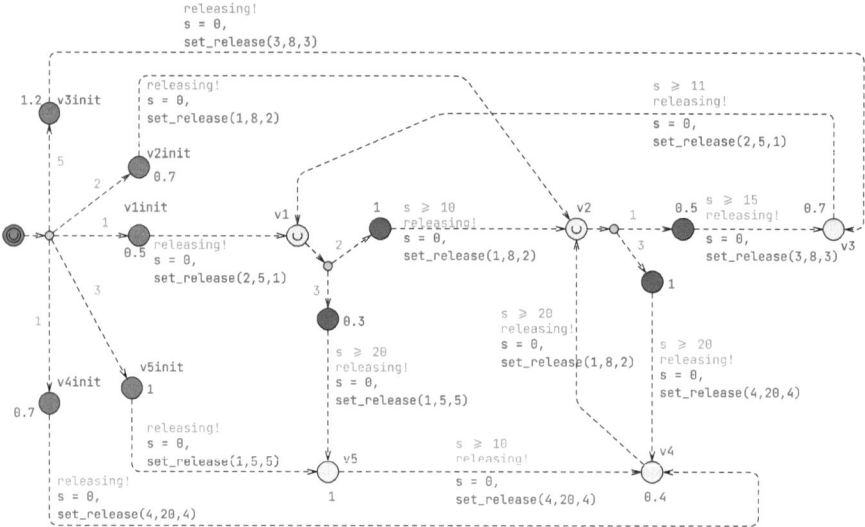

Fig. 3. A UPPAAL SMC template of an SDRT task. The template corresponds to the task presented in Fig. 2 and Table 2.

First, Fig. 3 shows the model of our running example. Three colors are used to help make visual sense of the model. Red are the locations used to determine which job is the first. The initial location, the left-most one, is committed so that no time can pass in that location. Therefore, its outgoing transition must be taken, but the edge is split into five different transitions. Each edge after the split has a relative weight, which is used to make a stochastic choice of which path to take, and these weights match those in Table 2. Matching to the same table, those locations have an exponential rate for the unbounded delay, and exponential distribution is by default used in UPPAAL SMC for delays when there is no upper bound. When a job is released, the `release!` channel sends a signal, and a clock `s` is reset to 0 such that minimum separation is respected. Moreover, the separation between jobs must respect the minimum separation, which the guard of clock `s` ensures. A helper function *set_release(...)* updates data structures behind the scenes with the execution demand, deadline, and job id. In our example, the yellow locations are the jobs, which are v_1 to v_5. Two yellow locations have blue helper locations to help determine which task is the next released. These splits also have weights matching those in Fig. 2, such that either the yellow job location or its blue helper location has a rate matching that of its outgoing edge.

The model of the scheduler under soft deadlines is shown in Fig. 4, which makes great use of stopwatches. There are two arrays of clocks, `worked[...]`, and `age[...]`, which track the amount of time a job has been processed and how old it is, respectively. Additionally, we have two arrays of integers for the upper bound of execution times `e[...]` and deadlines `d[...]`. There is the

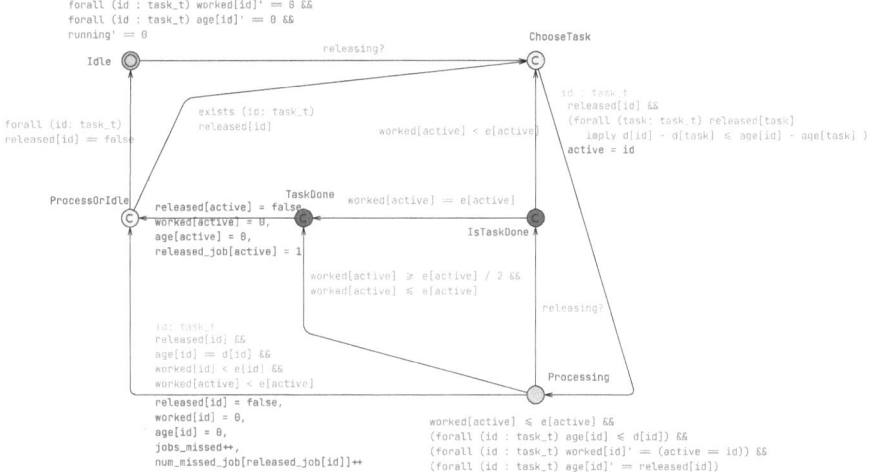

Fig. 4. A UPPAAL SMC template of a generic scheduler.

clock `running`, tracking the amount of time the processor is active. In the initial location `Idle`, no job is running, and the rate of all `worked[...]` and `age[...]` is zero, meaning that they are not progressing. In the location `processing`, the age of all active jobs progresses along the working time of the active jobs. Simultaneously, the age of an active job cannot exceed its deadline, and the active job's working time cannot exceed its upper bound on demand.

The scheduler acts on the incoming signal on the `release?` channel, where the scheduler will be in either `Idle` or `Processing`. The yellow locations are used to determine if any jobs have been released and, if so, which job should be executed. For now, the guard of the outgoing edge of `ChooseTask` ensures that the chosen job is one of those with the least time yet to complete, resulting in EDF. To use another scheduling policy, this guard must be changed. The blue locations determine if a running job has completed its execution demand. The edge from `Processing` to `TaskDone` is enabled when the working time of the job is in the range $[e/2, e]$, where e is the job's maximum execution demand. When there is an upper bound on the delay, UPPAAL SMC uses a uniform distribution between the upper and lower bound of the range to sample a delay. For the soft scheduling aspect, the edge on the lower left is taken when a job's age has reached its deadline but has yet to finish. In that case, the job is aborted, and counters reflecting missed deadlines are updated.

5 Simulations with Hard Deadlines

For our first analysis, we analyze a system consisting of 2 identical tasks of our running example. We are interested in the questions of feasibility, maximum response time, and expected response time. We employ both the symbolic model-checking of UPPAAL and the statistical model-checking of UPPAAL SMC. For feasibility, we employ the query E<> Scheduler.jobs_missed > 0 using symbolic model checking. In this query, we check if a trace exists where the process Scheduler increments its observer of missed deadlines. The property is not satisfied, and as the state space is over-approximated, we conclude that it is not possible to miss a deadline at all. The property took almost 400 s to verify.

Table 4. The deadline, supremum of response time, and the expected response time of every job in an SDRT system of 2 tasks.

Job Id	Deadline	Sup.	Exp.
Job 1	5	4	2.11 ± 0.006
Job 2	8	4	2.22 ± 0.011
Job 3	8	8	3.55 ± 0.012
Job 4	20	11	6.39 ± 0.011
Job 5	5	3	1.05 ± 0.005

Moreover, we use symbolic verification to obtain the supremum of the response times of the 5 different jobs and statistical model-checking for the expected response times. The results are shown in Table 4. To obtain the expected values, we conduct 10,000 simulations with a time horizon 10,000. The supremum query also uses over-approximation in the verification, so the supremums serve as upper bounds, and all supremums are below or at the jobs' deadlines. This also concludes that the system is feasible, but the expected response times are much lower (and some more than 50% lower) than those of the supremums. The spread of the observed response times is not shown in the table, but we can visualize the response times of any job to see the spread. An example is shown in Fig. 5, where the response times of job v_4 are shown. Even though the execution demand is in the range $[2, 4]$, the earliest response time bucket starts at 4.45, indicating that this job is almost sure to be blocked by another job. Besides that, the shape is, in this case, very similar to a normal distribution.

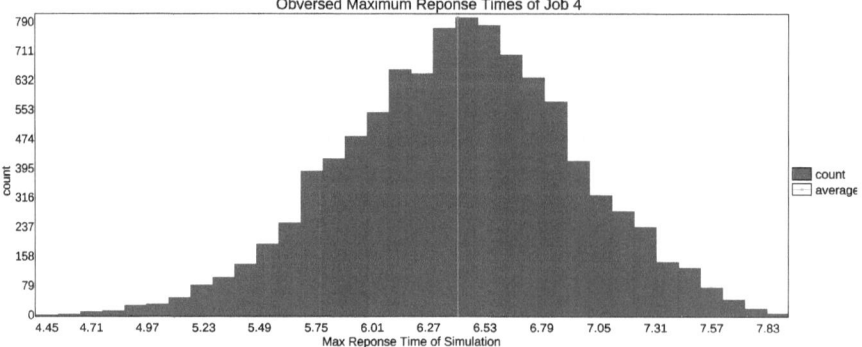

Fig. 5. Simulated response times of job v_4 using 10,000 runs.

6   Simulations with Soft Deadlines

To investigate the performance measures of an SDRT task system with soft deadlines, we again use our updated running example, which we have modeled using UPPAAL SMC. Instead of simulating 2 tasks, we simulate systems with varying numbers of task instances to observe changes in measures as the system's size increases. As shown in the previous sections, a system consisting of 2 tasks of the running example is feasible, but a system consisting of 3 such tasks is not. As for 2 tasks, we tried to use symbolic verification in UPPAAL but did not terminate within 17 h. How a deadline can be missed is shown in Appendix A using our DRT semantics, which demonstrates that when all 3 tasks release v_3 simultaneously, there is a demand of 9 during a time interval of 8. Therefore, systems of 3 tasks of the running example or more are infeasible. Assuming that deadlines are soft, we can investigate otherwise infeasible systems and their performance metrics.

We investigate each system's utilization, the number of jobs missing their deadline, and the number of jobs released. Each system has $\mathcal{N}$ identical instances of the running examples, each consisting of five jobs. The $\mathcal{N}$ range is [3..14], such that the largest system consists of 14 identical tasks. In all our evaluations, we make 10,000 simulations of the system, each with a horizon of 10,000 time units. The used scheduling policy is EDF.

First, we investigate the utilization and the ratio between missed deadlines and the total release amount. The utilization is shown in Fig. 6, and the ratio is shown in Fig. 7. For 3 tasks, the utilization is approximately 25%, and the miss/release ratio is 0. This means that a single deadline miss was not found in the system's 10,000 simulations, even though we know that one can occur. However, for a miss to occur, the execution time (sampled from the interval $[e/2, e]$) and the delay of releases must match such that the demand is higher than the length of a time interval. For 3 tasks, we then conclude that a missed deadline is a rare event.

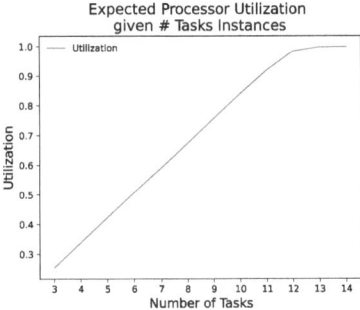
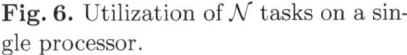
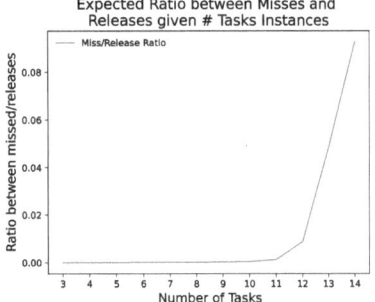

Fig. 6. Utilization of $\mathcal{N}$ tasks on a single processor.

Fig. 7. Ratio between the number of missed deadlines and released jobs for $\mathcal{N}$ tasks on a single processor.

When the number of tasks increases, the utilization increases linearly until it reaches 11–12 tasks, at which point the slope decreases. For the miss/release ratio, the value is approximately 0.5% for 11 tasks and below, but the ratio increases exponentially after that point. For 14 tasks, the ratio is almost 10%. The sharp increase in the miss/release ratio starts earlier than the utilization's decreasing slope.

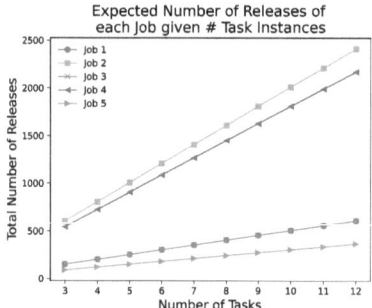

Fig. 8. Number of released jobs by job id for $\mathcal{N}$ tasks on a single processor.

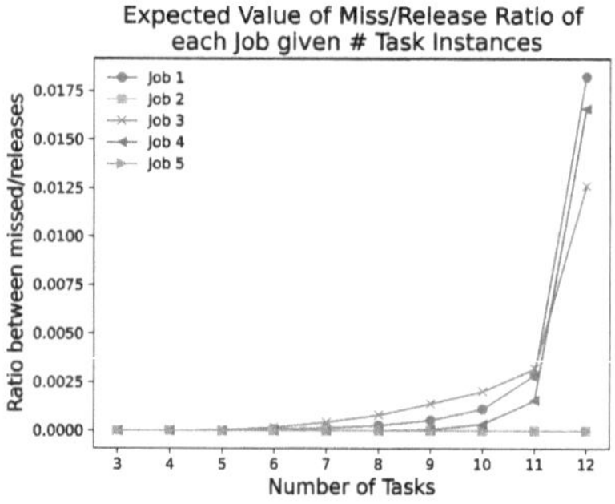

Fig. 9. Ratio between the number of missed deadlines and released jobs by job id for $\mathcal{N}$ tasks on a single processor.

The utilization and miss/release ratio are properties of the entire system, but we can also investigate the properties of the individual jobs. For example, what are the most released jobs, and are some jobs more likely than others to miss their deadline than others? We then investigate systems of 12 tasks and below, as this is before the sharp rise in the ratio of missed deadlines. In Figs. 8 and 9, we see the individual jobs' expected number of releases and the expected miss/release ratio of each job, respectively. We see that jobs 2 and 4 are released the most, but for 11 tasks and less, job 3 has the highest miss/release ratio.

It is somewhat surprising that job 3 is the one missing the most deadlines for systems of 11 tasks or less. Job 1 has the highest possible demand/deadline ratio of $2/5 = 40\%$, and job 4 has the highest possible demand of 4. Job 3's demand/deadline ratio is 37.5%, but its relative deadline is 8, which is a little more than jobs 1 and 5, both having a relative deadlines of 5. A plausible reason for job 3's high miss/release ratio might be that released jobs with a relative deadline of 5 do block the processor, and then job 3 will still have a demand of up to 3 with less time to execute. Interestingly, the realization that job 3 has the highest expectation of missed deadlines was not concluded by looking at execution demand and relative deadlines.

Now that we know that job 3 is most likely to miss deadlines, we can investigate the spread of the miss/release ratio of that job. Depending on what is deemed acceptable for the expected amount of missed deadlines, we can investigate the likely maximum load of that setting. For 12 tasks, job 3's ratio of missed deadlines is 1.2%. The frequency histogram in Fig. 10 shows the encountered miss/release ratios for job 3 in 10,000 simulations. In the worst case, more

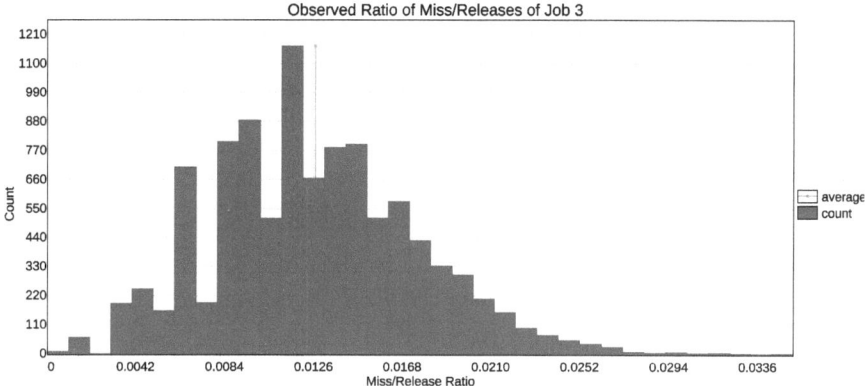

Fig. 10. Simulation results of ratio of the missed deadline and the number of releases for job v_3 across all 12 tasks.

than 3.3% of the job 3 releases missed their deadline, which is 2.75 times more than the expected ratio. However, only 13 simulations (out of 10,000) had a ratio above 3%. Whether or not this is acceptable depends on the scheduling system's use case, but these simulations can help one better judge whether or not a system fulfills some service criteria.

7   Conclusion and Future Work

In this paper, we presented the semantics of the Digraph Real-Time (DRT) Task Model and its expansion, the Stochastic Digraph Real-Time (SDRT) Task Model. We model the semantics of the SDRT task model using UPPAAL SMC, where we make a performance analysis of task systems of different sizes. We have shown how to obtain performance metrics for these systems, which include the holistic behavior of the system and the behavior of the individual jobs. The metrics include the expected values of miss/release ratios and the spread of the observed metrics. In our specific case, we observed that the job most likely to miss its deadline was neither the one with the highest demand/deadline ratio nor the highest relative deadline. Depending on the number of deadlines the system can afford to miss, a system with soft deadlines can have substantially more tasks than the feasible system of just 2 tasks. However, only statistical model-checking was tractable for systems of 3 tasks or more.

For future work, we want to test several scheduling policies other than EDF, such as Fixed-Priority scheduling policies. Additionally, we want to expand the work for performance analysis of multi-core systems. In such a setting, we can define different costs of using the cores, and the goal would be to dual-optimization of minimizing deadlines missed and the accumulated cost.

Acknowledgments. This work was supported by the S4OS Villum Investigator Grant (37819) from VILLUM FONDEN.

A   Deadline Miss of 3 Tasks

We have a task set $\mathcal{T}^3 = \{\tau^1, \tau^2, \tau^3\}$. Each task is defined as the task shown in Fig. 1, so the structure of the tasks are identical. To refer to a job of a given task, we superscript the job, s.t. v_3^2 means job v_3 of task τ^2. The scheduling policy is EDF. The proof shows what would happen if all three tasks release the job v_3 as soon as the system is started. The job v_3 has an execution demand of 3 and a relative deadline of 8.

Proof

$$(\emptyset, \emptyset, \mathtt{idle}, 0) \xrightarrow{release_{\tau 1}}_{0, \mathcal{T}^3}$$

$$(\{(v_3^1, 0, 8)\}, \{(v_3^1, 8)\}, (v_3^1, 0, 8), 0) \xrightarrow{release_{\tau 2}}_{0, \mathcal{T}^3}$$

$$(\{(v_3^1, 0, 8), (v_3^2, 0, 8)\}, \{(v_3^1, 8), (v_3^2, 8)\}, (v_3^1, 0, 8), 0) \xrightarrow{release_{\tau 3}}_{0, \mathcal{T}^3}$$

$$(\{(v_3^1, 0, 8), (v_3^2, 0, 8), (v_3^3, 0, 8)\}, \{(v_3^1, 8), (v_3^2, 8), (v_3^3, 8)\}, (v_3^1, 0, 8), 0) \xrightarrow{process}_{3, \mathcal{T}^3}$$

$$(\{(v_3^2, 0, 8), (v_3^3, 0, 8)\}, \{(v_3^1, 8), (v_3^2, 8), (v_3^3, 8)\}, (v_3^2, 0, 8), 3) \xrightarrow{process}_{3, \mathcal{T}^3}$$

$$(\{(v_3^3, 0, 8)\}, \{(v_3^1, 8), (v_3^2, 8), (v_3^3, 8)\}, (v_3^3, 0, 8), 6) \xrightarrow{deadline\ miss}_{2, \mathcal{T}^3}$$

$$(\{(v_3^3, 2, 8)\}, \{(v_3^1, 8), (v_3^2, 8), (v_3^3, 8)\}, \mathtt{miss}, 8)$$

This proves that the task set $\mathcal{T}^3$ is infeasible in a hard real-time scheduling setting.   □

References

1. Amnell, T., Fersman, E., Mokrushin, L., Pettersson, P., Yi, W.: TIMES: a tool for schedulability analysis and code generation of real-time systems. In: Larsen, K.G., Niebert, P. (eds.) FORMATS 2003. LNCS, vol. 2791, pp. 60–72. Springer, Heidelberg (2004). https://doi.org/10.1007/978-3-540-40903-8_6
2. Baruah, S.K.: The non-cyclic recurring real-time task model. In: Proceedings of the 31st IEEE Real-Time Systems Symposium, RTSS 2010, San Diego, California, USA, 30 November–3 December 2010, pp. 173–182. IEEE Computer Society (2010). https://doi.org/10.1109/RTSS.2010.19
3. Behrmann, G., David, A., Larsen, K.G.: A tutorial on UPPAAL. In: Bernardo, M., Corradini, F. (eds.) SFM-RT 2004. LNCS, vol. 3185, pp. 200–236. Springer, Heidelberg (2004). https://doi.org/10.1007/978-3-540-30080-9_7
4. Boudjadar, A., et al.: Statistical and exact schedulability analysis of hierarchical scheduling systems. Sci. Comput. Program. **127**, 103–130 (2016). https://doi.org/10.1016/j.scico.2016.05.008
5. Boudjadar, A., et al.: Hierarchical scheduling framework based on compositional analysis using Uppaal. In: Fiadeiro, J.L., Liu, Z., Xue, J. (eds.) FACS 2013. LNCS, vol. 8348, pp. 61–78. Springer, Cham (2014). https://doi.org/10.1007/978-3-319-07602-7_6
6. Boudjadar, A., Kim, J.H., Larsen, K.G., Nyman, U.: Compositional schedulability analysis of an avionics system using UPPAAL. In: Sahnoun, Z. (ed.) Proceedings of the 1st International Conference on Advanced Aspects of Software Engineering,

ICAASE 2014, Constantine, Algeria, 2–4 November 2014. CEUR Workshop Proceedings, vol. 1294, pp. 140–147. CEUR-WS.org (2014). https://ceur-ws.org/Vol-1294/paper16.pdf

7. Bulychev, P., et al.: Uppaal-SMC: statistical model checking for priced timed automata. arXiv preprint arXiv:1207.1272 (2012)

8. Cassez, F., Larsen, K.: The impressive power of stopwatches. In: Palamidessi, C. (ed.) CONCUR 2000. LNCS, vol. 1877, pp. 138–152. Springer, Heidelberg (2000). https://doi.org/10.1007/3-540-44618-4_12

9. Chadli, M., et al.: High-level frameworks for the specification and verification of scheduling problems. Int. J. Softw. Tools Technol. Transf. **20**(4), 397–422 (2018). https://doi.org/10.1007/S10009-017-0466-1

10. Dertouzos, M.L.: Control robotics: the procedural control of physical processes. In: Rosenfeld, J.L. (ed.) Information Processing, Proceedings of the 6th IFIP Congress 1974, Stockholm, Sweden, 5–10 August 1974, pp. 807–813. North-Holland (1974)

11. Fersman, E., Krcál, P., Pettersson, P., Yi, W.: Task automata: schedulability, decidability and undecidability. Inf. Comput. **205**(8), 1149–1172 (2007). https://doi.org/10.1016/j.ic.2007.01.009

12. Han, P., Zhai, Z., Nielsen, B., Nyman, U., Kristjansen, M.: Schedulability analysis of distributed multicore avionics systems with UPPAAL. J. Aerosp. Inf. Syst. **16**(11), 473–499 (2019). https://doi.org/10.2514/1.I010715

13. Lipari, G., Palopoli, L.: Real-time scheduling: from hard to soft real-time systems. CoRR abs/1512.01978 (2015). http://arxiv.org/abs/1512.01978

14. Liu, C.L., Layland, J.W.: Scheduling algorithms for multiprogramming in a hard-real-time environment. J. ACM **20**(1), 46–61 (1973). https://doi.org/10.1145/321738.321743

15. Mikučionis, M., et al.: Schedulability analysis using Uppaal: Herschel-Planck case study. In: Margaria, T., Steffen, B. (eds.) ISoLA 2010. LNCS, vol. 6416, pp. 175–190. Springer, Heidelberg (2010). https://doi.org/10.1007/978-3-642-16561-0_21

16. Stigge, M., Ekberg, P., Guan, N., Yi, W.: The digraph real-time task model. In: 2011 17th IEEE Real-Time and Embedded Technology and Applications Symposium, pp. 71–80. IEEE (2011)

A Closer Look at Pseudo-polynomial Time and Its Use in Real-Time Scheduling Theory

Sanjoy Baruah[1][(✉)] and Pontus Ekberg[2]

[1] Washington University in St. Louis, St. Louis, USA
baruah@wustl.edu
[2] Uppsala University, Uppsala, Sweden
pontus.ekberg@it.uu.se

Abstract. Amongst Wang's contributions to real-time computing are those in which he and his collaborators have pushed the boundaries of pseudo-polynomial time schedulability analysis: developing expressive task models for which schedulability analysis can be done using algorithms that have pseudo-polynomial running time. In this note we revisit these contributions in the light of more recent work that provides additional context within which to view Wang's results, and investigate further directions in which his contributions can be extended.

1 Wang's Contributions to Real-Time Schedulability Analysis

Wang and his research collaborators have played a major role in obtaining solutions to the **schedulability analysis** problem, one of the foundational problems studied in real-time scheduling theory. The schedulability analysis problem may be described as follows:

GIVEN (i) the specifications of the computational demands of, and the timing constraints upon, a workload; (ii) the platform upon which this workload is to be executed; and (iii) the run-time scheduling algorithm that will be used, DETERMINE (prior to run-time) whether the workload is guaranteed to always meet all its timing constraints in all runtime scenarios permissible by the specification.

The workload is often modeled as a collection (called a *task system*) of independent recurrent tasks executing upon a shared computing platform. In the widely-studied *sporadic task model*, for instance, each task τ_i is characterized by a *worst-case execution time* (WCET) parameter C_i, a *relative deadline* D_i, and a *period* T_i (each $\in \mathbb{N}$). Each such τ_i releases a potentially unbounded sequence of *jobs*, with successive job releases separated by a duration no smaller than T_i units, during any particular execution of the system; each job released by τ_i may need to execute for up to C_i time units and must complete execution within a duration D_i following its release time. The shared platform upon which

S. Graf et al. (Eds.): Festschrift Wang Yi, LNCS 15230, pp. 120–134, 2025.
https://doi.org/10.1007/978-3-031-73751-0_10

the system is to be implemented may be a *uniprocessor* one or it may comprise *multiple processors* that may be *identical* or *heterogeneous*; furthermore, processors are said to be *preemptive* if an executing job can be interrupted and have its execution resumed later at no cost or penalty, or non-preemptive otherwise. A variety of scheduling algorithms have been studied, amongst the most common of which are the *Fixed-Priority* (FP) [26,27,31] and *Earliest-Deadline First* (EDF) [17,31] algorithms. (FP and EDF scheduling are discussed further in Sects. 4.1 and 4.2.)

In earlier times the limited availability of computation meant that schedulability analysis algorithms were restricted to have worst-case running times that are low-degree polynomials in the size of their inputs in order to be considered "efficient." A famous early example of such an efficient algorithm is the utilization-based FP schedulability test [31] for implicit-deadline sporadic task systems[1] upon preemptive uniprocessors. This utilization-based test is approximate rather than exact in the sense that it is sufficient but not necessary; indeed, polynomial-time exact schedulability-analysis algorithms are scarce (one exception is the utilization-based EDF schedulability test for implicit-deadline sporadic task systems upon preemptive uniprocessors). This is not surprising: most schedulability-analysis problems, including FP and EDF schedulability analysis of sporadic task systems upon preemptive or non-preemptive uniprocessor or multiprocessors, have been shown to be NP- or coNP-hard and hence unlikely to admit to exact polynomial-time schedulability tests (e.g., [5,7,18,19,21,23,29,30]).

As computing capabilities increased over time, schedulability analysis algorithms with *pseudo-polynomial* running times came to be considered efficient. Early examples of efficient algorithms of this kind include Response-Time Analysis (RTA) [3,16,26,27,42,43], an exact FP-schedulability test for constrained-deadline sporadic task systems upon preemptive uniprocessors, Processor-Demand Analysis (PDA) [6,7,29], an EDF-schedulability test for sporadic task systems, also upon preemptive uniprocessors, that is pseudo-polynomial time for bounded-utilization systems.

The emergence of this consensus within the safety-critical real-time computing community that pseudo-polynomial running time equates to efficiency spurred the real-time scheduling theory community to ask: *what is the most general workload model* for which preemptive uniprocessor schedulability analysis remains doable in pseudo-polynomial running time? Wang and his team made very significant contributions in this area, proposing a variety of increasingly expressive models – see Fig. 1 – that demarcate a precise boundary between

---

[1] Some terminology: an *implicit-deadline* sporadic task system is a sporadic task system in which each task τ_i satisfies the additional constraint that $D_i = T_i$, while each task in a *constrained-deadline* sporadic task system satisfies $D_i \leq T_i$. The ratio (C_i/T_i) of task τ_i is called its *utilization*; a *bounded-utilization* system is one for which the cumulative utilization is a priori bounded by some constant that is strictly smaller than 1. A *utilization-based* schedulability test determines schedulability by comparing the cumulative utilization of all the tasks in the system to some limit.

efficiency and intractability by identifying the most expressive models for which schedulability-analysis can be done in pseudo-polynomial time and the least expressive models for which it cannot (assuming $P \neq NP$).

In particular, they established that EDF schedulability analysis of bounded-utilization task systems upon preemptive uniprocessors can be done in pseudo-polynomial time for task systems represented using all of the models depicted in Fig. 1 with the exception of the two most general ones (EDRT [39] and Timed Automata with Tasks [24]). For FP-schedulability upon preemptive uniprocessors, pseudo-polynomial time algorithms are known to exist only for the Liu & Layland [31] and constrained-deadline sporadic [32] task models. The existence of pseudo-polynomial time FP-schedulability tests is still open for the non-cyclic GMF model [34], while all other models in Fig. 1 were shown to be strongly coNP-hard by Stigge [37], and so do not have such tests unless $P = NP$.

Our perception of what constitutes an efficient algorithm for schedulability analysis continues to evolve [1], and some recent research in the real-time scheduling community is exploring ways of moving beyond the pseudo-polynomial time barrier. Many such investigations (see, e.g., [4,11,12,15,46]) seek to transform a schedulability-analysis problem to some other form such as an integer linear program (ILP), which can then be solved by an ILP solver. Although solving an integer linear program is itself computationally intractable (it is strongly NP-complete to decide if any feasible solution exists), excellent off-the-shelf solvers exist that, by incorporating a combination of expert techniques, special-purpose heuristics, and highly optimized implementation, are able to handle surprisingly large problem instances in reasonable amounts of time.

Does this emerging acceptance of ILP representations as adequately efficiently solvable imply that all schedulability-analysis problems can now be considered to be efficiently solvable? By no means: while it is known that solving an ILP (specifically, determining whether a feasible solution exists), is an NP-complete problem as mentioned above, computational complexity theory defines various additional complexity classes that are widely presumed to encompass problems beyond NP or coNP (akin to NP being believed to contain problems beyond P – i.e., unsolvable by polynomial-time algorithms). Demonstrating the hardness of a schedulability analysis problem for one of these complexity classes would strongly suggest that it cannot be efficiently solved, even with a highly optimized ILP solver. The complexity class NP^{NP} (commonly denoted as Σ_2^P) is an example: it is widely conjectured that $NP \subsetneq \Sigma_2^P$ and $coNP \subsetneq \Sigma_2^P$. Woeginger [45] explains the implications: "*If you hit a Σ_2^P-complete problem, then there is no way of formulating it (in polynomial time) as an integer program (of polynomial size)*" and goes on to state that "*Σ_2^P-complete problems are much, much, much, much, much harder than any problem [...] that can be attacked via ILP solvers.*"

Summarizing the discussion above, until quite recently notions of efficiency in schedulability analysis appear to have been centered around these three beliefs:

1. Schedulability-analysis algorithms that have pseudo-polynomial running times are accepted as being efficient; Wang and his colleagues have made sig-

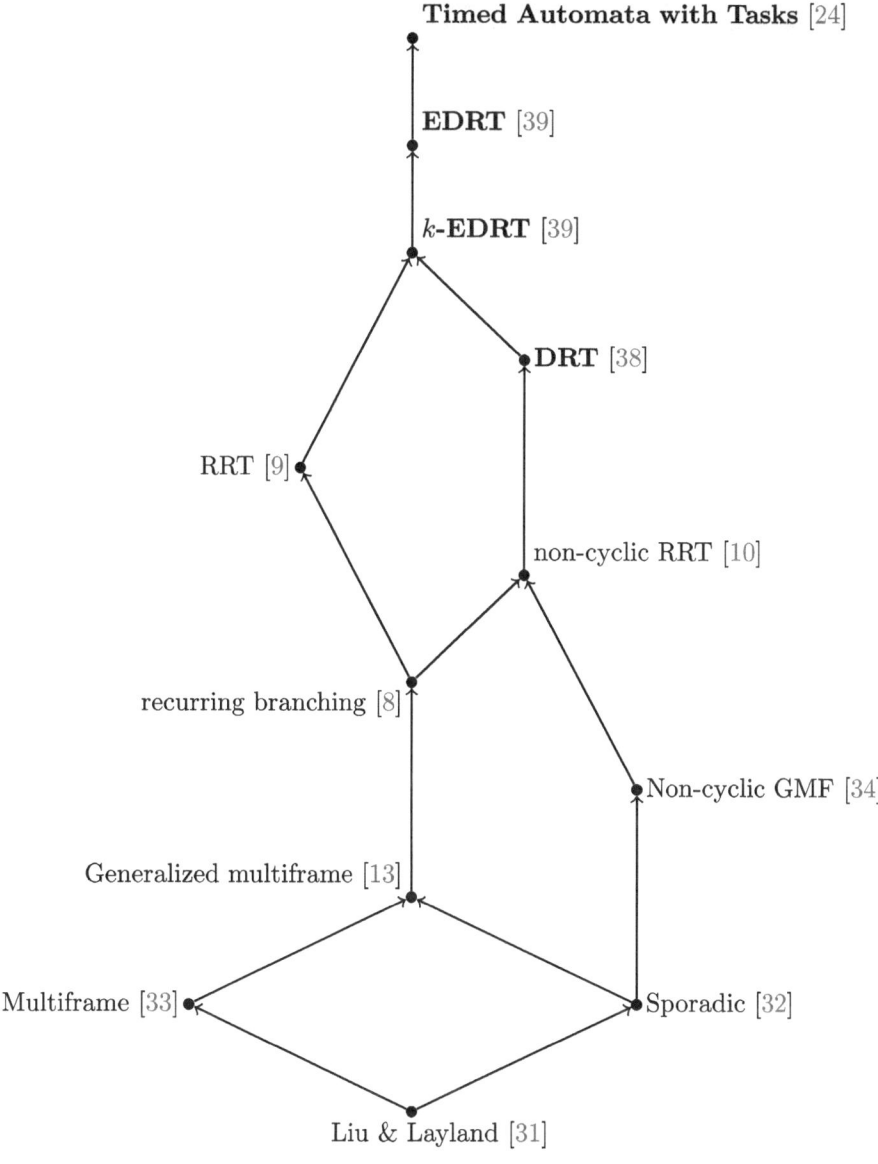

Fig. 1. Models for recurrent real-time tasks (the highlighted models have been proposed by Wang and his collaborators). Arrows point from less expressive models to more expressive ones; models not connected by a path have incomparable expressiveness. Wang and his collaborators proved that the k-EDRT model is the most general one for which preemptive uniprocessor EDF-schedulability analysis can be done in pseudo-polynomial time, and the sporadic model the most general one for which preemptive uniprocessor FP-schedulability analysis can be done in pseudo-polynomial time. This figure is adapted from [41].

nificant contributions in developing very general task models for which such efficient algorithms exist for preemptive uniprocessor EDF schedulability-analysis.

2. More recently, "polynomial-time + ILP-solver" algorithms – algorithms that have polynomial running time and are additionally allowed to make calls to an ILP solver – are also coming to be considered efficient (although less so than algorithms with pseudo–polynomial running times without needing an ILP solver).

3. Showing a problem to be hard for a complexity class believed to contain problems not in NP or coNP shows it to be truly intractable (as stated above, it is considered to be "much, much, much, much, much harder" [44] than any problem in NP or coNP).

However, recent research [1, page 4] somewhat blurs the third of these beliefs:

Observation 1 (From [1]) *If* C *is a complexity class contained in* EXP *and* C *is closed under polynomial-time reductions, then there exist* C-*complete problems with pseudo-polynomial time solutions.*   □

(Here EXP is the exponential-time analog of complexity class P: it is the complexity class of all decision problems that are solvable using exponential-time algorithms. A complexity class C is said to be closed under polynomial-time reductions if whenever problem X is in C and problem Y can be reduced to problem X in polynomial time, then problem Y is also in C.)

It immediately follows from Observation 1 that showing a problem to be Σ_2^P-hard does not necessarily rule out the possibility of there being a pseudo-polynomial-time algorithm for solving it – pseudo-polynomial time algorithms may exist for solving problems that belong to any complexity class $\subseteq$ EXP. This fact motivates us to also take a closer look at the first of these three beliefs: we make a case that not all pseudo-polynomial algorithms should be considered equally tractable, and, in Sect. 2 below, propose a finer-grained classification within the class of pseudo-polynomial time algorithms.

2   A Finer-Grained Notion of Pseudo-polynomial Time

The fundamental reason for why pseudo-polynomial time algorithms are considered efficient for scheduling problems is that the numerical parameters in such problems tend to have a direct physical interpretation, often as a measure of time, and therefore do not grow without bound in meaningful instances. Even so, numerical values found in input instances can quickly grow much larger than the instance size as measured in bits. In real-time scheduling problems, time may be measured in milliseconds, microseconds, or even CPU clock cycles, and numerical values can easily range into the thousands or millions even for "small" instances. If we expect to see instances where the largest numerical value N is much larger than the total input size n, then clearly the efficiency of a pseudo-polynomial time algorithm is often dominated by its scaling with respect to N

rather than to n. Still, in the real-time scheduling theory literature at least, we seldom see much attention paid to which polynomial scaling applies with respect to N.[2] Motivated by the above observations we define the following more fine-grained notion of pseudo-polynomial time, where the particular dependence (e.g., linear or quadratic) on the largest numerical parameter is made explicit.[3]

Definition 1 (Pseudo-f). *An algorithm's running time is pseudo-f if it is $O(n^k \times f(N))$, where n is the size of the representation of the problem instance, N is its largest numerical parameter value, k is a constant, and f is some function.* □

It follows from this definition that an algorithm's running time is pseudo-polynomial if and only if it is pseudo-f for some polynomial f. We will say that an algorithm with pseudo-f running time is *pseudo-linear* if $f(N) \in O(N)$, *pseudo-quadratic* if $f(N) \in O(N^2)$, etc.

A simple observation to make is that the notion of pseudo-f is unaffected by any logarithmic factors in f:

Theorem 2. *If $f(N) = \log^a(N) \times N^b$ and $g(N) = N^b$ for constants a and b, then an algorithm's running time that is pseudo-f is also pseudo-g.*

Proof. With any standard representation of numbers we have $\log(N) \in O(n)$, where N is the largest numerical parameter and n is the size of the input. If the running time is pseudo-f, then for some k it is

$$O(n^k \times f(N)) = O(n^k \times \log^a(N) \times N^b) \subseteq O(n^{k+a} \times N^b) = O(n^{k+a} \times g(N))$$

and is therefore also pseudo-g.   □

Despite being insensitive to logarithmic factors, Definition 1 provides meaningful distinctions not just between algorithm running times, but also between the complexity of problems. We see below that any difference in polynomial degree between f and g differentiates pseudo-f from pseudo-g, and the problems that can be solved correspondingly.

Theorem 3. *For all $a > b > 0$, there are problems that can be solved in time $O(\mathsf{poly}(n) \times N^a)$, but not in time $O(\mathsf{poly}(n) \times N^b)$, where n is the size of the input and N is the value of its largest numerical parameter.*

Proof. Let $c = (a+b)/2$ and let S be a problem that can be solved in time $O(2^{an})$, but not in time $O(2^{cn})$. (We know that such S exist by the Time Hierarchy Theorem [25].) Let

$$S' \stackrel{\text{def}}{=} \left\{ (x,y) \mid x \in S \wedge y = 2^{|x|} \right\}$$

---

[2] The authors of this paper are most certainly guilty of having, in multiple previous works, declared success as soon as a pseudo-polynomial time algorithm has been found for the problem under study.

[3] This definition is a generalization of one that appeared in [1].

and we will see that S' is the problem we are looking for. It is evident that y is the largest number in any instance $(x, y) \in S'$.

First, we can solve S' in time $O(\mathsf{poly}(n) \times N^a)$ as follows. Given (x, y) we check that $y = 2^{|x|}$ and if so we use the $O(2^{an})$ algorithm for S to check that $x \in S$ in time $O(2^{a|x|}) = O(y^a)$.

Second, we cannot solve S' in time $O(\mathsf{poly}(n) \times N^b)$. Suppose for the purpose of contradiction that we could, then we could solve S as follows. Given an instance x of S we reduce to instance $(x, 2^{|x|})$ of S' in polynomial time. Then we use the algorithm for S' to determine if $(x, 2^{|x|}) \in S'$ (and hence $x \in S$) in time

$$O\big(\mathsf{poly}(|x| + |y|) \times y^b\big) = O\big(\mathsf{poly}(|x|) \times 2^{b|x|}\big) \subsetneq O\big(2^{c|x|}\big),$$

thereby contradicting the assumption that S cannot be solved in time $O(2^{cn})$. □

Corollary 1. *More problems can be solved in pseudo-quadratic time than in pseudo-linear time, and in pseudo-cubic time than in pseudo-quadratic time, etc.* □

3   A Notion of Scaling Invariance of Pseudo-polynomial Time

In addition to being able to differentiate pseudo-polynomial time algorithms based on their polynomial dependence on the numerical values found in inputs (as in Definition 1), we would also like to differentiate pseudo-polynomial time algorithms based on whether their running time is invariant to simple scaling of such values.

Preferably, a pseudo-polynomial time algorithm should take longer time to run only when there are more complicated relationships between the values of numerical parameters in the input, and not when those numerical parameters grow without their internal relationships changing. This is a natural property of many problems with pseudo-polynomial time algorithms. For example, it is not inherently harder to evenly partition boxes of sizes 1000, 2000, and 3000, than to partition boxes of sizes 1, 2, and 3.

In the context of scheduling problems, if numerical parameters represent time, this translates into whether a pseudo-polynomial time algorithm is sensitive to the *unit* used for specifying timing parameters. For example, we would like such an algorithm to have the same running time for a particular input instance regardless of whether time is given in units of milliseconds, microseconds or 1/17'ths of a second, assuming that everything else remains unchanged and that numerical values are still integer.

The following definition attempts to capture this notion of invariance of a pseudo-polynomial time algorithm.[4]

---

[4] This definition (though not the analysis following it), appeared in [1]. There it was called *robust* pseudo-polynomial time, but we prefer the term used here as "robust" is an overloaded word.

Definition 2 (Scale-Invariant Pseudo-Polynomial Time). *An algorithm is* scale-invariant *pseudo-polynomial if it runs in time that is polynomial in n and in N/G, where n is the size of the input, N is its largest numerical parameter, and G is the greatest common divisor of all its numerical parameters.* □

By combining this definition with Definition 1 we will also refer to algorithms as being *scale-invariant pseudo-linear* if the dependence on N/G is linear, etc.

We note that it seems useful to retain some flexibility regarding which numerical parameters to include in the computation of the greatest common divisor G in Definition 2. For instance, in a multiprocessor scheduling problem with a multitude of numerical parameters denoting time (deadlines, periods, execution times) and a single numerical parameter denoting the number of processors, it may make sense to include only the parameters that share a unit (i.e., the parameters representing time), but not the processor count, when calculating G.

Not all pseudo-polynomial time algorithms are scale invariant, and in the following we see that this differentiates computational problems as well.

Theorem 4. *There are problems that can be solved in pseudo-polynomial time, but not in scale-invariant pseudo-polynomial time.*

Proof. This follows from a simple padding argument. Let S be an EXP-complete problem that is naturally encoded without using numbers, say *Generalized Go*, which was proven to be EXP-complete by Robson [35].[5] Say that S can be solved in time

$$O\big(2^{n^k}\big). \tag{1}$$

Then let

$$S' \stackrel{\text{def}}{=} \Big\{ (x,y) \mid x \in S \land y = 2^{|x|^k} \Big\}$$

be another problem created by padding instances x of S by exponentially large numbers y, where k is the constant from Eq. 1. A reduction from S to S' is clearly in polynomial time, so S' is EXP-hard. We can also solve S' in pseudo-polynomial time by first checking that $y = 2^{|x|^k}$ and then use the algorithm for S to check $x \in S$ in time $O(2^{|x|^k}) = O(y)$.

However, since we consider instances of S to have no numbers in them, the only number in an instance (x,y) of S' is y. Therefore y/G, where G is the GCD of numbers in (x,y) is simply $y/y = 1$. A *scale-invariant* pseudo-polynomial time algorithm for S' must therefore run in time $\mathsf{poly}(n, N/G) = \mathsf{poly}(|x|+|y|, y/y) = \mathsf{poly}(|x|+|y|)$, which is impossible by the Time Hierarchy Theorem since S' is EXP-hard. □

---

[5] Sorry, Wang, that's with traditional Japanese rules. Generalized Go with Chinese rules is not known to be EXP-complete. [36]

128 S. Baruah and P. Ekberg

In real-time scheduling problems, a lack of scale invariance of a schedulability test could stem from a reliance on discrete schedules (e.g., that jobs can only be released at integer time points or executed for an integer number of time units at a time)[6], or from scheduling decision based on things such as absolute time points or number of time units executed. In other cases, however, there seems to be little reason for why a pseudo-polynomial time schedulability test could not in principle be made scale invariant. The following natural property seems self-evident.

Proposition 1. *Let $\mathcal{J}$ be a sequence of independent jobs, each specified by release time, deadline and execution time, in a setting where scheduling does not have to be discrete. Let $\mathcal{J}$ be scheduled by a scheduler that, if it bases any scheduling decisions on the jobs' parameters or remaining execution times, only does so on the relative ordering of those values (e.g., as with EDF, which considers the relative ordering of deadlines). If $\mathcal{J}'$ is another sequence of jobs that differs from $\mathcal{J}$ only in that its jobs have their parameters uniformly scaled by some factor, then the scheduler would meet all deadlines of $\mathcal{J}$ if and only if it would meet all deadlines of $\mathcal{J}'$.*

Most common scheduling algorithms fit the above description and would simply generate scaled, but otherwise identical, schedules from job sequences $\mathcal{J}$ and $\mathcal{J}'$. This is easily seen to include schedulers such as EDF, FP and FIFO.

The above proposition immediately generalizes to task systems where, if task system Γ' is a uniformly scaled version of task system Γ, then any job sequence released by Γ' is a uniformly scaled version of a job sequence released by Γ. This includes basic periodic and sporadic task systems.

Corollary 2. *Let Γ be a task system of periodic or sporadic tasks not limited to discrete behaviors, and let Γ' be an identical task system, but with uniformly scaled task parameters. Then schedulers such as EDF, FP and FIFO would correctly schedule Γ if and only if they correctly schedule Γ'.*

We note that if a scheduling algorithm has the above properties of producing identical, but scaled, schedules on scaled inputs for a given setting, then a schedulability test for it could be made scale invariant by simply dividing every task parameter by the GCD before applying the test.

4   A (Very) Brief Survey of Some Schedulability Algorithms

In this section we take a quick look at three schedulability problems and corresponding schedulability tests from the real-time scheduling literature. These tests are pseudo-polynomial time algorithms; we classify them further on the basis of Definitions 1 and 2.

---

[6] In some settings this is a very important distinction. For example, in the popular *mixed-criticality* scheduling model some task systems are schedulable if job releases are restricted to integer time points, but become impossible to schedule correctly if they are not (see [22, Claim 2]).

4.1 Response-Time Analysis

Response-time analysis (RTA) [3,16,26,27,42,43] is the classical schedulability test for Fixed-Priority (FP) scheduling, which computes the worst-case response time of each task and compares it with the deadline. In the basic setting of independent sporadic or synchronous periodic tasks with constrained deadlines scheduled on a preemptive uniprocessor, if the smallest positive fixed point R_i to

$$R_i = C_i + \sum_{\tau_j \in \text{hp(i)}} \left\lceil \frac{R_i}{T_j} \right\rceil \times C_j$$

is such that $R_i \leq T_i$, where $\text{hp}(i)$ is the set of tasks with higher priority than τ_i, then R_i is the worst-case response time of task τ_i. The fixed-point iteration

$$R_i^{n+1} = C_i + \sum_{\tau_j \in \text{hp(i)}} \left\lceil \frac{R_i^n}{T_j} \right\rceil \times C_j \tag{2}$$

is known to find the smallest positive fixed point R_i if started with an initial value that is at most R_i. Since for schedulability we are interested only in knowing if $R_i \leq D_i$ for each task, we can immediately stop the fixed-point iteration if we encounter a $R_i^n > D_i$. Assuming integer task parameters, the number of iterations of Eq. 2 before converging or reaching $R_i^n > D_i$ is therefore bounded by D_i. From this follows the well-known result that determining whether $R_i \leq D_i$ can be done in time $O(|\text{hp}(i)| \times D_i)$ using RTA, and the entire task system's schedulability can then certainly be determined in time $O(n^2 \times N)$, where n is the size of the task system and N the largest task parameter value. From Definition 1 we have then that RTA is not only pseudo-polynomial in this setting, but is in fact pseudo-linear.

Just a little closer inspection of Eq. 2 reveals that the number of iterations is also bounded by $\sum_{\tau_j \in \text{hp(i)}} \lceil D_i/T_j \rceil$, which is $O(n \times N/G)$, where G is the greatest common divisor of all numerical task parameters. From Definition 2, we have then that RTA is also scale-invariant pseudo-linear.

We note that RTA in the form above does not work for task systems with arbitrary deadlines (where we may have $D_i > T_i$). It has been extended by Lehoczky [28] to work in such settings, but that variant of RTA takes exponential time and it is not known if the schedulability problem with arbitrary deadlines can be solved in pseudo-polynomial time at all in the general setting.

4.2 Processor-Demand Analysis

Processor-demand analysis (PDA) [6,7] is a schedulability test for Earliest Deadline First (EDF) scheduling of independent synchronous periodic or sporadic tasks on a preemptive uniprocessor. EDF-schedulability in this setting can be solved in linear time for task systems with implicit deadlines using a simple utilization test [31], but with constrained or arbitrary deadlines PDA is the canonical test. According to PDA, a task system Γ is EDF-schedulable if and only if

$$\sum_{\tau_i \in \Gamma} \left(\max \left(\left\lfloor \frac{t - D_i}{T_i} \right\rfloor + 1, 0 \right) \right) \times C_i \leq t \qquad (3)$$

for all time-window sizes $t \in \mathcal{T}(\Gamma)$, where $\mathcal{T}(\Gamma)$ is the so-called *test set* for Γ.

The EDF-schedulability problem is strongly coNP-complete [20], and so the size of the test set is not pseudo-polynomial in general. However, if the task system's utilization, $\sum_{\tau_i \in \Gamma} C_i/T_i$, is bounded by some constant c, where $c < 1$, then a valid test set is

$$\mathcal{T}(\Gamma) = \left\{ 0, 1, \ldots, \frac{c}{1 - c} \times \max_{\tau_i \in \Gamma} \{T_i - D_i\} \right\}.$$

In this case we have that $|\mathcal{T}(\Gamma)|$ is of pseudo-polynomial size, and indeed it is easy to see that PDA in this case meets the requirements of Definition 1 to be pseudo-linear. Bounding the utilization to something less than 100% (using, say, $c = 0.99$) is not particularly limiting, and good engineering practice is anyway to not utilize the processor to its limits at 100%.

We can note that the above pseudo-polynomial version of PDA is not scale invariant, as per Definition 2, as scaling all task parameters by some integer factor would cause the test set to grow by the same factor. A common optimization applied to PDA is to include only the points t where $t \equiv D_i \pmod{T_i}$ for some $\tau_i \in \Gamma$ in the test set (those are exactly the points at which the left-hand side of Eq. 3 is discontinuous). By applying this optimization, the size of the test set remains the same if a uniform scaling is applied to the task parameters, and PDA becomes scale-invariant pseudo-linear as per Definition 2.

The fact that both PDA and RTA (as seen in Sect. 4.1) are scale-invariant pseudo-linear in common settings may go some way to explain their practical efficiency.

4.3   Semi-clairvoyant Scheduling of Mixed-Criticality Tasks

We will now take a look at a more recent schedulability test for what is called semi-clairvoyant scheduling [2] of mixed-criticality tasks with graceful degradation [14]. In this scheduling problem we have a set of regular sporadic tasks, but each task is marked as having either high or low criticality. The tasks with high criticality come with alternative implementations that may have longer execution times (for handling extraordinary or critical situations), while the tasks with low criticality come with alternative implementations that may have lower execution times (as lower-quality backup implementations that consume less resources in critical scenarios). The arrival of any job from a high-criticality task may trigger a critical scenario and result in the use of, from that time point onwards, the alternative implementations of all new jobs from all tasks.

In [14], an exact EDF-schedulability test was described for this scheduling problem, which builds on PDA as described in Sect. 4.2 and also assumes bounded utilization. Instead of quantifying over a single pseudo-polynomially sized test set, as in PDA, this test requires two universal quantifiers and has the following general form (we skip the details of the expressions here, they are available in [14, Theorem 7]):

$$\forall t \in A, \forall s \in B : \mathrm{dbf}(t, s) \leq t,$$

where A and B are pseudo-linearly sized sets, and $\mathrm{dbf}(t, s)$ is a simple function that can be evaluated in linear time (essentially a generalization of the left-hand side of Eq. 3).

The extra quantification, compared to PDA, serves the purpose of testing all the possibilities as to which job triggers critical behavior, and there seems to be no obvious way to get rid of it. The effect is that this schedulability test is not pseudo-linear, though it can be seen to be pseudo-quadratic.[7] Some sort of additional quantification over time points in a time interval, as seen here, is not an uncommon pattern of schedulability tests and seems a likely cause of a number of slower-than-pseudo-linear pseudo-polynomial time schedulability tests in the literature.

The test described above is also not scale invariant, as in Definition 2, because one of the sets that is quantified over grows with an increased uniform scaling of task parameters. It is not trivial to see in the proofs presented in [14] that it does not have to be so, and it may seem as if the test strategy employed inherently lacks scale invariance. However, a higher-level reasoning similar to that of Corollary 2 shows that EDF-schedulability must be unaffected if all task parameters were uniformly scaled in this setting, and so the test can in fact easily be made scale invariant by first dividing all parameters by the GCD.

5   Concluding Remarks

The real-time scheduling community has long considered the availability of pseudo-polynomial time algorithms as one of the important delimiters between tractable and intractable problems. This largely holds true because numerical parameters in such problems tend to represent physical time, and therefore do not grow without bound. Wang has been part of several important works that have pushed the boundary of what can be analyzed in pseudo-polynomial time, and via complexity analysis found where that boundary lies exactly (for example in [20, 38–40]).

Recent research [1] has investigated some ways in which the pseudo-polynomial time boundary can be blurred. In this note we have looked closer at

---

[7] A pseudo-quadratic test is certainly much better than a full-blown exponential-time test, but we should also expect that this test can be much slower than the pseudo-linear PDA that it builds upon. The authors of [14] did however not dwell on this fact, and instead happily reported the success of finding a pseudo-polynomial time test for the problem without further discussion. The authors of [14] are also the authors of the current paper. *Nostra culpa.*

some of those ways, in particular by further classifying pseudo-polynomial time algorithms based on their particular polynomial dependency on the numerical variables, and based on whether their running time is invariant to scaling of those parameters. We anticipate that the findings reported here may spur additional research building upon Wang's works by extending his ideas and approaches to our finer-grained classification and by incorporating scale-invariance.

References

1. Agrawal, K., Baruah, S., Ekberg, P.: Rethinking tractability for schedulability analysis. In: 2023 IEEE Real-Time Systems Symposium (RTSS), pp. 1–12. IEEE Computer Society, Los Alamitos, CA, USA (2023). https://doi.org/10.1109/RTSS59052.2023.00011
2. Agrawal, K., Baruah, S., Burns, A.: Semi-clairvoyance in mixed-criticality scheduling. In: Proceedings of the Real-Time Systems Symposium (RTSS), pp. 458–468 (2019)
3. Audsley, N.C., Burns, A., Davis, R.I., Tindell, K.W., Wellings, A.J.: Fixed priority preemptive scheduling: an historical perspective. Real Time Syst. 8, 173–198 (1995)
4. Baruah, S.: An ILP representation of a DAG scheduling problem. Real Time Syst. Int. J. Time Crit. Comput. 58, 85 (2021)
5. Baruah, S., Howell, R., Rosier, L.: Algorithms and complexity concerning the preemptive scheduling of periodic, real-time tasks on one processor. Real Time Syst. Int. J. Time Crit. Comput. 2, 301–324 (1990)
6. Baruah, S., Howell, R., Rosier, L.: Feasibility problems for recurring tasks on one processor. Theor. Comput. Sci. 118(1), 3–20 (1993)
7. Baruah, S., Mok, A., Rosier, L.: Preemptively scheduling hard-real-time sporadic tasks on one processor. In: Proceedings of the 11th Real-Time Systems Symposium, pp. 182–190. IEEE Computer Society Press, Orlando, Florida (1990)
8. Baruah, S.: Feasibility analysis of recurring branching tasks. In: Proceedings of the Tenth EuroMicro Workshop on Real-time Systems, pp. 138–145. Berlin, Germany (1998)
9. Baruah, S.: Dynamic- and static-priority scheduling of recurring real-time tasks. Real Time Syst. Int. J. Time Crit. Comput. 24(1), 99–128 (2003)
10. Baruah, S.: The non-cyclic recurring real-time task model. In: Proceedings of the Real-Time Systems Symposium. IEEE Computer Society Press, San Diego, CA (2010)
11. Baruah, S., Bini, E.: Partitioned scheduling of sporadic task systems: an ILP-based approach. In: Proceedings of the 2008 Conference on Design and Architectures for Signal and Image Processing (2008)
12. Baruah, S., Bonifaci, V., Bruni, R., Marchetti-Spaccamela, A.: ILP-based approaches to partitioning recurrent workloads upon heterogeneous multiprocessors. In: Proceedings of the 2016 28th EuroMicro Conference on Real-Time Systems. ECRTS '16, IEEE Computer Society Press, Toulouse (France) (2016)
13. Baruah, S., Chen, D., Gorinsky, S., Mok, A.: Generalized multiframe tasks. Real Time Syst. Int. J. Time Crit. Comput. 17(1), 5–22 (1999)
14. Baruah, S., Ekberg, P.: Graceful Degradation in Semi-Clairvoyant Scheduling. In: Brandenburg, B.B. (ed.) 33rd Euromicro Conference on Real-Time Systems (ECRTS 2021). Leibniz International Proceedings in Informatics (LIPIcs), vol. 196, pp. 9:1–9:21. Schloss Dagstuhl – Leibniz-Zentrum für Informatik, Dagstuhl, Germany (2021)https://doi.org/10.4230/LIPIcs.ECRTS.2021.9

15. Baruah, S.K., Bonifaci, V., Bruni, R., Marchetti-Spaccamela, A.: ILP models for the allocation of recurrent workloads upon heterogeneous multiprocessors. J. Sched. (2018). https://doi.org/10.1007/s10951-018-0593-x
16. Burns, A., Tindell, K., Wellings, A.: Effective analysis for engineering real-time fixed priority schedulers. IEEE Trans. Softw. Eng. **21**(5), 475–480 (1995)
17. Dertouzos, M.: Control robotics : the procedural control of physical processors. In: Proceedings of the IFIP Congress, pp. 807–813 (1974)
18. Eisenbrand, F., Rothvoss, T.: Static-priority real-time scheduling: response time computation is NP-hard. In: Proceedings of the Real-Time Systems Symposium. IEEE Computer Society Press, Barcelona (2008)
19. Eisenbrand, F., Rothvoß, T.: EDF-schedulability of synchronous periodic task systems is coNP-hard. In: Proceedings of the Annual ACM-SIAM Symposium on Discrete Algorithms (2010)
20. Ekberg, P., Yi, W.: Uniprocessor feasibility of sporadic tasks with constrained deadlines is strongly coNP-complete. In: 2015 27th Euromicro Conference on Real-Time Systems, pp. 281–286 (2015)
21. Ekberg, P.: Models and Complexity Results in Real-Time Scheduling Theory. Ph.D. thesis, Uppsala University (2015)
22. Ekberg, P., Yi, W.: A note on some open problems in mixed-criticality scheduling. In: Proceedings of the 6th International Real-Time Scheduling Open Problems Seminar (RTSOPS) (2015)
23. Ekberg, P., Yi, W.: Fixed-priority schedulability of sporadic tasks on uniprocessors is NP-hard. In: 2017 IEEE Real-Time Systems Symposium, RTSS 2017, Paris, France, December 5-8, 2017. pp. 139–146. IEEE Computer Society (2017). https://doi.org/10.1109/RTSS.2017.00020
24. Fersman, E., Pettersson, P., Yi, W.: Timed automata with asynchronous processes: Schedulability and decidability. In: Tools and Algorithms for the Construction and Analysis of Systems. pp. 67–82. Springer Berlin Heidelberg, Berlin, Heidelberg (2002)
25. Hartmanis, J., Stearns, R.E.: On the computational complexity of algorithms. Trans. Am. Math. Soc. **117**, 285–306 (1965)
26. Joseph, M., Pandya, P.: Finding response times in a real-time system. Comput. J. **29**(5), 390–395 (1986)
27. Lehoczky, J., Sha, L., Ding, Y.: The rate monotonic scheduling algorithm: Exact characterization and average case behavior. In: Proceedings of the Real-Time Systems Symposium - 1989, pp. 166–171. IEEE Computer Society Press, Santa Monica, California, USA (1989)
28. Lehoczky, J.P.: Fixed priority scheduling of periodic task sets with arbitrary deadlines. In: Proceedings of the 11th Real-Time Systems Symposium (RTSS), pp. 201–209 (1990)
29. Leung, J.Y.T., Merrill, M.: A note on the preemptive scheduling of periodic, real-time tasks. Inf. Process. Lett. **11**, 115–118 (1980)
30. Leung, J.Y.T., Whitehead, J.: On the complexity of fixed-priority scheduling of periodic, real-time tasks. Perform. Eval. **2**, 237–250 (1982)
31. Liu, C., Layland, J.: Scheduling algorithms for multiprogramming in a hard real-time environment. J. ACM **20**(1), 46–61 (1973)
32. Mok, A.: Fundamental Design Problems of Distributed Systems for The Hard-Real-Time Environment. Ph.D. thesis, Laboratory for Computer Science, Massachusetts Institute of Technology (1983). Available as Technical Report No. MIT/LCS/TR-297

33. Mok, A.K., Chen, D.: A multiframe model for real-time tasks. In: Proceedings of the 17th Real-Time Systems Symposium. IEEE Computer Society Press, Washington, DC (1996)
34. Moyo, N.T., Nicollet, E., Lafaye, F., Moy, C.: On schedulability analysis of non-cyclic generalized multiframe tasks. In: Proceedings of the EuroMicro Conference on Real-Time Systems. IEEE Computer Society Press, Brussels (2010)
35. Robson, J.M.: The complexity of Go. In: Mason, R.E.A. (ed.) Information Processing 83, Proceedings of the IFIP 9th World Computer Congress, Paris, France, September 19-23, 1983, pp. 413–417. North-Holland/IFIP (1983)
36. Saffidine, A., Teytaud, O., Yen, S.J.: Go complexities. In: Plaat, A., van den Herik, J., Kosters, W. (eds.) Advances in Computer Games, pp. 76–88. Springer International Publishing, Cham (2015). https://doi.org/10.1007/978-3-319-27992-3_8
37. Stigge, M.: Real-Time Workload Models: Expressiveness vs. Analysis Efficiency. Ph.D. thesis, Uppsala University, Department of Information Technology (2014)
38. Stigge, M., Ekberg, P., Guan, N., Yi, W.: The digraph real-time task model. In: Proceedings of the IEEE Real-Time Technology and Applications Symposium (RTAS), pp. 71–80. IEEE Computer Society Press, Chicago (2011)
39. Stigge, M., Ekberg, P., Guan, N., Yi, W.: On the tractability of digraph-based task models. In: Proceedings of the EuroMicro Conference on Real-Time Systems. IEEE Computer Society Press, Porto, PT (2011)
40. Stigge, M., Yi, W.: Hardness results for static priority real-time scheduling. In: 2012 24th Euromicro Conference on Real-Time Systems, pp. 189–198 (2012).https://doi.org/10.1109/ECRTS.2012.13
41. Stigge, M., Yi, W.: Graph-based models for real-time workload: a survey. Real Time Syst. **51**, 602–636 (2015). https://doi.org/10.1007/s11241-015-9234-z
42. Tindell, K.W., Burns, A., Wellings, A.J.: An extendible approach for analysing fixed priority hard real-time tasks. Real Time Syst. Int. J. Time Crit. Comput. **6**, 133–151 (1994)
43. Wellings, A., Richardson, M., Burns, A., Audsley, N., Tindell, K.: Applying new scheduling theory to static priority pre-emptive scheduling. Softw. Eng. J. **8**, 284–292 (1993)
44. Woeginger, G.J.: When does a dynamic programming formulation guarantee the existence of a fully polynomial time approximation scheme (FPTAS)? INFORMS J. Comput. **12**(1), 57–74 (2000). https://doi.org/10.1287/ijoc.12.1.57.11901
45. Woeginger, G.J.: The trouble with the second quantifier. 4OR Quart J Oper Res **19**(2), 157–181 (2021). https://doi.org/10.1007/s10288-021-00477-y
46. Zheng, W., Zhu, Q., Natale, M.D., Vincentelli, A.S.: Definition of task allocation and priority assignment in hard real-time distributed systems. In: 28th IEEE International Real-Time Systems Symposium (RTSS 2007), pp. 161–170 (2007). https://doi.org/10.1109/RTSS.2007.40

Voting-Based Shortcuts through Random Forests for Obtaining Explainable Models

Alnis Murtovi$^{(\boxtimes)}$, Maximilian Schlüter, and Bernhard Steffen

TU Dortmund University, Dortmund, Germany
{alnis.murtovi,maximilian.schlueter,bernhard.steffen}@tu-dortmund.de

Abstract. In this paper, we introduce novel voting-based pruning strategies for the aggregation of Random Forests into decision tree-like explainable models. These strategies are designed to mitigate the enormous explosion in size during the aggregation process while minimizing the loss of accuracy. We explore four strategies ranging from strict semantics-preserving methods to more dynamic stochastic and machine learning models, which balance the trade-off between pruning aggressiveness and fidelity to the original Random Forest. We illustrate the impact of our approach with experiments covering an extensive set of popular datasets in this field.

Keywords: Tree Ensemble · Random Forests · Explainable AI · Algebraic Decision Diagrams · Interpretation

1 Introduction

Despite the recent exciting achievements based on Large Language Models, tree-based models, such as *Random Forests* [6] and *gradient boosted trees* [10], typically still outperform Deep Learning-based models on tabular data [3,13,23]. Characteristic for Random Forests is the low variance of their predictions in comparison to even very large learned individual decision trees. However, their underlying, majority-voting-based decision process obfuscates the reasons for a proposed classification. To increase trust in Random Forest-based classifications, heuristic explanation approaches like LIME [22] and SHAP [20] have been proposed. However, these approaches are insufficient to obtain guarantees like sufficiency or necessity of revealed reasons.

In contrast, the approach presented in [12] provides accurate explanations through *Algebraic Decision Diagram-based aggregation* (ADD aggregation): In essence, Random Forest are step-wise aggregated into a single, *semantically equivalent* decision tree, a structure that is accepted to be explainable [14]. Thus, these structures can be considered as *model explanations* that can, e.g., be used to formally verify properties of the underlying classifier [21]. Additionally, one can generate more concise *outcome explanations* in form of: (i) execution paths through these structures, i.e., the conjunction of the taken decisions [12], (ii)

S. Graf et al. (Eds.): Festschrift Wang Yi, LNCS 15230, pp. 135–153, 2025.
https://doi.org/10.1007/978-3-031-73751-0_11

logic explanations, i.e., necessary and/or sufficient conditions over the input to result in a specific classification [17, 18].

Although the ADD aggregation-based approach satisfactorily solves explainability and verification problems, it can lead to an exponential explosion in size, especially in intermediate models. The reason for these large intermediate ADDs is the required compositionality: The structure of the ADDs must be expressive enough, so that, given two ADDs, one can compute their sum without changing their classification behavior. It is easy to see that, just recording the 'winners' at the leaf of the ADDs, is not compositional, whereas it is sufficient for the final result which is only used for classification.

In this paper, we present four methods for reducing the explosion of the intermediate ADDs:

1. Two semantics-preserving optimizations that, given a voting vector, determine the outcome (win or lose) for a class based on sufficient available information.
2. One probabilistic optimization, that makes use of the training dataset and the trees of the Random Forest, to capture the voting behavior of the Random Forest, and decide whether enough information is present to determine the outcome.
3. A machine learning-based optimization in which a machine learning model is trained and queried to decide whether the given information is sufficient to decide whether a class is going to win or lose.

We analyze our proposed optimizations by answering the following research questions:

RQ1 How effective is the size reduction?
RQ2 Do the optimizations reduce the compile time required to construct the ADDs?
RQ3 How well do the heuristic optimizations preserve the accuracy of the original Random Forest?

Whereas the first two optimizations can be used for the explanation and verification of Random Forests without any loss, as they do not affect the classification function, the latter two change the classification behavior of the original Random Forest. Thus corresponding explanation or verification results are only approximations, but may, in contrast to explanations provided, e.g., by LIME, still be supported by softened sufficiency criteria. Alternatively, and this may be the even better solution, one could switch to using the reduced model itself which, provably, supports accurate explanation and verification.

This paper is dedicated to Wang Yi as part of his Festschrift. I, Bernhard, remember exactly when I met Wang first: at the first TACAS conference in 1995. He presented UPPAAL [1, 2, 24], and it was obvious that he was proud that UPPAAL outperformed renown tools like HyTECH [15] and Kronos [4]. Like for SMT and SAT solving, also here it is all about adequate heuristics, as is this paper. The lesson to learn is that one should not be scared away by worst case complexity. A few years later, Wang published [19] in the first issue of the international journal Software Tools for Technology Transfer (STTT), which I just had founded. With 3075 citations until today, this paper became the most cited STTT paper.

The structure of this paper is organized as follows: Section 2 provides an overview of Random Forests and ADDs, and briefly summarizes the approach originally introduced in [12]. Section 3 discusses the concept of *early termination*, which is fundamental to our proposed optimizations. Following this, Sect. 4 explores a probabilistic adaptation of early termination, which is the basis of our stochastic optimizations. In Sect. 5, we present two semantics-preserving optimizations, while Sect. 6 is dedicated to describing our probabilistic optimizations. The effectiveness of these optimizations is evaluated in Sect. 7. Finally, we conclude the paper in Sect. 8.

2   Background

For some natural number $n \in \mathbb{N}$, let $[n] := \{1, \ldots, n\}$ be the set of all natural numbers less than or equal to n. In this paper, we are only concerned with supervised classification tasks solved by Random Forests. In a supervised task, the Random Forest is trained over a *finite* set of samples, the training set, where for each sample the correct class, called ground truth, is known. Each sample consists of multiple feature (or attribute) valuations from the input domain $\mathbb{F} := F_1 \times \cdots \times F_l$ ($l \in \mathbb{N}$). The domain F_i of each feature is either *numerical* (e.g., $F_i = \mathbb{R}$) or *categorical* (e.g., $F_i \subset \mathbb{N}$ with $|F_i| < \infty$). In the first case, we assume that the features can always be linearly ordered, in the latter case this may not be the case. The data from the domain $\mathbb{F}$, including the training set, follows some (unknown) probability distribution D. For each sample $x \in \mathbb{F}$, the task is to predict its class $c \in \mathcal{C}$. For convenience, we may also identify the finite set of classes $\mathcal{C}$ with the first m natural numbers $[m]$ where $m := |\mathcal{C}|$.

2.1   Random Forests

Random Forests [6,9] are a tree ensemble model used in machine learning for classification and regression tasks. They consist of a finite collection of decision trees $T_1, \ldots, T_n$ (known as *forest*), where each individual decision tree is trained using the CART algorithm [5] on a *randomly* selected subset of the training data, drawn with replacement (*bagging*) [16]. A decision tree T_i is a full, binary tree with labeled edges. Its inner nodes represent predicates over the input space $\mathbb{F}$ and its terminal nodes store a prediction from $\mathcal{C}$. Predicates are logical formulas in form of a comparisons of some feature variable x_i from domain F_i against a constant value $z \in F_i$ ($i \in [l]$), i.e., of the form $x_i \leq z$ for numerical and $x_i = z$ for categorical attributes. Each edge label indicates whether the predicate of the outgoing node is satisfied or not. For evaluation, the input is passed through the tree by following the predicates evaluation until a terminal is reached. The value stored at the terminal is then the associated prediction of the tree for the input. In this regard a decision tree implies a unique total function $\mathbb{F} \to \mathcal{C}$.

To infer the prediction of a Random Forest, each decision tree T_i is evaluated on its own making a prediction for one class $c_i \in \mathcal{C}$. Then, the class which is predicted by most trees is the final prediction of the ensemble. This principle is called *majority vote*: Each tree T_i can vote for one class $c_i \in \mathcal{C}$ and the class with the most votes wins. When a tie occurs between multiple classes the one with the lowest index takes precedence. In the following, we associate with a Random Forest R the unique total function $\mathbb{F} \to \mathcal{C}$ that corresponds to this evaluation schema.

2.2 Algebraic Decision Diagrams

Algebraic Decision Diagrams (ADDs) are decision graphs over an abstract algebra (A, O) representing some function $\mathbb{F} \to A$. [1] In this paper we are mostly concerned with the algebra $((\mathbb{N} \cup \{\bot, \top\})^m, \{+\})$ of vectors over natural numbers and vector addition. ADDs extend 'classic' decision trees in two important ways: (i) they integrate the algebraic structure of their co-domain A into the decision structure, and (ii) they apply a set of semantics-preserving optimization techniques for an efficient representation [7].

Starting with optimizations, ADDs have a special graph structure that is key for their efficiency:

1. The graph structure is a Direct Acyclic Graph (DAG), allowing paths to be aggregated when they share equal prefixes or suffixes.
2. The predicates in an ADD have a fixed order in which they test the different features of an input vector. Thereby, graph isomorphy can detect many forms of semantic equivalence.
3. Isomorphic subtrees are identified by rerouting edges.
4. Redundant predicates are removed. E.g., when the left and right subtree of a predicate are isomorphic.

Additionally, based on the more expressive predicates used in this setting, predicates along a path can share semantic dependencies, e.g., when $x_2 \leq 3$ is followed by $-x_2 \leq 5$ along the same path the latter predicate is always false. Such paths are called *infeasible* and can be detected and eliminated using *infeasible path elimination* as, e.g., also applied in program analysis (specifically for ADDs see [12,21]).

ADDs support all operations of there underlying algebra. An algebra (A, O) consists of a carrier set A and a set O of operations over A. Operations $op \in O$ have a fixed arity and are closed under A. The operators O can be *lifted* onto ADDs [7].

---

[1] This is an extension of classic ADDs, which are defined over the domain $\{0, 1\}^n$. By allowing predicates over $\mathbb{F}$, we extend the expressiveness of ADDs at the cost of semantic dependencies along paths [12].

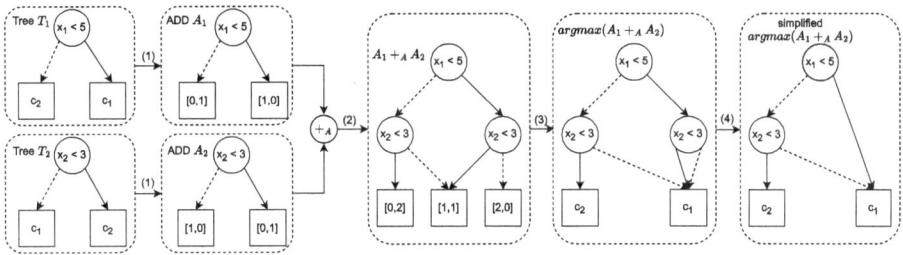

Fig. 1. Example of transforming a Random Forest with 2 trees $\{T_1, T_2\}$ to an ADD using the approach of [12].

Definition 1 (Lifting). *Given an operation $h \in O \subseteq A^r \to A$ of the algebra $(r \in \mathbb{N})$, it is possible to lift this operation on the ADD level such that for r ADDs $f_1, \ldots, f_r \colon \mathbb{F} \to A$ and all inputs $\boldsymbol{x} \in \mathbb{F}$ the following holds*

$$h_A(f_1, \ldots, f_r)(\boldsymbol{x}) := h(f_1(\boldsymbol{x}), \ldots, f_r(\boldsymbol{x}))$$

In particular, $h_A(f_1, \ldots, f_r)$ is an ADD itself.

The worst case complexity of computing $h_A(f_1, \ldots, f_r)$ is $\mathcal{O}(|f_1| \cdot \ldots \cdot |f_r|)$ including all optimizations.

2.3 Compiling Random Forests to Algebraic Decision Diagrams

Let us again consider a forest R comprised of $T_1, \ldots, T_n$ decision trees. As previously discussed, the evaluation of a forest follows the majority vote principle. According to [12], one can express this explicitly by considering ADDs over the vector space $\mathbb{R}^m$ representing the votes for each class. Map each class in $\mathcal{C}$ to a unique number in $[m]$. Then, update each terminal of each tree T_i ($i \in [n]$) to a unit vector $e_j \in \mathbb{N}^m$ that is one at the index j of the winning class and zero everywhere else. Convert this new tree into an ADD, called A_i, by applying the previously discussed optimizations. [2] Then, the evaluation of the Random Forest can be expressed as an addition of voting vectors and subsequent argmax:

$$A = \arg\max(A_1 +_A \cdots +_A A_n)$$

where A is a single ADD encoding the semantics of the Random Forest R:

$$R(x) = c_i \iff A(x) = i \quad \text{for all } x \in \mathbb{F}$$

Example 1. For a Random Forest with 2 trees, Fig. 1 illustrate its transformation to an ADD. First, the decision trees T_1 and T_2 are transformed to ADDs A_1 and A_2 (see step (1)). Here, the classes c_1 and c_2 are represented by vectors $[1, 0]$ and

---

[2] This conversion can increase the size of the ADD in comparison to the original decision tree.

$[0, 1]$. Next, A_1 and A_2 are used to construct $A_1 +_A A_2$ (see step (2)). For a given sample, this ADD returns the number of votes the classes received from the two decision trees. Finally, arg max is applied to ADD $A_1 +_A A_2$ (see step (3)). The voting vector $[1, 1]$ is replaced by c_1 as the lowest index takes precedence. We can observe that one node has two outgoing edges pointing to the same successor. Such redundancies are automatically removed and thus we obtain the ADD on the right in Fig. 1 (see step (4)).

3   Early Termination

Practically, the computation of $A_1 +_A \cdots +_A A_n$ is expensive. Without further optimizations, the running time for computing A is asymptotically $\mathcal{O}(|A_1| \cdot \ldots \cdot |A_n|)$, which is roughly equivalent to $\mathcal{O}(|A_i|^n)$ for some i.

In the state-of-the-art [12], first $A_1 +_A \cdots +_A A_n$ is constructed, i.e., an ADD that, given an input, computes the votes each class receives from all the decision trees. The argmax operation is applied only after this ADD is fully constructed. However, when counting the votes exactly, one keeps track of more information than is needed at the end. Thus, many distinctions made in $A_1 +_A \cdots +_A A_n$ are ultimately superfluous, as different voting vectors can lead to the same majority vote outcome. This can be measured empirically by considering the size of the ADD before and after applying the argmax function. In our evaluation described in Sect. 7, we constructed ADDs using the approach outlined in [12]. Figure 2 illustrates the ratio of the size of $A_1 +_A \ldots +_A A_n$ to that of the ADD following the application of the argmax. This ratio, which reaches as high as 141, indicates significant potential for optimization. By detecting such cases early, we reduce the size and computational effort for the intermediate products and thus speed up the whole process, avoiding unnecessary computations once the outcome is assured or probable.

Assume a setting with a Random Forest $R \colon \mathbb{F} \to [m]$ whose n decision trees have already been converted into the Algebraic Decision Diagrams $A_1, \ldots, A_n$. Further, assume that we have finished the first $k \in [n-1]$ aggregation steps, i.e., computed

$$P_k = A_1 +_A \cdots +_A A_k$$

Based on four different techniques, we will deduce from the current state of P_k how each *path/voting vector* might develop when aggregating the remaining $A_{k+1}, \ldots, A_n$ trees. In the next section, we will introduce a formal probability model for judging this development.

Let us briefly describe what we do once we determined that along some path π some class $i \in [m]$ will probably win or probably lose the majority vote. In both cases, we may stop counting the exact votes for this particular class i, as we are only interested in the outcome of the argmax, i.e., which class wins, but

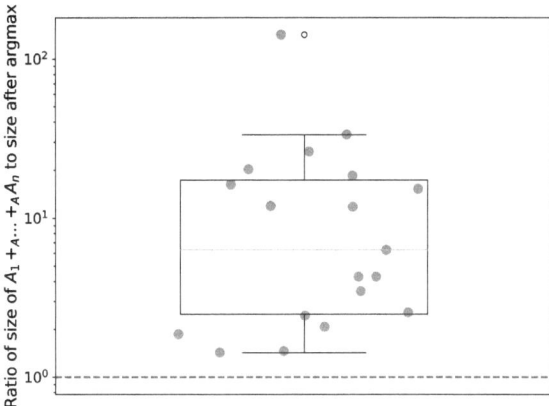

Fig. 2. Ratios between size of intermediate ADD before argmax to size of ADD after application of argmax.

not by which margin. We can express both cases algebraically by introducing the following persistent states ($z \in \mathbb{N}$):

$$\top + z = \top \qquad\qquad \bot + z = \bot$$

When a class is likely to win, we change its entry to $\top$ and all others to $\bot$. And when a class likely loses the majority vote, we update its entry to $\bot$.

When we stop counting the exact votes, we considerably reduce the state space of possible terminals nodes. Therefore, ADD reduction can eliminate redundant decisions in P_k that are only useful for exact counting, but are overly fine for tracking the classes.

Example 2. Figure 3 motivates the idea of replacing the entry of a class, that is likely to win, with $\top$ and all other entries with $\bot$. Let $A_1 \ldots, A_{20}$ be the decision trees of a Random Forest represented as ADDs. Consider the ADD on the left representing the result $A_1 +_A \ldots +_A A_{14}$ and that $A_{15} \ldots A_{20}$ still have to be added. In this ADD on the left, the predicate $x_1 < 5$ only exists to differentiate between $[13, 0, 1]$ and $[14, 0, 0]$. We already know that class c_1 is going to win as there are only 6 votes left that c_2 and c_3 could potentially receive. Replacing these voting vectors with $\top$ and $\bot$ entries leads to the ADD in the middle. There are two redundancies, that are automatically eliminated in our approach. First, the leaves are identical, so they can be merged into a single leaf. Second, after this merge, the edges of $x_1 < 5$ point to the same successor, so this predicate is redundant. Ultimately, the resulting ADD on the right has two fewer nodes than the initial ADD.

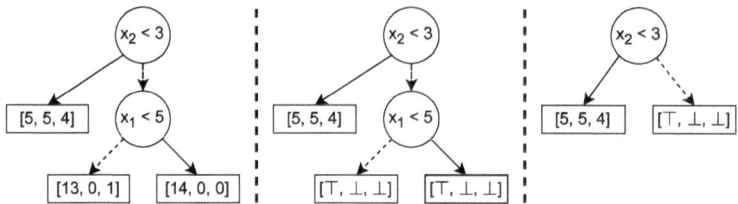

Fig. 3. Illustration of how setting entries to $\top$ leads to simplifications in the ADD.

Example 3. Figure 4 shows why solely replacing entries of classes that are likely to lose with $\bot$ is also helpful. Here, the ADD on the left represents $A_1 +_A \ldots +_A A_{21}$ and $A_{22} \ldots A_{30}$ still have to be added. Since c_3 and c_4 can at most receive 9 votes, they cannot catch up to class c_1 in and thus we replace their entries with $\bot$. The simplifications that can now be performed are analogous to the example in Fig. 4.

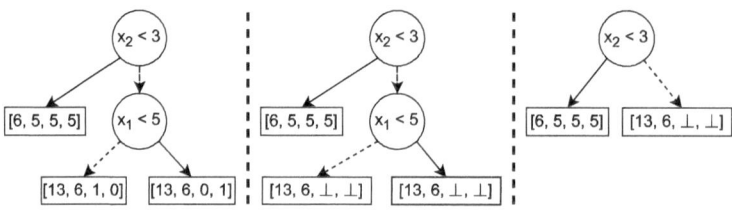

Fig. 4. Illustration of how setting entries to $\bot$ leads to simplifications in the ADD.

4   Stochastic Problem Description

As described in Sec. 2.3, each Tree (resp. ADD) has one vote and the class with the most votes wins. Before aggregation, votes are represented in the terminals of the ADDs as unit vectors, concretely, the unit vector e_i indicates a single vote for class i. After the votes of the first $k \in [n]$ ADDs have been added, the space of possible *voting vectors* can be described as

$$\Omega_k := \left\{ \omega \in \{0, \ldots, k\}^m \;\middle|\; \sum_{i=1}^{m} \omega_i = k \right\} \tag{1}$$

which contains $\binom{k+m-1}{k}$ distinct vectors. Based solely on this voting vector ω, one can estimate the probability that class i gets the most votes. For example, given a vector $[5, 1, 7]$ with two remaining votes, it is most probable that the third class will win. One can calculate this probability by examining the possible *outcomes* after the remaining $n - k$ votes have been collected:

$$w + \Omega_{n-k} = \left\{ w + v \,\middle|\, \sum_{i=1}^{m} v_i = n - k, v_i \in \mathbb{N} \right\} \subset \Omega_n$$

To judge how probable it is that class i wins given the votes w, one considers if class i wins in any possible outcome $w + \Omega_{n-k}$ weighted by the probability of reaching that outcome:

$$P(R = i \mid w) = \sum_{v \in \Omega_{n-k}} P(w + v \mid w) P(R = i \mid w + v) \tag{2}$$

For the outcomes $w' = w + v \in \Omega_n$, i.e., after all remaining votes have been collected, the probability that class i will win is straightforward

$$P(R = i \mid w') = \begin{cases} 1 & \text{if } \arg\max_j w'_j = i \\ 0 & \text{otherwise} \end{cases}$$

To compute Equation (2) in general, one still needs the underlying data distribution D to compute $P(w + v \mid w)$ exactly. For some cases, we will show in Sec. 5 that the probability is determined to be one or zero, in which case the outcome is assured. For other cases, we will discuss in Sec. 6 how the probability can be estimated.

Suppose that we have a probability function, we can now formalize the (pathwise) *early termination* procedure of Sec. 3. Consider a voting vector w of some terminal in P_k, then we define the two functions $\varphi_\top \colon \Omega_k \times [k] \to (\mathbb{N} \cup \{\top, \bot\})^m$ and $\varphi_\bot \colon \Omega_k \times 2^{[k]} \to (\mathbb{N} \cup \{\top, \bot\})^m$ as:

$$\left(\varphi_\top(w, j) \right)_i := \begin{cases} \top & \text{if } i = j, \\ \bot & \text{otherwise.} \end{cases}$$

$$\left(\varphi_\bot(w, J) \right)_i := \begin{cases} \bot & \text{if } i \in J, \\ w_i & \text{otherwise.} \end{cases}$$

Given a position j, the function $\varphi_\top$ can be used on a voting vector to indicate that the class at that position is predicted to win, by setting entry j to $\top$ and all other entries to $\bot$. Conversely, if the classes at positions J are expected to lose, $\varphi_\bot$ can be applied to replace these entries with $\bot$, demonstrating disinterest in the exact vote count.

We define a function $\psi \colon \Omega_k \times [0,1]^2 \to (\mathbb{N} \cup \{\top, \bot\})^m$ for early termination as:

$$\psi(w, \alpha, \beta) := \begin{cases} \varphi_\top(w, i) & \text{if } \exists! i : P(R = i \mid w) > \alpha, \\ \varphi_\bot(w, I) & \text{if } I = \{ i \mid P(R = i \mid w) < \beta \}, \\ w & \text{otherwise.} \end{cases}$$

Given a voting vector w and a probability function P that calculates the probability of class i winning given w, the parameters α and β serve as thresholds. These thresholds determine the necessary probability for a class to be considered likely to win or lose, respectively. Reasonable values satisfy $\beta \le 0.5 \le \alpha$.[3]

5   Semantics-Preserving Early Stopping

The first two optimizations concerns safe knowledge that can be inferred from the current voting vector w.

5.1   General Rules

When one class $i \in \mathcal{C}$ has more than half of the n total votes, it is guaranteed to win. Similarly, when a class i has less than $\lceil \frac{n}{m} \rceil - (n - k)$ votes, it cannot win. The first (resp. second) rule is sufficient to guarantee that the argmax of $w \in \Omega_k$ is always (resp. never) equal to i, independent of what votes $v \in \Omega_{n-k}$ might be added to w. Therefore, $P(R = i \mid w + v)$ is always equal to 1 (resp. 0), and with it the whole Equation (2).

Example 4. Given a Random Forest with $n = 10$ trees and $m = 3$ classes and the following voting vector $w = [6, 0, 0]$ $(k = 6)$. We know that the first class with 6 will definitely win because the other two classes can at most receive 4 votes. Therefore, applying our general rules to w results in $[\top, \bot, \bot]$.

Example 5. Given a Random Forest with $n = 10$ trees and $m = 3$ classes and the following voting vector $w = [v_1, v_2, 0]$ with $v_1 + v_2 = 8 = k$. We know that the third class can receive at most 2 votes and that $\max\{v_1, v_2\} \ge 4$ so the third class will definitely not win. Therefore, applying our general rules to w results in $[v_1, v_2, \bot]$.

5.2   Specific Rules

Extending the general rules, one can also incorporate the votes of the other classes. When $w_i > w_j + (n - k)$ for all $j \ne i$, then class i will win. Similarly, when $w_i + (n - k) < w_j$ for some j, then class i will definitely lose. The general rules imply the specific, but not vice-versa. Their proof is analogous.

Example 6. Given a Random Forest with $n = 10$ trees and $m = 4$ classes and the following voting vector $w = [4, 2, 2, 1]$ $(k = 9)$. While our general rules cannot be applied to this voting vector, our specific rules can, because there is only one remaining vote and no class can catch up to the class with 4 votes. Therefore, the application of specific rules to w results in $w = [\top, \bot, \bot, \bot]$.

---

[3] If multiple classes i satisfy $P(R = i \mid w) > \alpha$, one could either choose the one with the highest probability or wait for more votes in the hope that then the picture will be more clearly. Setting a value of $\alpha > 0.5$ mitigates this issue.

Example 7. Given a Random Forest with $n = 100$ trees and $m = 3$ classes and the following voting vector $\omega = [40, 25, 0]$ ($k = 65$). There are 35 votes left, and therefore our general rules cannot be applied, but our specific rules can be applied as we know that the class with 0 votes cannot catch up to the class with 40 votes. Applying our specific rules to ω results in $[40, 25, \perp]$.

6   Probabilistic Early Stopping

While the general and specific rules are always correct, they can only be applied when at least $k > \lfloor 0.5n \rfloor$ votes have been collected. If one wants to prune terminals early in the aggregation process (i.e., when $k \leq \lfloor 0.5n \rfloor$), it is impossible to preserve semantics as the outstanding votes can always change the winner. Instead, a probabilistic approach can be used that states which class is most likely to win. For that, one must make assumptions about the distribution of v. And even then, the sheer number of possible votes $v \in \Omega_{n-k}$, i.e., $\binom{n-k+m-1}{n-k}$, is so big that it quickly becomes practical infeasible to consider all of them.

6.1   Look-up Table

One way to estimate the probability $P(R = i \mid \omega)$ is to incorporate knowledge about how the votes for the decision trees of the Random Forest R are distributed on the training data. For that we create two tables W and L that track how many times a given voting configuration—a tuple (i, h, k) stating that class i received h out of k votes—has occurred on the training data and to what outcome it led after all votes have been considered. The table W tracks how many times the class i of the tuple won the final majority vote and L tracks how many times it lost.

Given a sample $x \in \mathbb{F}$, we can query each decision tree T_i of the Random Forest for its decision ($i \in [n]$). We obtain votes $V = (v_1, v_2, \ldots, v_n) \in C^n$, which we aggregate in a single vector whose i-th entry states how many trees voted for class c_i. Again, we define a family of these vectors each looking at the first $k \in [n]$ trees (i.e., the first k entries of V):

$$\omega^{\leq k} = \sum_{i=1}^{k} e_{v_i} \in \Omega_k$$

Note that $\omega^{\leq k}$ depends on x. By definition, it follows that the classification of x by R can be read from the values of the final vector of this sequence, i.e., when $k = n$:

$$R(x) = \arg\max_{i \in [m]} \omega^{\leq n}{}_i$$

Based on the series of voting vectors $\omega^{\leq 1}, \ldots, \omega^{\leq n}$ we fill out the tables W and L: For the class $i = R(x)$, we increment the n entries $(i, \omega^{\leq k}{}_i, k)$ ($k \in [n]$) in W by one. For all other classes $j \neq R(x)$, we increment the n entries $(j, \omega^{\leq k}{}_j, k)$

$(k \in [n])$ in L by one. We repeat this procedure for each sample in the training data.

When aggregating the trees, for each terminal with voting vector ω with $k = \|\omega\|_1$, we can estimate the probability that class i is going to receive the most wins, when it received h out of k votes (if $W(i, \omega_i, \|\omega\|_1) + L(i, \omega_i, \|\omega\|_1) > 0$):

$$P(R = i \mid \omega) \approx \frac{W(i, \omega_i, \|\omega\|_1)}{W(i, \omega_i, \|\omega\|_1) + L(i, \omega_i, \|\omega\|_1)}.$$

Using the look-up table, we define the corresponding probabilistic early stopping function, denoted as ψ_{LUT}, referring to $\psi(\omega, \alpha, \beta)$ with the above estimation of the probabilities. This function integrates the probabilistic assessments from this estimate to determine the stopping criteria based on the thresholds α and β.

6.2   Machine Learning Approach

One disadvantage of our look-up table is that it does not take into account the number of observations. If $W(i, h, k) = 1$ and $L(i, h, k) = 0$, we would estimate the probability that class i is going to win when it received h out of k votes to be 100%, even though we observed this only once on the training data.

Instead of constructing a look-up table by 'hand', one can, of course, train a machine learning model to predict $P(R = i \mid \omega)$. The ML model has three features:

- Feature 1: The class i.
- Feature 2: The total number of votes, i.e., $k = \|\omega\|_1$.
- Feature 3: The number of votes class i received.

We construct a new dataset from the existing tables W and L as follows: For each entry $W(i, h, k) = n_1$, we add n_1 samples to the dataset, where each sample consists of the input tuple (i, h, k) and is assigned an expected target of 1. Similarly, from table L, for each entry $L(i, h, k) = n_0$, we add n_0 samples with the same input tuple (i, h, k) but with an expected target of 0.

Let g denote the function that represents the output of our trained machine learning model. We approximate $P(R = i \mid \omega)$ for some intermediate voting vector $\omega \in \Omega_k$ with the prediction of the ML model:

$$P(R = i \mid \omega) \approx g(i, \|\omega\|_1, \omega_i).$$

Again, we define a probabilistic early stopping function using the trained ML model as ψ_{ML} referring to $\psi(\omega, \alpha, \beta)$ based on the above probability estimation.

Example 8. Given a Random Forest with 3 trees and two classes, given a sample where the decision trees predict the classes $V = (c_1, c_1, c_2)$, the training data would look as follows.

Table 1. Overview of datasets and the compiled ADD (#F = Number of features, #I = Number of test instances, #C = Number of classes, #T = Number of trees, #N = Number of nodes in the Random Forest, #P = Number of unique predicates, D = Maximum depth, %A = Accuracy of the Random Forest on test set).

Dataset	#F	#I	#C	#T	#N	#P	D	%A
ann-thyroid	21	1426	3	25	555	146	4	98
appendicitis	7	22	2	50	722	207	4	90
banknote	4	270	2	100	1998	614	4	97
ecoli	7	66	5	100	2532	379	4	90
glass2	9	33	2	25	445	159	4	87
ionosphere	34	70	2	15	247	101	4	87
iris	4	30	2	100	1200	94	4	93
magic	10	3781	2	25	747	349	4	82
mofn-3-7-10	10	205	2	100	2904	10	4	85
new-thyroid	3	43	3	100	1452	237	4	100
phoneme	5	43	2	100	2836	957	4	78
ring	20	1480	2	25	625	287	4	83
segmentation	19	42	7	15	329	148	4	92
shuttle	9	11600	7	50	1296	205	4	99
threeOf9	9	103	2	100	1364	9	4	100
twonorm	29	1480	2	15	465	225	4	90
waveform-21	21	1000	3	15	465	214	4	80
wine-recog	13	36	3	25	399	152	4	97
xd6	9	103	2	100	2904	9	4	90

Feature 1 (i)	Feature 2 (k)	Feature 3 $(w_i^{\leq k})$	Target
1	1	1	1
2	1	0	0
1	2	2	1
2	2	0	0
1	3	2	1
2	3	1	0

7   Evaluation

In this section, we evaluate the optimizations proposed in the previous sections by compiling Random Forests learned on a variety of datasets from the UCI Machine Learning Repository to ADDs. This evaluation aims to answer the three research questions introduced in Sect. 1.

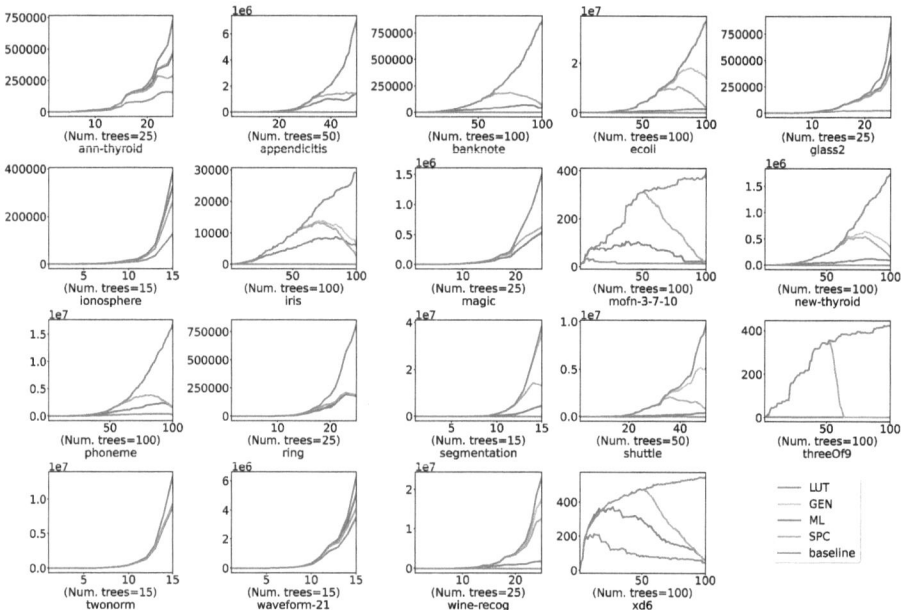

Fig. 5. Size of intermediate ADDs during the aggregation process.

7.1   Hardware, Software Setup and Benchmarks

We evaluated our approach on a machine with an Intel(R) Xeon(R) Gold 6152 CPU 2.10 GHz with 502GB of RAM. We use the decision diagram library *ADD-Lib* [11] for the construction of the ADDs. The Random Forests are learned using 80% of the dataset as the train set while 20% of the data is used as the test set. Table 1 gives an overview of the datasets used to learn the Random Forests and their properties. For all Random Forests we chose a maximum depth of 4 and an ensemble of either 15, 25, 50, or 100 trees.

We perform measurements with 5 different configurations:

- *baseline*: As our baseline we use the approach published in [12].
- *GEN*: The baseline approach enhanced with the general rules described in Sect. 5.1.
- *SPC*: The baseline approach enhanced with the specific rules described in Sect. 5.2.
- *LUT*: The baseline approach enhanced with the look-up table described in Sect. 6.1. We employ the function ψ_{LUT} with the thresholds set such that $\alpha = 1$ and $\beta = 0$.
- *ML*: We enhance the baseline approach with the machine learning approach described in Sect. 6.2. We decided to learn a XGBoost [8] model using the training data, that is generated as described in 6.2. The XGBoost model has been learned using 125 gradient boosted trees with a maximum depth of 4. We employ the function ψ_{ML} with the thresholds set such that $\alpha = 0.999$ and $\beta = 0.001$.

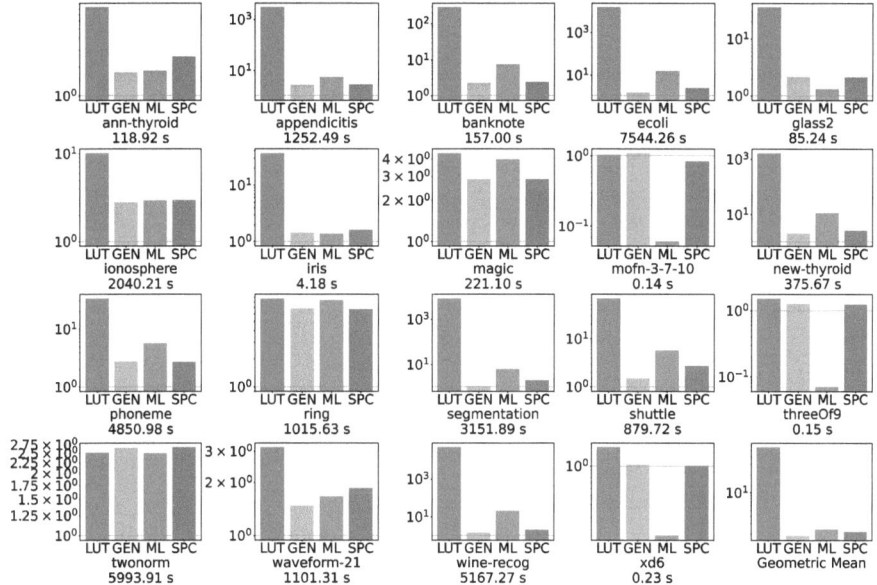

Fig. 6. Speedups over baseline for the transformation of the Random Forest to the ADD.

7.2   Experimentation Results

With this evaluation, we want to answer the research questions introduced in Sect. 1. **RQ1: Do our optimizations reduce the size of the voting ADDs?** The main motivation behind early stopping is to keep the size of the intermediate ADDs small. As the intermediate ADDs are larger than the majority vote ADD, reducing the size of the intermediate ADDs reduces peak memory usage.

To answer **RQ1** in more detail, we empirically take a look at the size of the intermediate ADDs after each join. Figure 5 gives an overview of the size of the vector ADD for each configuration after each join and infeasible paths have been eliminated. The y-axis represents the number of nodes of the ADD.

For *baseline*, we can observe that the number of nodes generally increases with the number of joined ADDs. Across all datasets, our four proposed optimizations consistently result in smaller intermediate ADDs. Specifically, we can observe that for *GEN* and *SPC* the size of the ADDs only goes down after at least half the trees have been joined as the general and specific rules cannot be applied earlier. In contrast, for *LUT* and *ML*, we can see for many datasets that they yield significant improvements even before half of the trees have been joined. This is attributed to the high probability of a class winning when it received a majority of the initial votes.

For many datasets, such as *banknote, ecoli, iris, mofn-3-7-10, new-thyroid, phoneme, threeOf9* and *xd6*, the size of the ADD actually decreases with an increase in the number of joined ADDs, as a result of our optimizations. Whereas

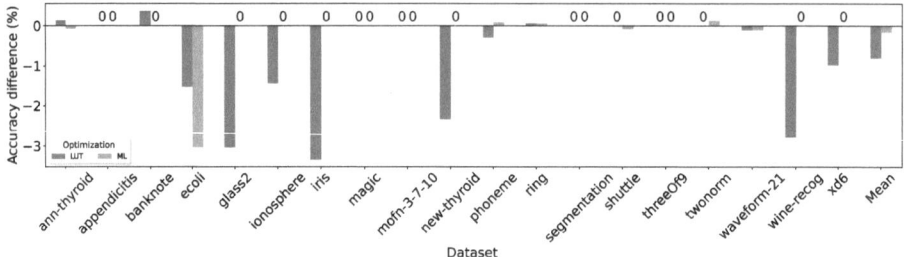

Fig. 7. Difference in test accuracy compared to the Random Forest.

for the remaining datasets, our optimizations ensure that the growth in ADD size remains more controlled compared to the size increases observed with the *baseline* ADD. Furthermore, when *LUT* is applied, the size of the ADD often remains stable or increases only marginally (compare *appendicitis, banknote, glass2, iris, mofn-3-7-10, new-thyroid, threeOf9*). These reductions in ADD sizes lead to significant reductions in peak memory usage.

RQ2: Do our optimizations reduce the time it takes to compile a Random Forest into an ADD? While we have observed that our optimizations are able to reduce the size of the intermediate ADDs, we also want to evaluate whether this size reduction translates into decreased execution times. As ADD aggregation is polynomial in the size of the ADDs, it is reasonable to assume that decreased intermediate ADD size also leads to improved execution times.

Figure 6 illustrates the speedups achieved by each of our optimizations over the baseline. For *LUT*, the time required to construct the lookup table and for *ML*, the overhead from training the XGBoost model are included in the execution time. Overall, we can observe that the size reductions do indeed lead to execution time improvements: the geometric mean speedups obtained by *LUT*, *GEN*, *ML*, and *SPC*, are 56.10×, 1.89×, 2.41×, and 2.19×.

For many datasets, *LUT* outperforms all other optimizations, achieving significant speedups of around 10^3 for *appendicitis* and *new-thyroid*. This is a result of the stable size of intermediate ADDs, which do not increase even as more ADDs are joined (see Fig. 5).

For datasets with more than 2 classes, *SPC* outperforms *GEN*. Ignoring the datasets with very low ADD construction time, *ML* is mostly competitive with *SPC* or outperforms it, but not by a significant margin.

ML performs poorly on *mofn-3-7-10, threeOf9* and *xd6* because the overhead incurred by learning the XGBoost model is greater than the time it takes to transform the Random Forest to an ADD (i.e., slower than the baseline approach).

RQ3: Do our probabilistic optimizations preserve the accuracy of the original Random Forest? Given the significant speed improvements observed with *LUT* and *ML*, it is necessary to examine their impact on the accuracy of the Random Forest. Figure 7 shows the difference in test set accuracy caused by the application of LUT and ML.[4] The mean difference in accuracy over all datasets for LUT and ML is -0.8% and -0.16%. For 5 datasets, both optimizations result in no loss of accuracy. For 6 of the remaining datasets, ML also does not lead to any loss of accuracy. For many datasets the loss in accuracy is relatively minor.

There are some datasets where loss in accuracy is larger than 1%. For these datasets the number of test samples (see Table 1) is less than 100. As a result, misclassifications of only a few samples will lead to a large difference in test accuracy.

In some cases, such as for *ann-thyroid*, *banknote* and *ring* our probabilistic approaches can even increase the accuracy on the test set. This can happen because the simplifications caused by our probabilistic approaches lead to better generalization on unseen data.

In general, there is a trade-off between performance, in terms of ADD construction time, and accuracy. By reducing the parameter α and increasing β, one can implement a more aggressive probabilistic early strategy, potentially achieving substantial performance gains. However, one has to be careful when adjusting these parameters as excessive decreases in α or increases in β could result in unacceptable losses in accuracy.

8   Conclusion and Future Work

In this paper, we have introduced four optimizations designed to enhance the method from [12] for converting Random Forests into ADDs. Our optimizations span from semantics-preserving techniques to more dynamic approaches involving stochastic processes and machine learning models. Our evaluation demonstrates the effectiveness of each optimization and reveals a trade-off between performance and accuracy. In future work, the probability $P(\omega + v \mid \omega)$ could be modeled by a *Dirichlet-multinomial distribution*. By doing so, however, one would ignore any specific facts about the dataset and the trees of the forest. Also, rather than using fixed values for α and β, a heuristic could be implemented that adjusts these parameters based on the training dataset and the characteristics of the learned Random Forest.

References

1. Bengtsson, J., Larsen, K.G., Larsson, F., Pettersson, P., Yi, W.: UPPAAL - a tool suite for automatic verification of real-time systems. In: Alur, R., Henzinger, T.A., Sontag, E.D. (eds.) Hybrid Systems III: Verification and Control, Proceedings of the DIMACS/SYCON Workshop on Verification and Control of Hybrid Systems, October 22-25, 1995, Ruttgers University, New Brunswick, NJ, USA. Lecture Notes in Computer Science, vol. 1066, pp. 232–243. Springer (1995). https://doi.org/10.1007/BFB0020949, https://doi.org/10.1007/BFb0020949

---

[4] Since *GEN* and *SPC* maintain the semantics of the Random Forest, their accuracy difference is always 0%.

2. Bengtsson, J., Larsen, K.G., Larsson, F., Pettersson, P., Yi, W.: UPPAAL in 1995. In: Margaria, T., Steffen, B. (eds.) Tools and Algorithms for Construction and Analysis of Systems, Second International Workshop, TACAS '96, Passau, Germany, March 27-29, 1996, Proceedings. Lecture Notes in Computer Science, vol. 1055, pp. 431–434. Springer (1996). https://doi.org/10.1007/3-540-61042-1_66, https://doi.org/10.1007/3-540-61042-1_66

3. Borisov, V., Leemann, T., Seßler, K., Haug, J., Pawelczyk, M., Kasneci, G.: Deep neural networks and tabular data: A survey. IEEE Transactions on Neural Networks and Learning Systems pp. 1–21 (2022). https://doi.org/10.1109/TNNLS.2022.3229161

4. Bozga, M., Daws, C., Maler, O., Olivero, A., Tripakis, S., Yovine, S.: Kronos: A model-checking tool for real-time systems. In: Computer Aided Verification: 10th International Conference, CAV'98 Vancouver, BC, Canada, June 28–July 2, 1998 Proceedings 10. pp. 546–550. Springer (1998)

5. Breiman, L.: Classification and regression trees. The Wadsworth & Brooks/Cole (1984)

6. Breiman, L.: Random forests. Mach. Learn. **45**(1), 5–32 (2001). https://doi.org/10.1023/A:1010933404324

7. Bryant, R.E.: Graph-based algorithms for Boolean function manipulation. IEEE Trans. Comput. **100**(8), 677–691 (1986). https://doi.org/10.1109/TC.1986.1676819

8. Chen, T., Guestrin, C.: Xgboost: A scalable tree boosting system. In: Krishnapuram, B., Shah, M., Smola, A.J., Aggarwal, C.C., Shen, D., Rastogi, R. (eds.) Proceedings of the 22nd ACM SIGKDD International Conference on Knowledge Discovery and Data Mining, San Francisco, CA, USA, August 13-17, 2016. pp. 785–794. ACM (2016). https://doi.org/10.1145/2939672.2939785, https://doi.org/10.1145/2939672.2939785

9. Cutler, A., Cutler, D.R., Stevens, J.R.: Random forests. Ensemble machine learning: Methods and applications pp. 157–175 (2012)

10. Friedman, J.H.: Greedy function approximation: a gradient boosting machine. Annals of statistics pp. 1189–1232 (2001)

11. Gossen, F., Murtovi, A., Zweihoff, P., Steffen, B.: Add-lib: Decision diagrams in practice. CoRR **abs/1912.11308** (2019), http://arxiv.org/abs/1912.11308

12. Gossen, F., Steffen, B.: Algebraic aggregation of random forests: towards explainability and rapid evaluation. International Journal on Software Tools for Technology Transfer pp. 1–19 (2021)

13. Grinsztajn, L., Oyallon, E., Varoquaux, G.: Why do tree-based models still outperform deep learning on typical tabular data? In: NeurIPS (2022), http://papers.nips.cc/paper_files/paper/2022/hash/0378c7692da36807bdec87ab043cdadc-Abstract-Datasets_and_Benchmarks.html

14. Guidotti, R., Monreale, A., Ruggieri, S., Turini, F., Giannotti, F., Pedreschi, D.: A survey of methods for explaining black box models. ACM Comput. Surv. **51**(5), 93:1-93:42 (2019). https://doi.org/10.1145/3236009

15. Henzinger, T.A., Ho, P.H., Wong-Toi, H.: Hytech: A model checker for hybrid systems. In: Computer Aided Verification: 9th International Conference, CAV'97 Haifa, Israel, June 22–25, 1997 Proceedings 9. pp. 460–463. Springer (1997)

16. Ho, T.K.: Random decision forests. In: Proceedings of 3rd international conference on document analysis and recognition. **1**, 278–282. IEEE (1995)

17. Huang, X., Izza, Y., Ignatiev, A., Silva, J.M.: On efficiently explaining graph-based classifiers. In: 18th International Conference on Principles of Knowledge Representation and Reasoning (KR 2021) (2021)

18. Izza, Y., Ignatiev, A., Stuckey, P.J., Marques-Silva, J.: Delivering inflated explanations. CoRR **abs/2306.15272** (2023). https://doi.org/10.48550/ARXIV.2306.15272
19. Larsen, K.G., Pettersson, P., Yi, W.: UPPAAL in a nutshell. Int. J. Softw. Tools Technol. Transf. **1**(1–2), 134–152 (1997). https://doi.org/10.1007/S100090050010
20. Lundberg, S.M., Lee, S.: A unified approach to interpreting model predictions. In: Guyon, I., von Luxburg, U., Bengio, S., Wallach, H.M., Fergus, R., Vishwanathan, S.V.N., Garnett, R. (eds.) Advances in Neural Information Processing Systems 30: Annual Conference on Neural Information Processing Systems 2017, December 4-9, 2017, Long Beach, CA, USA. pp. 4765–4774 (2017), https://proceedings.neurips.cc/paper/2017/hash/8a20a8621978632d76c43dfd28b67767-Abstract.html
21. Murtovi, A., Bainczyk, A., Nolte, G., Schlüter, M., Steffen, B.: Forest GUMP: a tool for verification and explanation. Int. J. Softw. Tools Technol. Transf. **25**(3), 287–299 (2023). https://doi.org/10.1007/S10009-023-00702-5
22. Ribeiro, M.T., Singh, S., Guestrin, C.: "why should I trust you?": Explaining the predictions of any classifier. In: Krishnapuram, B., Shah, M., Smola, A.J., Aggarwal, C.C., Shen, D., Rastogi, R. (eds.) Proceedings of the 22nd ACM SIGKDD International Conference on Knowledge Discovery and Data Mining, San Francisco, CA, USA, August 13-17, 2016. pp. 1135–1144. ACM (2016). https://doi.org/10.1145/2939672.2939778, https://doi.org/10.1145/2939672.2939778
23. Shwartz-Ziv, R., Armon, A.: Tabular data: Deep learning is not all you need. Inf. Fusion **81**, 84–90 (2022). https://doi.org/10.1016/J.INFFUS.2021.11.011
24. Yi, W., Pettersson, P., Daniels, M.: Automatic verification of real-time communicating systems by constraint-solving. In: Hogrefe, D., Leue, S. (eds.) Formal Description Techniques VII, Proceedings of the 7th IFIP WG6.1 International Conference on Formal Description Techniques, Berne, Switzerland, 1994. IFIP Conference Proceedings, vol. 6, pp. 243–258. Chapman & Hall (1994)

Reminiscences of a Real-Time Researcher

Thomas A. Henzinger[(✉)]

Institute of Science and Technology Austria (ISTA), Klosterneuburg, Austria
tah@ist.ac.at

Abstract. I give a personal account about the wave of new research activities that rose in the 1990s on the specification, verification, and control of real-time systems.

1 Introduction

Formal Methods met Real Time towards the end of the 1980s, and soon thereafter, the new couple met Control Theory. These encounters turned out to be highly productive; their lasting outcomes include the formal theory of *Timed Automata* [7,23][1], the system-analysis toolkit UPPAAL [40,65][1], and the annual interdisciplinary conference *Hybrid Systems: Computation and Control* [2,59][1]. In this short essay, I recall the first years of the budding research field from my subjective, unbalanced perspective.

2 Theory: Stanford and Weizmann 1986–91

I joined Stanford University in 1986 as a PhD student of Zohar Manna. At the time, Zohar worked with Amir Pnueli on a manuscript that later became the unfinished book series [68,69]. They modeled reactive programs as *transition systems* (today one might say *action systems*, as each Manna-Pnueli transition corresponds to a Lamport action [63], i.e., a binary relation on states), they specified temporal properties in *linear temporal logic*, and they developed *deduction rules* for proving temporal properties of reactive programs. My job was to add real time to the model and methodology.

Once—as a result of [75]—temporal logic had become popular in computer science, it became clear that there is a class of programs for which it is insufficient to prove that a reaction would happen "eventually" (using the temporal $\Diamond$ operator); rather, one sometimes needs a hard bound on the reaction time (effectively turning a liveness into a safety requirement [42]). Especially in real-time scheduling, the goal is to accomplish certain tasks by a deadline. This led to a popular view at the time that "actions take time," and that the time consumed by multiple actions is additive. Zohar, Amir, and I looked at time differently,

---

[1] The second references are examples illustrating that the original contributions have lasting impact.

For Wang, an early conspirator

S. Graf et al. (Eds.): Festschrift Wang Yi, LNCS 15230, pp. 154–164, 2025.
https://doi.org/10.1007/978-3-031-73751-0_12

through a clock that advances global time repeatedly (infinitely often) by one unit. Our *interleaving model of real time* [52] was rooted in the view of reactive programs as concurrent processes: rather than adding up the "durations" of actions [27], the real-time analysis of a program relates the program actions to the *tick* actions of an independent concurrent clock process. This is also the view advocated in [1] (using a global time variable *now*). A corresponding proof methodology was developed in my PhD thesis and published in [53]. We also characterized which properties over real-numbered time can be proved in the discrete-time *tick* model [54].

In 1987 Rajeev Alur joined Zohar's group at Stanford. Amir had become enamored with the usefulness of temporal logic for algorithmic verification— a.k.a. *model checking* [29,77]—if all state variables are boolean, i.e., in the "propositional" case [66]. He therefore encouraged Rajeev and me to look at real time also in the propositional setting. In 1988 we realized that various proposals at the time for extending propositional temporal logic with time [61,62] were unsuitable for model checking, because the resulting satisfiability problems are undecidable, no matter if time is interpreted over a discrete or dense time domain [11]. In 1989, while Rajeev and I joined Zohar for a semester at the Weizmann Institute in Rehovot, we identified a decidable logic, called *Timed Propositional Temporal Logic* (TPTL) [10], with boolean state and discrete time, whose time variables are bound by *freeze quantifiers* [41] (rather than first-order quantifiers) and whose constraints on time variables are limited to *difference bounds*. For example, the TPTL formula

$$\Box x.\ (p\ \rightarrow\ \Diamond y.\ (q\ \wedge\ y - x \leq 5))$$

requires that every p-state, whose time is "frozen" to x, is followed by a q-state whose time is at most $x + 5$. TPTL was the first real-time logic that can be used for model checking.

Independently, David Dill at Stanford had proposed an extension of finite-state machines with real-numbered *timers*, for modeling timing properties of asynchronous circuits [37]. Rajeev joined David to develop the theory of these *Timed Automata* (the value-decreasing timers were replaced by value-increasing *clocks*), one of the most successful formal methods of the last 35 years [6]. While the clock constraints of Timed Automata are also limited to difference bounds, unlike the satisfiability problem for TPTL, the emptiness problem for Timed Automata can be solved over real-numbered time. This makes model checking possible for real-numbered time if the system and the negated specification are represented by Timed Automata (or alternatively, the system is modeled by a Timed Automaton and the specification is expressed in a real-time extension of the branching-time logic CTL [3]). Timed Automata, however, cannot be complemented, which makes them unsatisfactory as specification language.

All this progress still left open the question of a decidable formalism that is interpreted over real-numbered time and closed under boolean operations. Together with another Stanford student, Tomás Feder, Rajeev and I provided the first such logic, called *Metric Interval Temporal Logic* (MITL) [8]. MITL achieves decidability over real-numbered time by foresaking "punctuality" constraints, such as the requirement that every p-state is followed by a q-state exactly 5 time units later. Logical decidability results that allow certain punctuality constraints over real-numbered time were later achieved by Joël Ouaknine, James Worrell, Patricia Bouyer, and Nicolas Markey [24,74].

3   Methods: Grenoble 1991

After finishing my PhD, I joined Joseph Sifakis for a semester-long postdoc in Grenoble. Joseph worked on a real-time extension of process algebra at the time [72,73]. When I arrived in Grenoble, he had already been introduced to Timed Automata by Costas Courcoubetis, a collaborator of David and Rajeev; also the 1991 REX workshop [36] played an important role in forming the community. The year before, the group of Edmund Clarke at CMU had announced *Symbolic Model Checking* (SMC) as a breakthrough in model checking very large state spaces [25]. SMC manipulates state sets that are represented "symbolically" (i.e., intensionally through constraints), rather than "explicitly" (i.e., extensionally through enumeration of the elements). For example, sets of boolean states can be represented symbolically by *Binary Decision Diagrams* (BDDs) or by SAT formulas[2].

Hence it was natural for Joseph and me to wonder what constraints and operators on state sets would be encountered when model checking Timed Automata, and how these operators can be computed symbolically, on constraints. Since timed automata have infinitely many states, no strictly enumerative method can succeed, and previous algorithms had been based on the *region graph* of a Timed Automaton, whose nodes represent state sets of a restricted form, namely, a boolean state together with a *clock region*, which is a set of clock states that agree on the integer parts and on the ordering of the fractional parts of all clock values [7]. For example, the constraint

$$1 < x \ \wedge \ y < 1 \ \wedge \ x - y < 1 \tag{†}$$

represents a triangle-shaped clock region for two clocks x and y. The region graph of a Timed Automaton is partly symbolic (using, e.g., *Difference Bound Matrices* to represent clock regions [37]), but too large to alleviate the state-explosion problem in model checking.

Joseph, his PhD student Xavier Nicollin, and I found it natural to make two adjustments to the model of Timed Automata. First, we introduced *clock invariants*: while a clock guard constrains when an automaton transition may happen, a clock invariant specifies when an automaton location must be left, i.e., when an automaton transition must happen. Second, we replaced traditional automata-theoretic liveness conditions (such as Büchi locations) with the single generic liveness condition that time must always advance by another unit (i.e., a Büchi condition on the progress of time). We then showed how Timed Automata

---

[2] Clarke and others used the term SMC synonymous with BDD-based model checking.

can be analyzed symbolically by manipulating *difference-bound zones*, which are boolean combinations of propositions and difference-bound constraints on clocks [55]. Clock regions correspond to minimal difference-bound zones; as an example that corresponds to an infinite union of clock regions, the difference-bound zone

$$1 < x \ \wedge \ 0 < x - y < 1$$

represents all clock states (x, y) that can be reached, by letting time progress, from a clock state in the triangle-shaped clock region (†). Using difference-bound zone analysis, we also showed how a Timed Automaton can be transformed, by strengthening its guards and invariants, into an equivalent model that can be executed, i.e., into a so-called *non-Zeno* automaton, for which every finite sequence of transitions can be extended to an infinite trajectory along which time diverges. This work was joined by Sergio Yovine, also a PhD student of Joseph, who implemented the constraint-based analysis of Timed Automata by building a new tool called KRONOS [30]. KRONOS was the first symbolic model checker for Timed Automata.

4 Tools: Cornell and Bell Labs 1992–95

After I was hired as Assistant Professor at Cornell University, I moved, like many researchers in the field, beyond timed systems towards hybrid systems. In 1991, Amir Pnueli, Oded Maler, Anil Nerode, and others propagated the combination of discrete and continuous dynamical systems for modeling hardware and software that interacts with the physical world [67,70]. Rajeev and I realized that this could be achieved by generalizing the clocks of timed automata to continuous variables whose evolution is governed by differential equations. We called the general model *Hybrid Automata* [5]; similar ideas were pursued independently by the researchers in Grenoble [71].[3] My first PhD student, Pei-Hsin Ho, implemented a symbolic model checker for the class of *Linear Hybrid Automata*, an extension of timed automata that can be analyzed using linear constraints on continuous state variables [16]. Our tool, named HYTECH, at first used linear constraints over the reals and later polyhedra for the symbolic representation and manipulation of continuous state sets [44,45]; it was developed further by Pei-Hsin together with my postdoc Howard Wong-Toi, also towards the abstraction-based analysis of nonlinear Hybrid Automata [46].

In 1993 a third competitor appeared on the scene for the constraint-based analysis of real-time systems: the tool TAB by Wang Yi and his PhD student Paul Pettersson introduced the on-the-fly analysis of products of timed automata [80]; its successor UPPAAL was developed further for multiple decades jointly by the groups of Wang Yi in Uppsala and Kim Larsen in Aalborg [22,64]. The remarkable triple of tools from that time—KRONOS [81], HYTECH [45], and UPPAAL [65]—had a pioneering impact on system analysis by separating operations on symbolic constraints on states from semi-algorithms[4] that approximate

---

[3] We joined forces for the journal paper [4].

[4] A *semi-algorithm* may not terminate; in verification it ensures soundness, but not completeness.

fixpoints by iterating these operations. The general methodology was later—in Berkeley—formalized as *Symbolic Transition Systems* (STS) [51]. The termination of fixpoint computations on STS is guaranteed by the existence of finite quotients: finite time-abstract bisimilarity quotients in the case of Timed Automata (namely, their region graphs) [7], and finite time-abstract similarity and untimed language equivalence quotients for certain classes of Hybrid Automata that lie between Timed and Linear Hybrid Automata [48,50]. These theoretical results led to a characterization of the decidability frontier for Hybrid Automata; they were proved by my second PhD student at Cornell, Peter Kopke, in collaboration with Pravin Varaiya at Berkeley and his student Anuj Puri. An introduction to the underlying modeling principles for systems with discrete and continuous transitions can be found in [14,15]; a summary of the corresponding decidability and undecidability results, in [43].

After graduating from Stanford, Rajeev joined Bell Labs at Murray Hill and, while at Cornell, I spent part of each summer there to continue our collaboration. Since deterministic Timed Automata (the most expressive complementable class of Timed Automata known at the time) were expressively incomparable with MITL, we were still on the lookout for a class of timed languages that could compete with the untimed regular languages in canonicity. Canonicity is supported by the decidability of verification questions, closure properties, the equivalence of different formalisms, and maximal expressivity [12]. An important milestone in our quest for real-time canonicity was the study—together with Limor Fix, who visited Cornell at the time—of *Event-Clock Automata* (ECA) [9], a class of Timed Automata that maintain deterministic clock values despite nondeterministic transitions. Later—in Berkeley—my postdoc Jean-François Raskin and his PhD advisor Pierre-Yves Schobbens showed that although ECA and MITL are very different formalisms, they are essentially expressively equivalent [58]. Hence they have a strong claim on defining what can be called the *Regular Real-time Languages*.

5   Agents: Berkeley 1996–2004

At the beginning of 1996 I moved to the EECS Department at the University of California, Berkeley, into the immediate neighborhood of leading control theorists such as Pravin Varaiya and Shankar Sastry. As control became software-based, their interest in hybrid systems grew, because a discrete controller of a continuous plant is a hybrid model with two agents: Controller and Plant. The budding hybrid-systems community had organized a series of workshops from 1992 to 1996 which brought together the formal methods and control communities [18–20,38]. In 1998 the community felt that it was time for a regular series of meetings, and thus the annual workshops—now ACM conferences—on *Hybrid Systems: Computation and Control* were born. The first installment was organized by Shankar and myself in Berkeley [59]. From a control point of view, a shortcoming of the "standard" formal-methods model of real time is that it distinguishes behaviors that differ only in the exact real-numbered time of events, which makes the modeling of measurement errors difficult. An early attempt to make the model "robust" was unsatisfactory [39,57]; see [56,79] for later treatments of the issue.

Before moving to the University of Pennsylvania, Rajeev visited UC Berkeley in 1996 for an extended period of time to work on a book project we later abandoned. Around the same time Orna Kupferman joined my group as postdoc. We became increasingly interested in the game-theoretic view of sequential synthesis and control—System versus Environment, or Controller versus Plant—and especially in its extensions, on one hand, to more than two players (i.e., multiple agents) [13,17,32], and on the other hand, to timed, hybrid, and stochastic systems. Rediscovering an old approach to sequential synthesis ("Church's problem") [26], Amir Pnueli and Roni Rosner had pioneered the computation of winning strategies in games for the synthesis of reactive programs [76], and Peter Ramadge and Murray Wonham had done the same for discrete-event control [78]. Gérard Hoffmann and Howard Wong-Toi applied the method to the control of real-time systems [60], and Eugene Asarin, Oded Maler, and Amir Pnueli developed the symbolic, constraint-based view of timed games for controlling real-time systems [21]. My Cornell student Peter Kopke was the first to solve games on certain hybrid state spaces in discrete time [49], and my Berkeley students Ben Horowitz and Rupak Majumdar did so for continuous time [47]. The issue of Zeno effects in timed games was addressed in [31].

I want to conclude with a final result that I consider to be the capstone of my research on symbolic transition systems. Together with Rupak and my postdoc Luca de Alfaro, we unified the design of symbolic algorithms for model checking and control, i.e., for system analysis and strategy synthesis [33,34]. This is achieved by iterating symbolic transition operators on single- and multi-player structures which are defined by different quantifier prefixes: given a zone Z, ($\exists$) which states have some transition into Z? ($\forall$) which states have all transitions lead into Z? ($\exists\forall$) in which state does Player 1 (e.g., the Controller) have a choice that, for all choices of Player 2 (e.g., the Plant), leads to a state in Z? etc. It is worth noting that also UPPAAL was developed to encompass the game-theoretic setting [40]. In fact, the symbolic view of games played on transition systems can be extended further to the quantitative analysis of probabilistic choices and the synthesis of quantitatively optimal strategies [35]; see [28] for a survey.

6   Conclusion

A look at recent proceedings of CAV, TACAS, or HSCC shows that formal methods for real-time systems are still an active area of research 35 years after the first results. Indeed, this field can serve as a role model for the mutual fertilization of theoretical insights and practical applications.

Acknowledgements and apologies. I thank all my collaborators over the years. None of the mentioned contributions would have been possible without them. I also apologize for all omissions. The selection of contributions in this essay reflects primarily my personal involvement rather than any measure of importance.

References

1. Abadi, M., Lamport, L.: An old-fashioned recipe for real time. In: *Real-Time: Theory in Practice, REX Workshop*, volume 600 of *Lecture Notes in Computer Science*, pages 1–27. Springer (1991)
2. Ábrahám, E., Mazo Jr, M. editors: *Proc. 27th Conference on Hybrid Systems: Computation and Control, HSCC*. ACM (2024)
3. Alur, R., Courcoubetis, C., Dill, D.L.: Model checking for real-time systems. In: *Proc. 5th Symposium on Logic in Computer Science, LICS*, pages 414–425. IEEE Computer Society (1990)
4. Alur, R., Courcoubetis, C., Halbwachs, N., Henzinger, T.A., Ho, P., Nicollin, X., Olivero, A., Sifakis, J., Yovine, S.: The algorithmic analysis of hybrid systems. Theor. Comput. Sci. **138**(1), 3–34 (1995)
5. Alur, R., Courcoubetis, C., Henzinger, T.A., Ho, P.: Hybrid automata: An algorithmic approach to the specification and verification of hybrid systems. In: *Hybrid Systems*, volume 736 of *Lecture Notes in Computer Science*, pages 209–229. Springer, (1992)
6. Alur, R., Dill, D.L.: Automata for modeling real-time systems. In *Automata, Languages and Programming, 17th International Colloquium, ICALP*, volume 443 of *Lecture Notes in Computer Science*, pages 322–335. Springer, 1990
7. Alur, R., Dill, D.L.: A theory of timed automata. Theor. Comput. Sci. **126**(2), 183–235 (1994)
8. Alur, R., Feder, T., Henzinger, T.A.: The benefits of relaxing punctuality. In: *Proc. 10th Symposium on Principles of Distributed Computing, PODC*, pages 139–152. ACM (1991)
9. Alur, R., Fix, L., Henzinger, T.A.: A determinizable class of timed automata. In: *Computer Aided Verification, 6th Conference, CAV*, volume 818 of *Lecture Notes in Computer Science*, pages 1–13. Springer (1994)
10. Alur, R., Henzinger, T.A.: A really temporal logic. In: *Proc. 30th Symposium on Foundations of Computer Science, FOCS*, pages 164–169. IEEE Computer Society (1989)
11. Alur, R., Henzinger, T.A.: Real-time logics: Complexity and expressiveness. In: *Proc. 5th Symposium on Logic in Computer Science, LICS*, pages 390–401. IEEE Computer Society (1990)
12. Alur, R., Henzinger, T.A.: Back to the future: Towards a theory of timed regular languages. In: *Proc. 33rd Symposium on Foundations of Computer Science, FOCS*, pages 177–186. IEEE Computer Society (1992)
13. Alur, R., Henzinger, T.A.: Reactive modules. In: *Proc. 11th Symposium on Logic in Computer Science, LICS*, pages 207–218. IEEE Computer Society (1996)
14. Alur, R., Henzinger, T.A.: Modularity for timed and hybrid systems. In: *Concurrency Theory, 8th Conference, CONCUR*, volume 1243 of *Lecture Notes in Computer Science*, pages 74–88. Springer (1997)
15. Alur, R., Henzinger, T.A.: Real-time system = discrete system + clock variables. Int. J. Softw. Tools Technol. Transf. **1**(1–2), 86–109 (1997)
16. Alur, R., Henzinger, T.A., Ho, P.: Automatic symbolic verification of embedded systems. In *Proc. 14th Real-Time Systems Symposium, RTSS*, pages 2–11. IEEE Computer Society, (1993)
17. Alur, R., Henzinger, T.A., Kupferman, O.: Alternating-time temporal logic. In: *Proc. 38th Symposium on Foundations of Computer Science, FOCS*, pages 100–109. IEEE Computer Society (1997)

18. Alur, R., Henzinger, T.A., Sontag, E.D. editors: *Hybrid Systems III: Verification and Control*, volume 1066 of *Lecture Notes in Computer Science*. Springer (1996)
19. Antsaklis, P.J., Kohn, W., Nerode, A., Sastry, S. editors: *Hybrid Systems II*, volume 999 of *Lecture Notes in Computer Science*. Springer (1995)
20. Antsaklis, P.J., Kohn, W., Nerode, A., Sastry, S. editors: *Hybrid Systems IV*, volume 1273 of *Lecture Notes in Computer Science*. Springer (1997)
21. Asarin, E., Maler, O., Pnueli, A.: Symbolic controller synthesis for discrete and timed systems. In: *Hybrid Systems II*, volume 999 of *Lecture Notes in Computer Science*, pages 1–20. Springer (1994)
22. Bengtsson, J., Larsen, K.G., Larsson, F., Pettersson, P., Yi, W.: UPPAAL: A tool suite for automatic verification of real-time systems. In: *Hybrid Systems III: Verification and Control*, volume 1066 of *Lecture Notes in Computer Science*, pages 232–243. Springer (1995)
23. Bose, S., Henzinger, T.A., Lehtinen, K., Schewe, S., Totzke, P.: History-deterministic timed automata are not determinizable. In: *Reachability Problems, 16th Conference, RP*, volume 13608 of *Lecture Notes in Computer Science*, pages 67–76. Springer (2022)
24. Bouyer, P., Markey, N., Ouaknine, J., Worrell, J.: The cost of punctuality. In: *Proc. 22nd Symposium on Logic in Computer Science, LICS*, pages 109–120. IEEE Computer Society (2007)
25. Burch, J.R., Clarke, E.M., McMillan, K.L., Dill, D.L., Hwang, L.J.: Symbolic model checking: 10^{20} states and beyond. In: *Proc. 5th Symposium on Logic in Computer Science, LICS*, pages 428–439. IEEE Computer Society (1990)
26. Büchi, J.R., Landweber, L.H.: Solving sequential conditions by finite-state strategies. Trans. AMS **38**(27), 295–311 (1969)
27. Chaochen, Z., Hoare, C.A.R., Ravn, A.P.: A calculus of durations. Inf. Process. Lett. **40**(5), 269–276 (1991)
28. Chatterjee, K., Henzinger, T.A.: Value iteration. In: *25 Years of Model Checking: History, Achievements, Perspectives*, volume 5000 of *Lecture Notes in Computer Science*, pages 107–138. Springer (2008)
29. Clarke, E.M., Emerson, E.A.: Design and synthesis of synchronization skeletons using branching-time temporal logic. In: *Logics of Programs, Workshop*, volume 131 of *Lecture Notes in Computer Science*, pages 52–71. Springer, (1981)
30. Daws, C., Olivero, A., Yovine, S.: Verifying ET-LOTOS programs with KRONOS. In: *Formal Description Techniques, 7th WG6.1 Conference, FORTE*, volume 6 of *IFIP Proceedings*, pages 227–242. Chapman & Hall (1994)
31. de Alfaro, L., Faella, M., Henzinger, T.A., Majumdar, R., Stoelinga, M.: The element of surprise in timed games. In: *Concurrency Theory, 14th Conference, CONCUR*, volume 2761 of *Lecture Notes in Computer Science*, pages 142–156. Springer (2003)
32. de Alfaro, L., Henzinger, T.A., Kupferman, O.: Concurrent reachability games. In: *Proc. 39th Symposium on Foundations of Computer Science, FOCS*, pages 564–575. IEEE Computer Society (1998)
33. de Alfaro, L., Henzinger, T.A., Majumdar, R.: From verification to control: Dynamic programs for omega-regular objectives. In: *Proc. 16th Symposium on Logic in Computer Science, LICS*, pages 279–290. IEEE Computer Society (2001)
34. de Alfaro, L., Henzinger, T.A., Majumdar, R.: Symbolic algorithms for infinite-state games. In: *Concurrency Theory, 12th Conference, CONCUR*, volume 2154 of *Lecture Notes in Computer Science*, pages 536–550. Springer (2001)

35. de Alfaro, L., Majumdar, R.. Quantitative solution of omega-regular games. In: *Proc. on 33rd Symposium on Theory of Computing, STOC*, pages 675–683. ACM (2001)

36. de Bakker, J.W., Huizing, C., de Roever, W.P., Rozenberg, G. editors: *Real-Time: Theory in Practice, REX Workshop*, volume 600 of *Lecture Notes in Computer Science*. Springer (1992)

37. Dill, D.L.: Timing assumptions and verification of finite-state concurrent systems. In: *Automatic Verification Methods for Finite-State Systems, Workshop*, volume 407 of *Lecture Notes in Computer Science*, pages 197–212. Springer (1989)

38. Grossman, R.L., Nerode, A., Ravn, A.P., Rischel, H. editors: *Hybrid Systems*, volume 736 of *Lecture Notes in Computer Science*. Springer (1993)

39. Gupta, V., Henzinger, T.A., Jagadeesan, R.: Robust timed automata. In: *Hybrid and Real-Time Systems, Workshop, HART*, volume 1201 of *Lecture Notes in Computer Science*, pages 331–345. Springer (1997)

40. Hasrat, I.R., Jensen, P.G., Larsen, K.G., Srba, J.: A toolchain for domestic heat-pump control using UPPAAL STRATEGO. Sci. Comput. Program. **230**, 102987 (2023)

41. Henzinger, T.A.: Half-order modal logic: How to prove real-time properties. In: *Proc. 9th Symposium on Principles of Distributed Computing, PODC*, pages 281–296. ACM (1990)

42. Henzinger, T.A.: Sooner is safer than later. Inf. Process. Lett. **43**(3), 135–141 (1992)

43. Henzinger, T.A.: The theory of hybrid automata. In: *Proc. 11th Symposium on Logic in Computer Science, LICS*, pages 278–292. IEEE Computer Society (1996)

44. Henzinger, T.A., Ho, P.: HyTech: The Cornell HYbrid TECHnology tool. In: *Hybrid Systems II*, volume 999 of *Lecture Notes in Computer Science*, pages 265–293. Springer (1994)

45. Henzinger, T.A., Ho, P., Wong-Toi, H.: HyTech: A model checker for hybrid systems. Int. J. Softw. Tools Technol. Transf. **1**(1–2), 110–122 (1997)

46. Henzinger, T.A., Ho, P., Wong-Toi, H.: Algorithmic analysis of nonlinear hybrid systems. IEEE Trans. Autom. Control **43**(4), 540–554 (1998)

47. Henzinger, T.A., Horowitz, B., Majumdar, R.: Rectangular hybrid games. In: *Concurrency Theory, 10th Conference, CONCUR*, volume 1664 of *Lecture Notes in Computer Science*, pages 320–335. Springer (1999)

48. Henzinger, T.A., Kopke, P.W.: State equivalences for rectangular hybrid automata. In: *Concurrency Theory, 7th Conference, CONCUR*, volume 1119 of *Lecture Notes in Computer Science*, pages 530–545. Springer (1996)

49. Henzinger, T.A., Kopke, P.W.: Discrete-time control for rectangular hybrid automata. In: *Automata, Languages and Programming, 24th International Colloquium, ICALP*, volume 1256 of *Lecture Notes in Computer Science*, pages 582–593. Springer (1997)

50. Henzinger, T.A., Kopke, P.W., Puri, A., Varaiya, P.: What's decidable about hybrid automata? In: *Proc. 27th Symposium on Theory of Computing, STOC*, pages 373–382. ACM (1995)

51. Henzinger, T.A., Majumdar, R., Raskin, J.: A classification of symbolic transition systems. ACM Trans. Comput. Log. **6**(1), 1–32 (2005)

52. Henzinger, T.A., Manna, Z., Pnueli, A.: An interleaving model for real-time. In: *Proc. 5th Jerusalem Conference on Information Technology*, pages 717–730. IEEE Computer Society (1990)

53. Henzinger, T.A., Manna, Z., Pnueli, A.: Temporal proof methodologies for real-time systems. In: *Proc. 18th Symposium on Principles of Programming Languages, POPL*, pages 353–366. ACM (1991)
54. Henzinger, T.A., Manna, Z., Pnueli, A.: What good are digital clocks? In: *Automata, Languages and Programming, 19th International Colloquium, ICALP*, volume 623 of *Lecture Notes in Computer Science*, pages 545–558. Springer (1992)
55. Henzinger, T.A., Nicollin, X., Sifakis, J., Yovine, S.: Symbolic model checking for real-time systems. In: *Proc. 7th Symposium on Logic in Computer Science, LICS*, pages 394–406. IEEE Computer Society, (1992)
56. Henzinger, T.A., Otop, J.: Model measuring for discrete and hybrid systems. Nonlinear Anal. **23**, 166–190 (2017)
57. Henzinger, T.A., Raskin, J.:. Robust undecidability of timed and hybrid systems. In: *Hybrid Systems: Computation and Control, 3rd Workshop, HSCC*, volume 1790 of *Lecture Notes in Computer Science*, pages 145–159. Springer (2000)
58. Henzinger, T.A., Raskin, J., Schobbens, P.: The regular real-time languages. In: *Automata, Languages and Programming, 25th International Colloquium, ICALP*, volume 1443 of *Lecture Notes in Computer Science*, pages 580–591. Springer (1998)
59. Henzinger, T.A., Sastry, S. editors: *Hybrid Systems: Computation and Control, 1st Workshop, HSCC*, volume 1386 of *Lecture Notes in Computer Science*. Springer, (1998)
60. Hoffmann, G., Wong-Toi, H.: The input-output control of real-time discrete-event systems. In: *Proc. 13th Real-Time Systems Symposium, RTSS*, pages 256–265. IEEE Computer Society (1992)
61. Jahanian, F., Mok, A.K.: Safety analysis of timing properties in real-time systems. IEEE Trans. Software Eng. **12**(9), 890–904 (1986)
62. Koymans, R.: Specifying real-time properties with metric temporal logic. Real Time Syst. **2**(4), 255–299 (1990)
63. Lamport, L.: *Specifying Systems: The TLA+ Language and Tools for Hardware and Software Engineers*. Addison-Wesley (2002)
64. Larsen, K.-G. , Pettersson, P., Yi, W.: Compositional and symbolic model-checking of real-time systems. In: *Proc. 16th Real-Time Systems Symposium, RTSS*, pages 76–87. IEEE Computer Society (1995)
65. Larsen, K.G., Pettersson, P., Yi, W.: UPPAAL in a nutshell. Int. J. Softw. Tools Technol. Transf. **1**(1–2), 134–152 (1997)
66. Lichtenstein, O., Pnueli, A.: Checking that finite-state concurrent programs satisfy their linear specification. In: *Proc. 12th Symposium on Principles of Programming Languages, POPL*, pages 97–107. ACM (1985)
67. Maler, O., Manna, Z., Pnueli, A.: From timed to hybrid systems. In: *Real-Time: Theory in Practice, REX Workshop*, volume 600 of *Lecture Notes in Computer Science*, pages 447–484. Springer (1991)
68. Manna, Z., Pnueli, A.: *The Temporal Logic of Reactive and Concurrent Systems: Specification*. Springer (1992)
69. Manna, Z., Pnueli, A.: *Temporal Verification of Reactive Systems: Safety*. Springer (1995)
70. Nerode, A., Kohn, W.: Models for hybrid systems: Automata, topologies, controllability, observability. In: *Hybrid Systems*, volume 736 of *Lecture Notes in Computer Science*, pages 317–356. Springer (1992)
71. Nicollin, X., Olivero, A., Sifakis, J., Yovine, S.: An approach to the description and analysis of hybrid systems. In: *Hybrid Systems*, volume 736 of *Lecture Notes in Computer Science*, pages 149–178. Springer (1992)

72. Nicollin, X., Richier, J., Sifakis, J., Voiron, J.: ATP: An algebra for timed processes. In *Programming concepts and methods, IFIP WG2.2 & WG2.3 Working Conference on Programming Concepts and Methods*, pages 415–442. North-Holland (1990)

73. Nicollin, X., Sifakis, J.: An overview and synthesis on timed process algebras. In: *Computer Aided Verification, 3rd Workshop, CAV*, volume 575 of *Lecture Notes in Computer Science*, pages 376–398. Springer (1991)

74. Ouaknine, J., Worrell, J.: On the decidability and complexity of metric temporal logic over finite words. Log. Methods Comput. Sci., 3(1) (2007)

75. Pnueli, A.: The temporal logic of programs. In: *Proc. 18th Symposium on Foundations of Computer Science, FOCS*, pages 46–57. IEEE Computer Society (1977)

76. Pnueli, A., Rosner, R.: On the synthesis of a reactive module. In: *Proc. 16th Symposium on Principles of Programming Languages, POPL*, pages 179–190. ACM (1989)

77. Queille, J., Sifakis, J.: Specification and verification of concurrent systems in CESAR. In: *Symposium on Programming, Fifth Colloquium*, volume 137 of *Lecture Notes in Computer Science*, pages 337–351. Springer (1982)

78. Ramadge, P.J., Wonham, W.M.: The control of discrete-event systems. Proc. IEEE **77**(1), 81–98 (1989)

79. P. Tabuada. *Verification and Control of Hybrid Systems: A Symbolic Approach.* Springer (2009)

80. Yi, W., Pettersson, P., Daniels, M.: Automatic verification of real-time communicating systems by constraint-solving. In: *Formal Description Techniques, 7th WG6.1 Conference, FORTE*, volume 6 of *IFIP Proceedings*, pages 243–258. Chapman & Hall (1994)

81. Yovine, S.: KRONOS: A verification tool for real-time systems. Int. J. Softw. Tools Technol. Transf. **1**(1–2), 123–133 (1997)

Author Index

A
Abate, Alessandro   64
Abdulla, Parosh Aziz   79
Andersson, Bjorn   18
Atig, Mohamed Faouzi   79

B
Baruah, Sanjoy   120

D
Das, Sarbojit   79

E
Ekberg, Pontus   120

F
Fersman, Elena   12

G
Gao, Yulong   64
Graf, Susanne   1

H
Hansson, Hans   8
Henzinger, Thomas A.   154

J
Johansson, Karl H.   64
Johnsen, Einar Broch   42
Jonsson, Bengt   79

K
Kobialka, Paul   42
Kristjansen, Martin   98

L
Larsen, Kim Guldstrand   98

M
Murtovi, Alnis   135

N
Norström, Christer   8

O
Olderog, Ernst-Rüdiger   23

P
Pettersson, Paul   1, 12
Pferscher, Andrea   42

S
Sagonas, Konstantinos   79
Schlüter, Maximilian   135
Seceleanu, Cristina   8
Steffen, Bernhard   1, 135

T
Tarifa, Silvia Lizeth Tapia   42

Z
Zhou, Can   64

S. Graf et al. (Eds.): Festschrift Wang Yi, LNCS 15230, p. 165, 2025.
https://doi.org/10.1007/978-3-031-73751-0